CHARLES COLSON

WITH ANNE MORSE

BURDEN OF TRUTH

Defending Truth in an Age of Unbelief

TYNDALE HOUSE PUBLISHERS, INC.
WHEATON, ILLINOIS

Library of Congress Cataloging-in-Publication Data

Colson, Charles W.
  Burden of truth : defending truth in an age of unbelief / Charles Colson.
    p.   cm.
  ISBN 0-8423-0190-9 (softcover)
  1. Christianity—20th century.   2. Apologetics.   3. United States—Moral conditions.   4. Church and social problems.   5. United States—Religion—1960-   I. Title.
BR526.C628   1997
239—dc21   97-8409

Printed in the United States of America

03   02   01   00   99
7   6   5   4   3

CONTENTS

ACKNOWLEDGMENTS

The most inspiring part of working for *BreakPoint* is hearing from our listeners. They range from professionals to schoolchildren. They tell us they are using the *BreakPoint* transcripts to prepare letters to the editor, teach adult Sunday School classes, and write essays for school.

One mother called to say that *BreakPoint* comes on at 7:30 in the morning and her ten-year-old son refuses to leave for school until he's heard the program. The most astonishing call came from a harassed father in a hospital delivery room. His wife was listening to *BreakPoint* while in labor and was so enthralled by the message that she insisted, between contractions, that he call for a transcript of that day's broadcast.

Together with Chuck, I would like to thank the people who make this program possible. Managing editor Anne Morse knows the alchemy for transforming any draft into radio style. Associate editor Roberto Rivera lends the program much of its intellectual punch. Research associate Kim Robbins goes beyond the call of duty in tracking down hard-to-find sources.

For several years Gary Fisher was *BreakPoint*'s executive producer, ably assisted by administrator Bonnie Burt and administrative coordinator Karen Scantlin. Recently Will Nance joined us as director of Wilberforce Communications, Kevin Raleigh as fulfillment manager, and Kathy Berry as administrative secretary. We are thankful to the *BreakPoint* volunteers, who give of their time generously to support the program, especially Jean Epley.

We also want to express our gratitude to various writers who have assisted us, either on staff or on contract, in preparing the commentaries included in this volume. Timothy Dailey was senior editor of *BreakPoint* for a brief but fruitful time. Gene Edward Veith has contributed drafts for several years, always with a thought-provoking angle. Susan Bauer keeps an alert eye on popular culture. Paul Nelson steers us on course with science topics. John Richard Pearcey was a major support to the program for several years. Others who helped prepare commentaries that appear in the following pages are: Frederica Mathewes-Green, John Hodges, Paul Thigpen, Beth Spring, Tom Johnson, John Sparks, and Mark Horne.

Our thanks to Ambassador Radio Agency and its capable staff, especially Mark Conner. Finally, we are grateful to our loyal listeners and supporters, whose generosity keeps *Break-Point* on the air. They convince us, day in and day out, that *BreakPoint*'s message is helping them think biblically about the world and work toward the creation of a vibrant Christian culture.

Nancy R. Pearcey
Executive Editor, *BreakPoint*
April 1997

INTRODUCTION

"Mr. Colson, how do we know there is truth?"

Standing before me was a spit-and-polish major at Camp Lejeune, North Carolina, where I had been invited to speak to two thousand marine officers about ethics. In this very place, many years ago, I once served as a young lieutenant. Now I had returned to urge a commitment to absolute moral standards. Otherwise, I argued, America will suffer an escalating cycle of crime, drug abuse, and family breakup.

It was at the end of my talk that the major strode up to the microphone. "You've made a good argument that absolute moral standards are necessary to prevent social decay," he said. "But that's a pragmatic argument. I want to know, sir: Is it true? Is there such a thing as moral truth—and if there is, how do we know it?"

I stared in astonishment at the officer. After speaking on the subject all across America, I had finally found someone who knew the key question: The most important question is not whether moral standards are useful in propping up society but whether they are true.

Many Christians contend for Christian values in order to knit together some threads of civility in a rapidly unraveling society—as I did that day at Camp Lejeune. At Prison Fellowship, we've crafted a moral case against crime: Crime is a moral disorder, and unless America adopts a moral response, crime will overwhelm us. Similar arguments can be made to help prop up the shattered social structures in every area of American life. A free society's way of sustaining social harmony is through a shared value system.

But we must recognize these are, at root, pragmatic arguments. And the pragmatic approach is not ultimately what will grip peoples' minds and hearts. Values must be rooted in truth.

David Klinghoffer went to the heart of the matter in a *Wall Street Journal* article. "A person doesn't accept a new, rigorous system of moral action because it might in the long run prop up civilized society," Klinghoffer wrote. No, a person submits to a demanding moral system "because he believes the system is, in a fundamental sense, true—very likely because he believes it is the will of God."

Precisely.

Today it has become more important than ever to frame arguments based on truth itself—that we owe allegiance to these moral standards, not just because they work well in society, but because they are true.

My search for someone who even knows the question started many years ago when I wrote an article contending that Harvard's much ballyhooed ethics program was doomed. My thesis was that ethics depend on absolutes and Harvard was thoroughly committed to philosophical relativism. Provoked by the article, the Harvard administration invited me to give a Distinguished Lecture at Harvard Business School.

I prepared by reading every book on ethics I could get my hands on. I studied the ethics course curriculum in depth and discovered that it was a four-week class in pure pragmatism. My view was confirmed by a Christian business executive who took it. When I asked him what he learned, he said the course had given him some great pointers. "I can sum it up like this," he told me. "When you're making a serious business decision, never do anything you think might end up in the newspapers."

Despite his apparent Christian maturity, this man didn't realize that he had consumed a blitz course in pragmatic ethics. No regard for absolute rights and wrongs; it's good business not to get in trouble—or even get bad press.

Harvard calls *this* ethics?

This was the course I set my sights on. The day I arrived for the lecture, Harvard's Aldrich Hall was packed. Hundreds of students and faculty were sitting at desks and in the aisles and standing against the walls. For forty-five minutes I dealt with the question posed by the great Russian novelist Fyodor Dostoyevsky: Can man be good without God?

My conclusion was no. I contended that absolute truth is essential for the formulation of ethics. Otherwise, right and wrong is up for grabs, determined subjectively. We humans are very unreliable, capable of infinite self-justification, as I discovered from my own experience in the Watergate scandal. Since Harvard is committed to relativism, it can teach only subjective values, which can never withstand the pressures of life.

Now, I assumed Harvard students might not take kindly to my assertion that they were wasting their time and money taking ethics courses at Harvard. So when I finished speaking, I braced myself for tough questions. But to my shock, not a single person threw out a tough, challenging question. As one Christian student later told me, "They didn't know what to ask." He meant that most of the students have never even thought about the issues—a troubling observation, if true.

I'm not picking on Harvard. I've had similar experiences speaking at my own alma mater, Brown University, as well as at Princeton, Yale, and other campuses. It wasn't until I returned to the place I had started my career—Camp Lejeune—that I found someone who raised the root question about the moral nihilism of our age. That young marine wanted to know: Is there truth? And is it knowable? Is there a right and wrong?

"Yes," I replied, "there are moral absolutes, and we know them because God has revealed them in Scripture." I then briefly shared my testimony—that we can know God through his Word.

"Further, our everyday experiences show us that there's an objective order," I argued. I took my pen out of my pocket and dropped it repeatedly onto the podium. It landed beside the microphone, the sound reverberating through the auditorium.

"When I let go of this pen, it falls every time," I said. "We call that the law of gravity. Now, if there are predictable consequences to physical acts, why shouldn't we assume there are predictable consequences to moral acts? If there's a physical law, there is also a moral law.

"There's an order to the moral universe, just as there is an order in the physical universe," I added. "God's revelation fits what we know from experience."

I watched as comprehension began dawning on the faces of the officers assembled in the auditorium. And yet the very idea of objective truth is alien to most of America's cultural and intellectual elites today. Moral relativism is now the reigning philosophy of American life—the idea that truth differs from culture to culture, or from group to group, or from person to person.

Widespread relativism explains why even students at Ivy League universities have been so apathetic to any moral challenge. As law professor Stephen Carter explained to me before my presentation at Yale, "Students today are taught that law is amoral—that moral issues like the ones you'll raise are irrelevant." Even dyed-in-the-wool secularists won't bother to debate, Carter warned me. "They'll listen to your point of view, acknowledge that you're entitled to it, but conclude that it's really of no consequence. They won't bother to argue because they don't think it matters."

This indifference to truth is at the root of the moral collapse in American life. Pollster George Barna discovered that nearly three-quarters of all Americans reject even the concept of absolute truth. In response to the question asked by the prophets of old—"how should we then live?"—the answer the postmodern American gives is "however I please." But when people no longer believe that standards of right and wrong are rooted solidly in a transcendent reality beyond their own wishes and needs, there is nothing to restrain their worst impulses.

The result is the social devastation of the kind we are witnessing in America today. Divorce and illegitimacy are dissolving the family; today, 76 percent of teenage births are out of wedlock. An increasing crime rate among juveniles threatens to shake the very foundations of our political order. Widespread pornography is rotting the soul of our society. Since we can't agree on any definition of common good, law itself becomes impossible. And the laws we do enact can't be enforced because they're not upheld by general and widely shared moral convictions.

As the social devastation spreads, our cultural leaders are abandoning the once fashionable Great Society approaches and are groping desperately for alternatives. Suddenly everyone is talking about morals, values, or virtue. Former education secretary Bill Bennett wrote *The Book of Virtues,* a hefty volume that reached the best-seller lists—and stayed there for years. Psychologist and radio talk-show host Laura Schlessinger routinely tells callers to grow up and accept their responsibilities—and her ratings have shot through the ozone layer.

This surprising new respect for morality may sound like music to our ears. But like the young major, we should be aware of the pragmatic spirit behind much of it: Many of our leaders view virtue and morality merely as useful ropes we can use to pull ourselves out of the social sinkhole we've fallen into.

When Christians argue for values, we should do so squarely on the basis of truth. Of course, truth is good for society as well, but our main appeal should be on the basis of truth—not just benefits. Otherwise, our case will become as weak and ineffectual as the Harvard ethics course. British historian Paul Johnson writes in *Enemies of Society* that the very essence of civilization is the quest for truth and the adaptation of our behavior to its laws. But, Johnson warns, "at all times civilization has its enemies, though they are constantly changing their guise and their weapons." These enemies are those who, "for whatever motive, deny, distort, minimize, exaggerate or poison the truth."

The great defensive art, Johnson says, is to detect and unmask truth's enemies before the damage they inflict becomes fatal.

This is precisely the purpose of this book, and of the *BreakPoint* radio program upon which it is based: to equip readers to recognize those who exchange the truth for a lie, to unmask their many disguises, to blunt their weapons and expose their distortions. We hope to challenge listeners to consider the claims of truth itself and to defend them, and ultimately to make the most effective apologetic of all: to submit to the demands of God's truth in our lives.

We write in the twilight of the second millennium and, some would argue, in the twilight of a great civilization. But this is no time for despair. The question today is no different from what it was two thousand years ago when Pontius Pilate sarcastically asked Jesus Christ, "What is truth?"

Today, many people no longer know the question—or if they do, they reject the answer. But the one who stood before Pilate two thousand years ago speaks today with the same firm and unshakable confidence. He is the one who responds, "I am the way, the truth, and the life."

Charles W. Colson

Anne Morse, *BreakPoint* editor

May 1, 1997

For more information on *BreakPoint,* and for a listing of stations in your area that carry the program, write us at P.O. Box 17500, Washington, D.C. 20041, or call Prison Fellowship at 800-995-8777.

Visit our Web site at www.breakpoint.org.

"I'm afraid that God is speaking but that no one's listening."

Dana Scully, *The X-Files*

One

WAR
OF THE
WORLDVIEWS

Taking On Dr. Death

....

Cardinal Maida's Project Life

"PUT up or shut up."

That's what Jack Kevorkian's attorney said to the local archbishop, Cardinal Maida, when Maida criticized Kevorkian's
deadly hobby of helping people commit suicide. Maida decided
he *would* "put up." He put up the assets of his archdiocese to
help people in crisis who might otherwise seek the services of
Dr. Death.

On the very day Kevorkian was helping his thirty-third
victim commit suicide, Cardinal Maida, the Archbishop of
Detroit, made a startling announcement: He would do "whatever it takes," he said, to provide alternatives for people considering suicide or abortion—and he pledged the funds of the
archdiocese to make good on his promise.

Cardinal Maida offered to pay the medical bills for the
terminally ill and for pregnant women willing to consider
alternatives to abortion. He then mobilized some thirty local
agencies, including hospices and counseling centers, to help
him keep his promise. "Before you pick up that telephone to
schedule [an abortion] or . . . a consultation with Jack Kevorkian, call Project Life," Maida told the people of Detroit. "There
are options and people who care."

Kevorkian and his supporters sneered at Project Life, calling
it a "publicity gimmick." But the sick and suffering of Detroit
have taken Cardinal Maida at his word. More than six hundred

people have called Project Life since the hot line was set up in July 1996. Depressed people thinking of killing themselves received counseling and medical care. Women considering abortion made adoption plans instead. People suffering terminal illnesses were referred to hospices for long-term care.

Detroit residents who did *not* call the hot line were given something as well: a lesson in true Christian compassion. Cardinal Maida wasn't just putting his dollars where his doctrine was, as the *Detroit News* put it. He was reminding a confused world what *real* compassion looks like (*Detroit News,* 10 July 1996).

Euthanasia groups claim that when people are suffering, helping them kill themselves is the only "compassionate" response. In the same way, the abortion lobby says that abortion is the "compassionate" choice when babies are unwanted.

But these definitions are cheap substitutes for the real thing. It's easy to hook up a terminally ill man to an IV full of lethal drugs. *Real* compassion is caring for him for months or even years—and, as Mother Teresa put it so well, "letting him see Jesus in the midst of his suffering."

It's easy to spend ten minutes aborting the baby of a desperate teenager. *Real* compassion is assisting that teen through nine months of pregnancy and helping her after the baby's birth, or supporting her through the process of putting the baby up for adoption.

What an impact the church could have if every evangelical congregation and diocese dared to do what Cardinal Maida is doing. It would reduce the rates of abortion and suicide more than any pro-life laws we might ever enact.

Churches, pastors, laypeople, my advice to you is: Go and do likewise. Follow the example of this determined and faithful cardinal. He's proven that he's willing to put his money where his mouth is—and at the same time powerfully demonstrate the love of Christ to people in need.

The Kissing Bandit

A Republic of Rules

A SEXUAL predator was caught stalking the streets of Lexington, North Carolina. He was described as male, about three and a half feet tall, with glasses, blond hair, and a cute grin. He was known to kiss little girls.

I'm talking about Johnathan Prevette, a first grader accused of sexual harassment for pecking a classmate on the cheek. For all the publicity the case received, few understand its deeper significance. It illustrates what happens when old-fashioned moral restraints fall away: They are replaced by what we might call a puritanism of procedures.

When Johnathan's teacher caught him kissing a classmate, she suspended him for a day and banished him from a class ice-cream party. Later, the principal handed Johnathan's mother a copy of the school's sexual-harassment policy, required by federal education law.

When the story of the pint-sized Lothario hit the airwaves, the public was appalled at the school board's draconian response. The Lexington school district was flooded with outraged calls. People sent Johnathan money and told him to buy himself some ice cream to make up for the party he missed. It was the case of the kiss heard round the world.

Of course, procedural puritanism didn't start in elementary schools. Colleges now enforce strict procedures governing the relations between the sexes. For example, at Antioch College in Ohio, date rape became such a problem that the college required students to give each other verbal consent during each stage of a sexual encounter.

In the business world, fear of sexual-harassment lawsuits has led companies to develop complex policies dictating rules covering all sorts of potential situations between men and women.

There was a time when Americans didn't need detailed guidelines to regulate behavior between the sexes. Prior to the sexual revolution, the most important factor in restraining male sexuality was simple morality. America's moral tradition granted women great dignity. Moral restraints on men spelled out what it meant to give women sexual respect.

If the moral tradition didn't impress men, other factors often did. In the 1995 film *Clueless,* a father collars a boy who's taking out his sixteen-year-old daughter and says, "If anything happens to my daughter, I've got a .45 and a shovel." Young men respected their dates because they knew they had to answer to the young lady's father.

The sexual revolution dissolved all these moral and social conventions. The prophets of this revolution thought that by throwing out traditional moral restraints, they were setting women free to enjoy their sexuality. But it didn't quite work out that way. As we now know, the only thing the sexual revolution set free was men's worst impulses.

Instead of rolling back the revolution, we've tried to regulate it with convoluted sexual-harassment codes. The results have been absurd, as Johnathan Prevette's punishment demonstrates.

How can we bring back respect for women? By bringing back a moral tradition that *teaches* respect for women. Parents need to teach their sons that women should be treated with dignity.

And then we ought to tell schools that when it comes to a couple of six-year-old children, a kiss is still just a kiss.

Killing Trees

....

Taking Environmentalism to Extremes

A SIX-YEAR-OLD girl nestled down happily in a new bed. Just before her mother turned out the lights, the little girl turned strangely sad. "I really love my new bed," she said, "but—it's *wood.* They killed trees to make my bed!"

Killed trees? It used to be that we spoke of trees being cut down—not murdered in cold blood. But if the extreme environmental movement has its way, we'll all be feeling guilty about even the responsible use of nature.

Especially our children. The story of the six-year-old girl was told by Nancy Bray Cardozo in *Audubon* magazine. There is a concerted effort today to bombard kids with a litany of dire predictions about ozone holes, vanishing rain forests, and the extinction of endangered species. They hear about it at school. They read about it in books. They even watch it on Saturday-morning cartoons. A survey by the Center for Media and Public Affairs discovered that nine out of ten Saturday-morning cartoons evoke frightening scenarios of impending environmental disaster. And guess who the cartoon villain is? It is a businessman or, even worse, a scientist, portrayed as pillaging the earth (*Audubon,* January/February 1994).

The result, writes Cardozo, is that "children feel like intruders in nature, destined to destroy their world."

Behind this radical view of nature is the age-old worldview

of pantheism: the belief that the universe as a whole is divine. As British author John Fowles writes, "We think, what a miserable little worm or what a horrible flea, but you get to the point where you realize it's all one . . . what Christians call pantheism." As a result, Fowles writes, "all species are equal."

But are humans really on the same level as the lowly worm? Nonsense. History itself refutes the claim that fleas and worms are equal with humanity. Humanity has always exercised powers that no other part of nature has. The Bible explains this uniqueness better than any other system of thought. It teaches that human beings are unique because we are indelibly stamped with the *imago Dei,* the image of God. We are commanded to be responsible stewards over his creation—not to plunder and needlessly destroy but to guard and protect.

Christians believe that the world has value because it is God's creation. As his creation it deserves to be treated with respect. In Psalm 50:10 the Lord says, "Every animal of the forest is mine," and the Old Testament warns against the mistreatment of animals.

At the same time, there is a real difference between humans and the rest of creation, which serves as the gracious provision of God for the human race. The apostle Paul tells us that God "richly provides us with everything for our enjoyment" (1 Tim. 6:17).

We need to instill in our children the biblical perspective of responsible stewardship. Only then can they resist a pantheistic ideology that denies humanity its proper place in God's creation. Help them understand that humans have the privilege of utilizing nature for legitimate purposes.

And yes, that includes wooden beds for little girls to sleep in.

Toy Terrorists

....

Saving Children from Sexism

CHILDREN'S birthday parties may never be the same.

Just imagine a little girl tearing open her gift: a Teen Talk Barbie doll. The little girl pulls the string to make Barbie talk, only to hear her snarl, "Attack!" and "Eat lead, Cobra!"

Now picture a little boy unwrapping *his* birthday present: a GI Joe with machine gun and grenades. When the boy pulls the string, he's stunned to hear a feminine voice chirping, "I love to shop with you," and "Let's plan our dream wedding."

This is exactly what happened to several children not long ago, thanks to the work of a group that calls itself the Barbie Liberation Organization. The group switched the voice boxes of hundreds of Barbie dolls and GI Joe action figures. It was a media stunt designed to warn children of the dangers of gender-based stereotyping.

I'll be the first to admit that Barbie and GI Joe are both vacuous, one-dimensional figures. But the very fact that the switched voice boxes sound wrong to our ears signals that some differences between the sexes are not due to cultural conditioning alone. It's a simple biological fact that women's voices *are* higher pitched than men's.

That rather obvious fact signals other, more important, differences—differences underlying that interdependent unit, the family. Women do bear and care for young children. Men do work hard to support their wives and children. This interdependence is not just cultural, it is built into the fabric of our biology and our character.

Radical feminists and other gender benders don't want to acknowledge the differences that make men and women interdependent. Their goal is radical autonomy—and that means each individual must be regarded as completely self-sufficient. Differences are denied or played down.

What the radicals fail to see is that they are promoting blatant disrespect for the distinctive contributions of each gender—with disastrous consequences. Disrespect for women's unique child-bearing functions has undercut their motivation to embrace motherhood across our culture. Abortion is partly a rejection of bearing children. Use of day care is partly a rejection of *raising* children.

On the other side, downplaying the male contribution has prompted a massive exodus of men from family life. In America today, men's lack of commitment to the family is a major social crisis. Because of divorce and desertion, between 1960 and 1980 there was a striking 43 percent reduction in the amount of time men spend in a family environment where young children are present.

David Blankenhorn, of the Institute of American Values, says, "Never before in our nation's history have so many children grown up without a father's presence and provision." And studies show that children without fathers are more likely to grow up in poverty, to have school problems, to commit crimes (*New York Times,* 20 June 1992).

So far be it from me to recommend Barbie dolls or GI Joes, with their exaggerated femininity and masculinity. But I do believe they're a lot less harmful to children than radical egalitarianism.

There's a *reason* Barbie sounds funny talking like GI Joe. And it reminds us of the rich interdependence God created as the basis for family life.

A "Liberal" Education

....

Darwinism and Our Kids

A NEWSPAPER editor once boasted that he had spearheaded efforts to remove the Ten Commandments from the walls of local classrooms. The editor was proud of his success in promoting a more "liberal" education.

Yet moments later, he was bemoaning crime in the schools—the epidemic of cheating and fighting. "Perhaps," I suggested, "you ought to put a sign on the wall—telling kids not to steal." The editor stared at me and then turned away without uttering a word. For, of course, he had worked hard to *remove* just such a sign—one that said, "You shall not steal"—along with the rest of the Ten Commandments.

What this editor failed to see is that the liberal approach to moral education is closely linked to increasing crime and disorder. As Phillip E. Johnson explains in *Reason in the Balance,* liberal education is based on the philosophy of naturalism: that there is no God. The implication is that morality is based not on God's commandments but on individual choices. Every person's goals in life are intrinsically as good as every other person's, and no one has a right to "impose" morality on anyone else—not even on his or her own children.

What does this philosophy mean for education? It means schools should *not* train children in particular character traits, like courage or honesty. Instead, schools should maximize a child's ability to choose for himself, after critical consideration of competing alternatives.

This explains modern sex education, for example, where students are not taught to restrain their sexual impulses until marriage. Instead they're taught a wide range of sexual practices, with the message that "Only you can judge what's right for you."

Yet, ironically, if you walk down the hall to the science classroom, you'll find educators employing exactly the *opposite* method. There they have no qualms about teaching that there is one and only one right way to think—namely, to embrace Darwinism. Evolution is not open to question, nor are students invited to judge for themselves whether it is true or not.

Why such a sharp discrepancy in teaching styles?

The answer is that science is taught in absolute terms because it is regarded as giving the truth about what "really exists." And what "really exists" is nature alone; there is no God. Naturalism in science then becomes the basis for liberalism in morality: If there is no God, then kids should be taught to make up their own minds about moral questions.

Is it any real surprise that some of them make up their minds to cheat and fight? No wonder schools are becoming battlegrounds. You and I need to help people see the underlying philosophies at war in public education. The Darwinism taught in science courses is regarded as the factual basis for the philosophy of naturalism. And naturalism in turn means that morality is taught as nothing more than individual choice.

When God is kicked out of science courses, eventually his commandments will be taken off classroom walls—and out of students' hearts.

Crimes? What Crimes?

···

The Grand "Sez Who?"

DUSAN TADIC, a café owner and part-time policeman, sat uneasily in a blue chair draped with a United Nations emblem. He was charged with the murder, rape, and torture of Bosnian Muslims as part of a campaign of "ethnic cleansing." He has the dubious distinction of being the first person to be tried for war crimes since the end of World War II.

Tadic isn't the only one who should be uneasy. His case raises an awkward question for the modern world: Is law—especially international law—possible in a world that rejects the idea of absolute truth?

In a delightful bit of irony, the United Nations tribunal that tried Tadic and his comrades was convened on the fiftieth anniversary of the Nuremberg trials—the same trials that made the term *crimes against humanity* part of our lexicon. Nuremberg set an important legal and moral precedent: that there exists a standard of decency legally binding on all nations, irrespective of culture, creed, or history. By charging Nazi leaders with "crimes against humanity," the United States implicitly rejected notions of moral and cultural relativism. Instead, we declared a universal moral standard—one that supersedes political boundaries and national sovereignty.

Today, fifty years later, do we still accept the idea of a universal standard, binding on all nations? What gives the international community the moral authority to sit in judgment on Dusan Tadic—or anyone else?

The answer is that there no longer *is* any moral authority because the leading nations of the world have rejected the basis for that authority—ultimately, the law of God. Without a basis in divine law, human law is only a matter of opinion, imposed by force.

The late legal scholar Arthur Leff put it this way: Without the ultimate warrant of divine revelation, all claims to authority are vulnerable to the "grand 'sez who?'" Genocide is wrong, we say. To which Tadic and his ilk respond, "Sez who?" Massacring civilians is wrong, we say. Sez who? If it's merely my opinion versus yours, claims to international justice are really nothing more than power plays.

This is a vivid illustration of what Berkeley law professor Phillip Johnson, in *Reason in the Balance,* calls the "modernist impasse." The modern mind demands freedom from moral restraints for *individuals* but then demands a strong moral code for *society* in order to justify punishing barbarians like Tadic.

That conjuring trick just won't work. You can't deny a transcendent moral order when it's inconvenient and then try to pull one out of a hat when you *do* need one.

The modernist impasse provides Christians with a wonderfully effective apologetic. When people are horrified by the bloodbath in Bosnia, we can explain that they are implicitly acknowledging an objective moral standard that underlies all human laws. By condemning the Serbs, they are implying the existence of a standard that judges our own lives as well.

The need for just laws challenges each individual to search his *own* heart. We must acknowledge that our own moral failings are just as much a violation of a transcendent order as the failings of the barbarians we abhor—and that we are just as much in need of divine mercy and forgiveness.

Two

WHOSE LAW IS IT, ANYWAY?

Tough Love with a Vengeance

....

Sister Connie's Boot Camp

CYNTHIA didn't know it, but she had just confronted the woman reporters nicknamed "the nun from hell."

"Do you want to take me on? Come on, I'm ready," invited Sister Connie, a tough sixty-one-year-old nun with a black patch over one eye.

Cynthia, a prostitute and drug addict, took a second look at her steely faced opponent and realized she had met her match. She reluctantly agreed to obey the strict rules of the homeless shelter Sister Connie runs.

Sister Connie opened St. Martin dePorres House of Hope for Women twelve years ago in the heart of Chicago's south side. Her nearest neighbors are gang members and drug dealers. It's a tough neighborhood.

But Sister Connie, who has dodged bullets and taken knife wounds in the course of her work, is even tougher. And her shelter is, as the nun bluntly puts it, not a place where homeless women are coddled.

The residents must accept a strict regimen that includes rising at 6:30 A.M. Mothers must clean both their children and their rooms before breakfast. Classes in parenting and life skills are mandatory. So are daily twelve-step programs for substance abusers. Women who don't have a high school diploma must work toward one. And if Sister Connie suspects residents are hiding drugs, she's not above calling in a SWAT team to bust her own shelter.

It's tough love with a vengeance—and it works. Only 4 percent of the women who pass through Sister Connie's boot camp ever end up back in the shelter system. By comparison, nearly 40 percent of those who pass through Chicago's shelter system as a whole return seeking help.

Sister Connie's secret is simple: She attaches moral demands to the assistance she gives.

The most common cause of homelessness, Sister Connie believes, is a lack of personal responsibility. Thanks to public assistance, her clients almost always receive enough money to pay their rent; they simply refuse to. Instead, Sister Connie says, that money often goes up in smoke in the form of crack cocaine.

By contrast, Sister Connie's approach meets the biblical definition of compassion: to suffer *along with* the homeless. It means getting personally involved with people who truly need help. That's something no government check can do.

If assistance is to make a long-term difference, it has to come with moral strings attached. It involves requiring people to learn how to behave responsibly. That's what Sister Connie demands of everyone who walks through her door. And it works: Today Cynthia works as a restaurant cook, rents her own apartment, and supports her own children. She's made it, and her success at turning her life around is a shining example of why private charity works where government handouts fail.

We aren't all as tough as the so-called nun from hell, who chews up drug addicts for lunch and spits them out with job skills and dignity. But you and I ought to reach out with the love of Christ and get personally involved in tough-love programs in our own neighborhoods. Programs that offer *real* solutions to poverty.

Programs with moral strings attached.

Welfare Entrepreneur

....

Biblical Welfare Reform

GOVERNMENT records show that a Brooklyn woman is the proud mother of seventy-three children, giving birth under fifteen different names, including Shirley, Jane, Patricia, and Celeste.

This woman is definitely a candidate for the *Guinness Book of World Records*—not for the number of children she has borne but for breaking all records for welfare fraud. It turns out that she forged baptismal certificates and succeeded in cheating welfare out of nearly $450,000.

New York City officials are still trying to determine her real name and the true number of her children.

It seems obvious that anyone with enough ingenuity to finagle the government out of $450,000 is competent to hold a job—and shouldn't be on the dole in the first place. In fact, welfare reform primarily targets people who are *capable* of working but refuse to.

And their numbers are growing. Lawrence Mead of the Kennedy School of Government says that until the '60s, most poor people worked. Poverty was due largely to *external* factors, such as low wages, racial discrimination, and lack of opportunity.

But today labor unions have pushed wages and benefits up; laws have outlawed racial discrimination. In surveys, only a fraction of the poor say they lack job opportunities.

Instead, most poverty today seems rooted in the *internal* attitudes and behavior of the poor themselves. Chronic poverty tends to accompany dysfunctional life choices that undercut the motivation to work, such as dropping out of school, teen pregnancy, drug abuse, and crime.

To deal with this new kind of poverty, we need a new

approach to welfare. Or rather, an *old* approach. Nineteenth-century America suffered many of the same social pathologies plaguing today's inner cities, but back then the Christian church organized most charity work. Volunteers nursed the sick, housed abandoned women, helped the jobless find work.

Church-based charity was nothing like the free handouts of the modern welfare system. Instead, all able-bodied adults were required to do some form of work. Homeless men chopped wood in return for dinner. Women sewed or cooked in return for a safe place to sleep. Teen mothers were taught to care for their babies and find jobs. Drug and alcohol addicts were expected to get clean and sober up.

This biblical approach to charity fostered responsible behavior. Instead of turning the poor into passive recipients, it granted them the dignity of doing worthwhile work.

In 2 Thessalonians Paul writes that those who refuse to work should not receive free handouts. Paul wasn't being hard-hearted; he simply knew that charity without obligation is demeaning. No matter how down-and-out people are, they're happier if they are making a worthwhile contribution.

Politicians like to grandstand about reforming welfare, but you and I need to demand reform based on biblical principles of charity. We should not treat the poor as passive and incompetent but as talented people made in the image of God, capable of making an important contribution.

Let's face it: If those talents are not channeled into constructive work, they're likely to be used for destructive, and even illegal, schemes.

Like the Brooklyn woman who found ways to invent seventy-three children.

Brother, Can You Spare a Billion?

....

Ending Corporate Welfare

WHEN you hear the term *welfare recipient,* you probably picture someone who lives in public housing and buys groceries with food stamps.

I'll bet you never thought of Ronald McDonald and the Pillsbury Dough Boy as welfare recipients, but the fact is, both the McDonald's Corporation and the Pillsbury company are among hundreds of companies that receive what is known as corporate welfare. It's a form of "public assistance" that costs taxpayers billions of dollars a year.

A study by the Cato Institute reveals just how massive corporate welfare has become. For example, the McDonald's Corporation received half a million dollars this year to promote chicken nuggets in foreign markets. Pillsbury received $3 million to advertise its muffins and pies overseas. The Du Pont Company received $1.6 million to develop something called a "thin film fabrication" project. And automotive giants GM, Ford, and Chrysler will guzzle up $246 million to develop new cars (*American Enterprise,* July/August 1995).

What are rich corporate giants doing on the dole in the first place? Companies like McDonald's and Pillsbury receive funding under the guise of boosting American products overseas. Of course, what they're *really* doing is boosting their *own* products. Government money helps other companies develop technologies they can't—or won't—pay for on their own.

For example, Armstrong World Industries received $1.8 million from the U.S. Commerce Department to develop a new type of pipe installation used in plumbing and heating systems.

Companies like Xerox, IBM, Kodak, and GE also received millions of dollars for research.

But if these research projects have merit, why can't the companies attract *private* investors—or put their *own* money on the line? And if private investors don't think the ideas are worth the financial risk, why should *taxpayers* be asked to gamble *their* money?

The fact that companies are willing to risk taxpayer money—but not their own—points up the glaring problem with welfare: It tends to encourage and reward imprudent behavior. That's as true for billion-dollar companies that throw taxpayer money into risky projects as it is for individuals who spend their government checks on drugs and alcohol.

Worst of all, in order to give handouts to those "needy" corporate giants, the government must take money from families, who sacrifice their *own* projects to pay for them. Projects like funding a child's college education, adding a room onto their home, or even taking the kids to McDonald's for Happy Meals.

Welfare reform has become one of the hottest debates of the day, and I for one am glad to see our lawmakers reconsider wasteful programs that do more harm than good. But we can't just get tough on individuals who have come to depend on government largesse. We have to come down just as hard on corporate giants who never saw a handout they didn't like.

You and I need to tell our representatives that it's time to end corporate welfare—that we ought to get Ronald McDonald and the Pillsbury Dough Boy off the dole for good.

A Twisted Tale

Blocking the Way out of Poverty

YOU'D hardly expect to find an inner-city teenager running her own business. But that's exactly what Monique Landers was doing.

That is, until the government shut her down.

Monique received training through the National Foundation for Teaching Entrepreneurship, an organization that helps inner-city teenagers start businesses. Teens who might otherwise be dealing drugs or having welfare babies are instead learning how to develop a business plan and market a product.

The foundation has taught ghetto teens to become desktop publishers, baby-sitters, and stereo component installers. Monique, who lives in Wichita, started a business washing and braiding hair. With family members and friends as customers, she founded an enterprise called "A Touch of Class" and was soon earning one hundred dollars per month in profits. She was even honored by the foundation as one of the five Outstanding High School Entrepreneurs.

Considering the odds against kids like Monique, you'd think everyone would be thrilled about her achievement. But the *government* wasn't happy at all. Columnist Walter Williams reports that the Kansas State Cosmetology Board ordered Monique to close shop.

The board warned that it is illegal for her to touch anyone's hair for a profit without a license—and that if she did not stop immediately, she would be subject to "a fine or imprisonment in the county jail or both" (*New Pittsburgh Courier,* 2 December 1993).

The trouble is that getting a license is quite a barrier for an impoverished teenager. It requires one year of cosmetology school, costing anywhere from $2,500 to $5,500. That's if you can *find* a school that teaches cornrow braiding, which is rare. Even then, the minimum age for a license is seventeen. Monique is fifteen.

Why do licensing laws exist in the first place? Licensing makes sense for high-skill professionals like doctors or dentists, when we put our life and health in someone else's hands. But low-skill jobs like braiding don't involve any health hazards. In these jobs, the real effect of licensing is to shut the poor out of economic competition.

In Monique's case, more than 100 cosmetologists went howling to the cosmetology board to complain. Were they really concerned about the *safety* of their customers—or about *losing* customers? The answer is obvious.

In *Prosperity and Poverty,* Calvin Beisner argues that licensing for low-skill jobs effectively blocks the poor from climbing onto the bottom rungs of the economic ladder. When that happens, Beisner argues, licensing laws actually violate the eighth commandment against stealing. You see, taken in a broad sense, stealing means anything that prevents us from making legitimate use of our property—not just physical property but also our human capital: skills, time, and motivation.

Preventing people from using their human capital to earn a living is unjust. It's morally equivalent to taking money out of their pockets *after* they've earned it.

Christians who want to help the poor should think beyond giving to charity. We should also work against unnecessary laws that block the poor from climbing out of poverty.

And maybe we should think about creating our *own* programs for turning poor teens into productive entrepreneurs.

Human Cages

....

Death of the Great Society

THE NEWS photos were dramatic: They showed four high-rise buildings being blown sky-high—the destruction of a public-housing project in Newark, New Jersey. One photo, taken just as the explosives were ignited, showed the buildings tilting precariously, dust billowing on all sides. In the second photo, the buildings had been reduced to massive piles of rubble.

This demolition project is not just another urban renewal program. It has a much deeper significance. It echoes the death sentence of the Great Society. As the mayor of Newark put it, the explosion represents "the end of an American dream that failed."

The Great Society grew from the dream that government social planning could eliminate poverty and solve our country's social problems. Modern social philosophers were inspired by the scientific optimism of the Enlightenment. They dreamed of finding what they called a "social physics," a set of laws governing the way individuals interact, just as the laws of physics govern the way atoms interact. They hoped to use rational scientific planning to map out the ideal society.

In the '50s and '60s, those dreams took flesh as they were backed by government funding. Public housing was one of the brainstorms of that era. Great, hulking structures were erected, where the style itself reflected the modernist vision: The buildings were scientifically functional, constructed of steel and concrete. Their lines were stark and impersonal, their only goal utilitarian: to warehouse as many people as efficiently as possible.

The result was not homes but human cages.

But humans are not animals and they cannot live in cages.

25

Soon the walls were defaced by graffiti, the elevators stopped working, and criminals stalked the hallways. With no safe places to play, children huddled in gangs.

The housing projects designed with such scientific care turned into seedbeds of crime and misery. Residents hated them. When the Newark housing project was blown up, former residents watched and cheered.

This was not the first time a housing project was blown up. The trend started with the Pruitt-Igoe project in St. Louis in 1972. That explosion sent social planners into shock. Historian Charles Jencks even considers the destruction of the St. Louis project the end of the modern era.

In other words, what we're seeing is not just the demolition of a few old buildings. We're seeing the collapse of modernist social philosophy—the idea that society can be redesigned according to an abstract "social physics."

Today most people agree that the Great Society has failed. Several states are experimenting with new approaches to poverty and welfare. This is a marvelous opportunity for Christians to promote a truly biblical social philosophy—one that treats people not as social atoms to be engineered but as image bearers of God, with dignity and responsibility.

Our most fundamental beliefs are reflected even in the buildings we design. The secular world's fascination with modern science led ultimately to cages. You and I need to argue for a biblical understanding of humans made in God's image and develop humane social policies.

Otherwise, even our best schemes may end up once more as piles of rubble.

Reweaving Loose Threads

....

Can We Mend Our Social Disorder?

IN THE shadow of the Capitol in Washington are a pair of monuments few tourists ever visit. But they ought to—because within their walls are clues to how we can reweave our badly frayed social fabric.

Both of these monuments are homeless shelters. One is a symbol of failure. The other is a beacon of hope.

The monument to failure is largely run with government funds, and the rules are very loose: No drug testing, except in extreme cases; residents aren't held responsible for their behavior, and neither is the staff. A few years ago, a *60 Minutes* exposé revealed staff members dealing in crack and selling donated food.

Just a few blocks away is another shelter, the Gospel Mission, run by the Reverend John Woods. Here there are strict rules and random drug tests. Along with the "three hots and a cot," the Gospel Mission offers homeless men "services" that are even more important: unconditional love and spiritual renewal.

One drug addict came to the Gospel Mission after failing in several government-run programs. "Government programs don't place anything within you," he told the *Washington Post*. "I needed a spiritual lifting . . . and Reverend Woods [was] like God walking into [my] life" (*Washington Post*, 14 April 1996).

Which shelter is more successful in rehabilitating men? The Gospel Mission enjoys a twelve-month drug rehabilitation rate of about 66 percent. By contrast, government-run treatment programs are considered successful if they have a success rate of about 10 percent.

The difference is dramatic, and it's evidence that when it

comes to solving our worst social scourges, even the best-funded bureaucracies fail. But private, faith-based ministries that not only feed the body but also nourish the soul—these are the programs that truly change lives.

The late Christian law professor Jacques Ellul warned against believing that government is the instrument to create an ideal society. Social engineering is destructive because it requires the state to take over functions from other institutions—and that weakens those institutions.

As Senator Dan Coats explains, under liberal policies, "fathers were replaced by welfare checks, private charities were displaced by government spending, [and] religious volunteers were dismissed as 'amateurs'" (*Policy Review*, January/February 1996).

Today, most Americans agree that these skewed policies must be reformed, but state action alone can't rebuild the rubble. Revival must come from cultural institutions themselves.

Boston University economist Glenn Loury gives a wonderful illustration of what I mean. Loury writes that welfare policies, with their perverse incentives, have pulled on the loose threads of the social fabric, causing it to unravel. Pushing back on those threads won't reweave the fabric. It can be mended only by the character-forming institutions of civil society: family, church, and voluntary associations.

As Loury puts it, no incentive scheme to inspire responsible parenting works as well as believing that parents are God's stewards for their children. No deterrent to teen pregnancy is as strong as believing that "your body is the temple of the Holy Spirit." And no affirmative-action law unites the races as effectively as the conviction that "God is no respecter of persons" (*Washington Post*, 17 December 1995).

Real change comes from the heart—and habits of the heart are most susceptible to being influenced by those closest to us.

Politically Incorrect?

....

When Government Decides

A SIMPLE newspaper ad cost a woman thousands of dollars in legal bills and fines. No, the ad was not lewd or indecent. Beverly Schnell simply wanted to find a tenant to help remodel her 100-year-old home in return for lower rent. As a Christian, she hoped to offer the job to a fellow believer. So she advertised for a "mature Christian handyman."

State officials were aghast. A clear case of sexual and religious discrimination, they decreed—and imposed fines and fees totaling eight thousand dollars.

In today's multicultural world, advertising for a "handyman" is a gender crime. Trying to help a fellow believer is a religious crime.

Across America, government coercion is steadily ratcheting up. Why is this happening? In *Postmodern Times,* Gene Edward Veith says it stems from postmodernism, a philosophy that detects oppression everywhere—especially of blacks, women, Native Americans, and other minorities.

In our relativistic world, the only moral imperative left is to protect these so-called oppressed groups.

Postmodernism has adopted the social philosophy of cultural determinism—teaching that everyone is a product of his or her culture. The individual is merely a web of social forces. Being a woman or an African American or whatever has become more important than being an individual human being.

This represents a stunning turnaround in Western thought. For centuries the Western mind—inspired by the biblical teaching of individual salvation—has nurtured a heritage of individual rights and dignity. But today that heritage is being cast off. Postmodernism puts a higher premium on collective group identity.

All blacks are expected to believe the same things—otherwise they are "white inside." All women are supposed to support feminist ideology—otherwise they are trapped in "false consciousness."

And by outlawing an ad for a Christian handyman, the government itself is now enforcing political correctness.

The *Wall Street Journal* tells a chilling story about a young Capitol Hill staffer who underwent his periodic five-year clearance review. Later he discovered that during the review the FBI grilled his neighbors to find out whether he had ever told a racist joke—whether he ever said anything indicating prejudice.

The FBI officials weren't asking about *public* speech, they were asking about his *private conversations.* In other words, today your job in government may depend on whether anyone anywhere feels you have demeaned their race, gender, or ethnic background.

This could easily become open season for misunderstanding and even blackballing. Just consider how widely people differ in what they consider demeaning or offensive. From time immemorial women have told jokes about men—and men have reciprocated in kind. But now the *government* will decide which jokes reveal "incorrect" opinions.

You and I need to be aware that postmodernism is not just one more "ism" on the intellectual horizon. It has become a powerful force shaping our culture—and even our legal rights. Reducing individuals to their social group is a direct attack on the biblical teaching of individual dignity—and an insidious move toward tyranny.

Your Land or Your Liberty

Why Property Rights?

IMAGINE you're an entrepreneur planning to build your own business—but first the government demands that you to hand over 10 percent of your land. That's exactly what happened to Florence Dolan in Tigard, Oregon.

The story illustrates just how important property rights are to America's entire system of freedoms.

Dolan owns a thriving plumbing and electric supply business, and she applied for permits to expand the buildings. City officials agreed to give her the permits—under one condition: Dolan would have to turn over a tenth of her property to the city for storm drainage and a bike path.

Now Florence Dolan is as civic-minded as anyone else, but this forced "tithe" to the city government struck her as out of line. She took the case to court, and it went all the way to the United States Supreme Court before she finally won her point.

The irony is that the case should not have been necessary in the first place. After all, the Fifth Amendment protects citizens against government seizure of private property. The amendment includes what is called a "takings clause," which says that whenever the government takes away private property for public use, it must compensate the owner at a fair market value.

Beginning with New Deal legislation in the 1930s, however, government regulatory agencies began to disregard the takings clause. The Supreme Court refused to intervene, declaring that property rights are less important than other constitutional rights such as freedom of speech and of the press.

But the Court could not have been more wrong. The truth is that property rights actually *undergird* other crucial rights. To understand why, we need only look at places like the former Soviet Union.

The late Soviet dictator Leonid Brezhnev ordered citizens to register with the state whenever they purchased typewriters, copying machines, and even carbon paper. Why? So that authorities could trace the production of underground literature, such as newspapers and Bibles. Regulation of private property was one tool the Soviet government used to track Christians and other dissidents and throw them behind bars.

In other words, by depriving citizens of the right to private property, the Soviets were able to deprive them of freedom of religion, freedom of speech, and freedom of the press.

Back in 1775, the Virginia patriot Arthur Lee saw this connection clearly. He wrote: "The right of property is the guardian of every other right, and to deprive a people of this is in fact to deprive them of their liberty."

Scriptural teaching supports the importance of private property when it is acquired and used according to God's law. In fact, two of the Ten Commandments specifically protect the right to property: You shall not steal, and you shall not covet anything that belongs to your neighbor.

So we ought to fight vigorously when the government tries to take away property without compensation, because the right to private property is not just about protecting your home or business.

As Arthur Lee said two hundred years ago, it's also the "guardian" of all other freedoms.

Is Capitalism Christian?

The Revolutionary Michael Novak

THE 1996 Templeton Prize for Progress in Religion was awarded to my friend Michael Novak. And the "progress" he inspired spread all around the globe.

It was Novak's vision of a free society that inspired Czechoslovakian dissidents to throw off communism. His writings were studied by leaders of the Solidarity movement in Poland. They're even echoed in the writings of the pope.

What is this remarkable message? Simply that the free market of capitalism is morally superior to the controlled economy of socialism. A free market is based on a biblical vision of human nature, Novak teaches. It respects individual initiative and unleashes human creativity, by which we reflect the character of the Creator himself.

In other words, Novak has reconnected markets and morals.

This is a revolutionary accomplishment. Since the last century, it was communism that claimed to have a moral vision for a just society. Even though actual Communist regimes are always tyrannical, the moral vision of communism has continued to attract idealists around the world.

Capitalism, on the other hand, has been regarded as a purely pragmatic system. Even Adam Smith, capitalism's founder, did not present it as a means of creating a just society. Instead, he presented it as a practical means of controlling self-interest—of providing a socially useful channel for an antisocial impulse. Hardly a stirring vision to engage the hearts of social reformers.

But Novak has articulated the moral basis of capitalism. A free market expresses a high view of human dignity, Novak argues, because it requires individuals to be creative and responsible. It does not set apparatchiks over everyone telling them what to do.

A free market requires self-sacrifice and delayed gratification, as entrepreneurs invest their time and money into enterprises whose rewards are not immediate.

A free market requires sensitivity and courtesy to others because if you don't please the customer, you're out of business.

Most of all, free markets are an effective tool for helping the poor. Historically, free economies have the best record of empowering the poor to climb out of poverty.

These things may seem obvious to you and me—especially since communism lost the Cold War—yet intellectual leaders in academia, journalism, and the arts are still heavily left-leaning. To be sure, they've been forced to concede that capitalism works better on a *practical* level—that it produces more consumer goods—yet they still maintain that socialism is superior in its *moral* vision for a just society.

This is why we need to continually defend the moral basis of free-market capitalism. As Novak so brilliantly demonstrates, capitalism rests inescapably on the high view of human creativity and responsibility expressed in the Bible.

You can acquaint yourself with Novak's seminal work by reading his book *The Spirit of Democratic Capitalism*. The world desperately needs to know that in a just society, markets depend on morality.

Blame the Babies

....

How Governments Cause Poverty

Do babies cause poverty? You'd certainly think so, listening to some politicians. "Population growth often contributes to . . . poverty and economic disparity," Al Gore has said. The vice president even blamed "population pressures" for the tragedy in Rwanda (*Vital Speeches,* 1 October 1994).

Ironically, Rwanda proves exactly the *opposite.* It's true that it was the most densely populated country in Africa before the current civil war erupted. But Rwanda was just "about to reap a copious harvest" when the killing started. The war drove the farmers off the land, and the crops were left to wither in the fields (*U.S. News & World Report,* 12 September 1994).

So the sick and starving refugees we see in news photos are not the outcome of overpopulation; they're the result of bitter tribal hatred between the Hutu and the Tutsi peoples, erupting in a battle for political power.

In fact, the top causes of poverty worldwide have more to do with politics than with sheer numbers of people. Robert Cassan, an Oxford economist, points out that war and wrong-headed government policies far outweigh population as causes of poverty (*Newsweek,* 12 September 1994).

If *bad* government policy can create poverty, then *good* government policy ought to be able to help create wealth and raise the standard of living. The Bible teaches that a good government exercises two primary functions: It restrains evil, and it is a "minister . . . for good" (Rom. 13:4, KJV).

How do these two functions apply in the economic sphere?

Restraining evil includes such things as enforcing property rights, clamping down on corruption, and enforcing laws on contracts. No one can carry on business transactions in a society where people cannot trust one another—where graft and corruption are the rule and contracts are made only to be broken.

In short, government's role in restraining evil is to enforce the law—to hold people accountable to their obligations. The government acts as a referee, making sure there's a level playing field and that people follow the rules.

Government's role in ministering for good means contributing to the general economic welfare, such as keeping taxes low and maintaining a sound currency. For example, if you're a Third World craftsman who makes blankets to sell but the government takes half your profit in taxes, it doesn't make sense to weave very many blankets.

Government can also help the economy thrive by keeping its own house in order and practicing fiscal responsibility. But we need to go beyond criticizing the wrong answers: We also need to educate ourselves and our neighbors on the right way for governments to alleviate poverty.

The best way wealthy nations like America can assist developing nations is by encouraging sound ideas for creating wealth. Ideas that destroy poverty, not babies.

Patent Wars

Is Life a Commodity?

IT WAS a race to the patent office.

In 1993, two research teams, working independently, both announced the discovery of a gene that causes colon cancer. A company called Human Genome Sciences isolated a mutant gene that appears only in families suffering an inherited form of colon cancer.

Immediately, the company applied for a patent on the gene. But at the same time a competing patent application was filed jointly by three universities, whose scientists had worked together to discover the same gene. It was a patent war—with the winner reaping royalties any time the gene is used for research or therapy.

But wait a minute. Doesn't it strike us as odd that a part of the human body can be patented in the first place?

Patents are generally granted for mechanical or chemical inventions. They're a way of rewarding people for the time and expense of inventing a new product—a toaster, computer, or cleaning product. But today the United States Patent and Trademark Office gives patents for plants and animals genetically engineered in the laboratory—as if they, too, were mechanical inventions.

How did patents come to be applied to living things? It all began in 1972, when an Indian microbiologist named Chakrabarty took several bacteria that eat oil and combined their genes to create a superbacterium, designed to devour oil slicks produced by tanker spills. Chakrabarty applied for a patent on his oil-eating bacterium, but the patent office said no. The case went to court, and the judge issued a ruling that is nothing short of astonishing. "The fact that micro-organisms are alive," the judge declared, is "without legal significance."

Think for a moment what that ruling means: It denies any legal significance to the difference between a living organism and a machine.

That conclusion was so repugnant to many people that the case went all the way to the Supreme Court. But in 1980 the justices upheld the lower court's ruling. "The relevant distinction," they said, is "not between living and inanimate things" but whether living products can be seen as "human-made inventions."

With a stroke of the pen, the justices redefined living things as mechanical inventions.

This represents a momentous change in American legal philosophy. Living things have been reduced to the legal status of a car or lawn mower.

And it didn't stop with plants and animals. Today human tissue is often patented as well, when used in laboratory research. And several patents are pending on human genes—the latest being the patent pending over the gene that causes colon cancer.

The fact that life has been legally redefined as a commodity ought to disturb us deeply. As Christians we believe that God created life and that it demands our profound respect. But, as Senator Mark Hatfield puts it, current patent laws treat "life as mere chemical manufacture and invention, with no greater value or meaning than industrial products" (*Congressional Record*, 28 April 1992).

You and I need to educate ourselves on the moral and legal issues surrounding genetic technology. Genetic engineering has great potential for healing illness and saving lives. But it could also do irreparable damage . . . if it destroys respect for the life God created.

Fevered Fantasies

Pollution and Moral Will

THE POPULATION question seems to bring out the doomsayers. At the 1994 United Nations' International Conference on Population and Development, held in Cairo, Norway's prime minister urged all countries to cut their population rates "for the sake of the earth." A dark image loomed of a world devastated by too many people.

But is overpopulation devastating the earth? Are people the problem?

The answer is clearly no. The densely populated countries of the world are not the ones destroying the environment. In fact, a dense population often brings together the knowledge needed to develop environmentally safe technologies.

Take Sudan. It is one of the most sparsely populated countries in the world. Yet much of Sudan's farmland has been destroyed. Why? Because farmers there don't know how to control erosion. When the land becomes unfarmable, the farmers simply move on and leave the devastated land behind.

But in a more densely populated country like the United States, farmers don't have the option of just moving on. As a result, they're spurred on to discover new ways to take better care of the land. For example, a new method of plowing has been developed that cuts only a narrow slit in the ground to plant the seeds, drastically reducing erosion. In another innovation, the use of satellite maps has enabled what is called "precision farming," allowing fertilizers to be applied much more accurately and reducing the rate of pollution from fertilizer runoff.

The point is that a larger population can actually bring together more human capital to *solve* the problems we all face—to develop the technologies needed to take good care of the environment.

Of course, people do not always come up with environmentally safe technologies, which is why our air and rivers are often polluted. But that's not a matter of population per se; it's a matter of moral vision. Every nation must make fundamentally ethical decisions about what kind of technology to develop: We must all be willing to say no to harmful technologies and to invest the time and creativity to develop technologies that truly nurture the creation.

If that word *nurture* sounds familiar, it should. In Genesis, human beings are commanded to nurture, or care for, the world God created. Christians ought to be at the forefront in strengthening our country's moral will to create technologies that enhance instead of destroy the natural world. We need to keep our eyes firmly on the real issue: the *moral* dimension to development.

Liberating Haiti

....

Without Firing a Shot

WHEN the United States threatened to invade Haiti, the military-backed provisional president of Haiti gave a surprising response: He called on the gods of voodoo to protect his tiny country. In a televised speech, the president invoked Agawou, the voodoo god of strength.

You and I probably hear about voodoo more often in jokes than in serious political discourse, but in Haitian culture, it is a powerful force. According to Lawrence Harrison, formerly with the U.S. Agency for International Development, many of Haiti's most intractable social and economic problems stem from its commitment to the voodoo religion.

The key to a nation's well-being, Harrison says, is not primarily geography, natural resources, or ethnic background. Instead, the key is culture, and at the heart of culture is religion. Religion shapes a people's most fundamental outlook on life— their values and attitudes.

Though Haiti is nominally Catholic, even the educated classes are still strongly influenced by voodoo, a concoction of traditional African folk religions brought to the island in the seventeenth century by slaves. Voodoo is a form of animism: It attributes events to hundreds of spirits who reside in the trees, the fields, the villages. The religion centers on magical ceremonies performed by voodoo priests, aimed at placating or influencing the spirits.

But religion is not defined by its rituals alone; every religion also leads to an overall worldview. According to Wallace Hodges, a Baptist missionary working in Haiti, voodoo leads to a view of the world that contrasts sharply with Christianity.

For example, Christianity holds every individual morally accountable for his actions. But Voodoo attributes good and evil to the spirits—a belief that dissolves any sense of personal accountability. According to Hodges, when a worker steals a jug of milk from the missionary hospital, he has no sense of shame or guilt. Instead, the thief's attitude is, if the spirits gave me the opportunity, they must have *meant* for me to steal the jug.

This dissipation of moral responsibility makes Haitian society vulnerable to mistrust and exploitation—from the corrupt bureaucrat to the ruthless businessman.

So it's true that Haiti is in need of liberation today, but not by a military invasion. Instead, Haitians need to be set free from a false religion that encourages corruption while *dis*couraging active responsibility for one's life.

The lesson for you and me is to look behind the headlines, which often treat only the political and economic dimensions of current events. Scripture teaches that the most fundamental dimension to human life is religious.

When you read news accounts about Haiti, take a moment to pray for that destitute country. Pray that God will bring the light of the gospel to dispel its spiritual darkness.

Certainly, a nation's well-being is affected by things like geography and natural resources. But what determines whether a nation can make *use* of those resources is its religion—which in turn shapes its values and worldview. Proverbs 23:7 says, "As [a man] thinketh in his heart, so is he" (KJV). And as a *nation* believes in its heart, so is its destiny.

Send Those Riverboats Back

Gambling and Its Discontents

STAND on the banks of the Mississippi River these days, and you're likely to see a quaint stern-wheeler riverboat chugging its way up from New Orleans—bringing slot machines and blackjack tables to places like Iowa and Indiana.

Yes, gambling has spread beyond Las Vegas and is spilling across America's heartland.

Nearly every state in the Union now has some form of legalized gambling. Lawmakers welcome casinos as a shortcut to increased tax revenues, new jobs, and urban renewal.

This is an astonishing turnabout. Just twenty-five years ago, gambling was considered a vice, pursued in seedy back rooms and run by the Mafia. Today the casino business has been taken over by major corporations like Hilton and Holiday Inn. It's managed by executives in pinstripes and accountants with MBAs. Gambling halls are being redesigned as colorful theme parks modeled on Walt Disney World.

Today gambling is advertised as good fun for the whole family. Just think, kids can enjoy rides and amusements while Dad and Mom hit it big . . . or, more likely, gamble away the family savings.

That's the side no one wants to think about, of course. But

the truth is that gambling exacts steep social costs—costs that lawmakers ought to be weighing very seriously.

As gambling becomes respectable, more people are falling into the trap of compulsive gambling. Hot lines for gambling addicts are reporting a dramatic increase in calls.

Many casinos have posted signs threatening to prosecute parents who leave their children in the car. Parents were literally abandoning their children outside for hours as they lost all track of time in a gambling haze.

Then there's the problem of crime. People coming to gamble have money with them, and criminals know it. The Atlantic City police department figures that each casino brings with it, on average, one thousand crimes a year, from petty theft to assault.

Juvenile delinquency climbs, too, as parents are enticed into spending evenings and weekends away from their families, leaving youngsters unsupervised.

What makes gambling so addictive?

I believe it's a symptom of the decline of the work ethic. Many people today are less willing to invest in hard work, education, and savings to get ahead. We are more easily tempted by the promise of getting something for nothing.

It's a trend that's especially devastating to the poor. In a Chicago ghetto, a colorful billboard showing a lottery ticket says, "This Could Be Your Ticket Out." Notice that the prize is dangled before those who *spend* their money on lottery tickets, not those who work and save. A lot of welfare checks are buying lottery tickets instead of food for the dinner table.

As Christians we ought to be demanding that our lawmakers clamp tighter limits on gambling. Gambling creates no new wealth. It manufactures nothing useful. And it imposes a heavy social cost in crime and family dysfunction.

Let's work and pray that all our lawmakers will make a sober assessment of this ancient vice.

And that they'll begin sending those riverboat casinos chugging right back down the Mississippi . . . empty-handed.

Today's "Little Platoons"

Schools in Self-Government

THE BRUTAL storms of the 1994 winter would have cost one little girl her life—if it hadn't been for a host of volunteers.

Three-year-old Michelle Schmitt had been on a waiting list for a liver transplant for two long, frustrating years. Finally the electrifying news came: A transplant was available. Michelle had only a few hours to fly from Louisville, Kentucky, to a hospital in Omaha, Nebraska.

Every minute counted. But heavy snows had shut down the entire city. A helicopter ambulance service offered to pick up Michelle and fly her to the Louisville airport, where a runway was being cleared, if she could get to a county airfield.

But driving to the county airfield would eat up precious hours. That's when Southeast Christian Church came to the rescue. Church members had already helped raise money to cover the costs of the transplant operation. Now they had a brilliant thought: Let's not bring Michelle to the helicopter; let's bring the helicopter to Michelle. The aircraft could land on the church parking lot.

Members ran door-to-door, asking for help. Neighbors hurried to the church parking lot, shovels on their shoulders, to clear off a landing pad. Soon Michelle was on her way. The transplant operation was a complete success, and a little girl's life was saved.

The members of Southeast Christian Church have my vote as 1994's model volunteers. They were acting both as Christians *and* in a distinctively American spirit. The American founders did not believe governments could create virtue; government attempts to make people good are inherently coercive. Instead, our Constitution rests on the premise that virtue comes from citizens themselves—acting through smaller groups, such as the family, church, community, and voluntary associations.

These are what English statesman Edmund Burke called the "little platoons." They create the arena where virtue is best cultivated: both the disposition to be good and the impulse to *do* good. The little platoons are the roots of social order, where the art of self-government is practiced.

Historically, Americans have always impressed outsiders with their habit of volunteerism. In the nineteenth century, the French writer Alexis de Tocqueville marveled that Americans form associations for everything—to start libraries, send out missionaries, build hospitals and schools. By contrast, Tocqueville remarked, in his own France there were not ten men doing what ordinary Americans do routinely.

As Christians we need to grasp the broad cultural impact of the ministries we devote our time to. Volunteerism is more than individual acts of justice and kindness, important though they are. When the members of Southeast Christian Church save the life of a little girl, or when you and I give up our Tuesday nights to visit a prisoner, in a very real sense we're helping to maintain the distinctive character of our society—preserving America's richest heritage.

We are strengthening the "little platoons" that foster virtue and are the bedrock of America's freedom.

A Victory for the Baby

....

An Immigrant's Lesson

RITA WARREN is a sixty-eight-year-old immigrant who grew up in Italy, and this Italian has taught her Virginia neighbors a lesson in protecting American freedom.

For years, every Christmas, Mrs. Warren traveled from Fairfax, Virginia, to Washington, D.C., to set up a nativity scene at the Capitol. Because Mrs. Warren sat by her crèche all day long and then took it home at night, the display was considered a form of free speech, not a public display.

But in December 1995, Mrs. Warren took a different tactic. That summer, the Supreme Court had ruled that the Ku Klux Klan had the right to erect a cross in a public park in Columbus, Ohio. Such displays are permissible, the court said, if public property is designated as a forum for public expression.

Well, if the Klan had the right to a public display, Mrs. Warren decided, then so did she. This elderly, soft-spoken woman got as tough as any ACLU lawyer: She threatened to sue Fairfax if city officials didn't permit her to display her crèche on public property.

And she won. The city designated an area near city hall for public displays and gave Mrs. Warren permission to set up her crèche there.

Mrs. Warren was ecstatic. As she told the *Washington Times,* "It's a victory for . . . the little baby in the cradle and for all the people of Fairfax City."

Well, not *all* the people. The grinches at the ACLU muttered and fumed, trying to figure out some way to get rid of Mrs. Warren's crèche.

But if they decide to take Rita Warren on, they'll have quite a fight on their hands, because this is one woman who takes religious freedom seriously.

Rita Warren still remembers vividly the day fifty years ago when Mussolini's henchmen marched into her junior-high classroom in Italy and stripped the cross off the wall. In its place, they hung pictures of Mussolini and Hitler. Instead of reciting the Lord's Prayer, the children were forced to salute the two dictators.

The memory was burned into Rita's mind and stayed there long after she immigrated to the U.S. in 1947. It taught her that citizens must fight to protect their religious freedoms.

"I am not a religious fanatic," she says, "but maybe if we Italians had put up a fight years ago, we could have avoided that horrible war" (*Washington Times,* 8 December 1995).

Unlike Rita Warren, too many Americans think we can strip the public square of all religious influences and replace them with a neutral secularism. But as the Italians discovered, when you get rid of God, another ideology will spring up in his place—one far less benevolent.

We ought to thank people like Rita Warren for reminding us how fiercely our religious freedoms have to be guarded.

Even if it means single-handedly taking on city hall to do it.

Three

CLASSROOM CACOPHONY

Park Your Brains at the Door

Parents and Public Schools

PUBLIC schools of America, beware! Education is "under siege" by a vast conspiracy of censorship—spearheaded by religious fanatics.

At least, that's how a 1993 report tells it.

The report is an annual project of People for the American Way (PAW), an ultraliberal organization that styles itself as a civil liberties watchdog group. But the report invites the suspicion that the group is much less concerned about civil liberties than about banishing Christian values from the public arena.

According to PAW, 347 times in the 1992–1993 school year parents actually had the temerity to question what their children were reading in school. Most of the concerns focused on books containing high levels of profanity, violence, or occult phenomena.

For example, many of the parents objected to a series of scary storybooks by Alvin Schwartz that centered on gruesome plots. One story, called "Wonderful Sausage," tells of a jolly butcher who grinds up his wife into bratwurst and eats her. Not surprisingly, parents were a bit upset.

Another story, titled "Just Delicious," features a woman who goes to a mortuary, steals another woman's liver, and feeds it to her husband.

Many parents objected to Lois Duncan's *Killing Mr. Griffin,* a book about students who kidnap and murder their teacher. Isn't it odd that teachers would defend the right of students to read that one?

PAW lists these examples with a great deal of hand-wringing, decrying them as censorship by fundamentalist, archconservative Christian groups. Ironically, the charges are proven false by the details of the report itself.

Only about a fifth of the complaints could be traced to conservative groups. Most came from individual parents or teachers. Several of the complaints even came from *liberal* groups.

Black parents objected to racist attitudes in Mark Twain's *Huckleberry Finn*. Native American groups objected to Laura Ingalls Wilder's classic *Little House on the Prairie* for its depiction of American Indians.

Somehow almost no news accounts picked up these examples. Most portrayed the PAW report as evidence of a frightening wave of censorship from the religious right.

Perhaps the most disturbing thing about the report is the underlying assumption that any parent who wants input into his own child's education is automatically a censor. Don't forget that by the time educational materials reach your child's classroom, they have *already* been "censored": They have passed through an intensive selection process carried out at several levels by educators, librarians, and other professionals.

Why is it OK for professionals to review school materials, but not the child's own parents?

Teachers and administrators often urge parents to get more involved in school, but it seems all they really want parents to do is run bake sales and raise money for band uniforms. Schools are often highly suspicious of parents who express any moral or intellectual views about what their children are learning.

If schools really want parents to get involved, they need to stop accusing concerned parents of being censors. They need to listen to parents' ideas—and stop telling them to park their brains at the schoolhouse door.

Postmodern Prose

Trashing the Classics

A FEW years ago, a British schoolteacher achieved notoriety by refusing to let her students attend Shakespeare's *Romeo and Juliet.* Her objection? The play is "too heterosexual," the teacher complained.

In the age of gay rights, portraying a normal heterosexual romance is apparently no longer politically correct.

Examples of political correctness are often so egregious, we may be tempted to dismiss them as mere educational high jinks. But that would be a mistake. As law professor Phillip Johnson explains in his new book *Reason in the Balance,* political correctness, or postmodernism, is the logical result of ideas held by many ordinary Americans.

In a nutshell, postmodernism says there are no universal truths valid for all people. Instead, individuals are locked into the limited perspective of their own race, gender, or ethnic group. That's why even classic literature like *Romeo and Juliet* is being deconstructed for its treatment of sex and gender.

Yet ironically, even though postmodernism insists that there's no ultimate truth, it actually rests on a very definite conviction about ultimate truth: It rests on the philosophy of naturalism, the belief that nature is all that exists. From elementary school on, Americans are taught that the universe needs no God to explain it, that Darwinian evolution is enough to explain where we came from. Our educational system is committed lock, stock, and barrel to naturalism.

If there is no God, then obviously we have to throw out the idea that God has revealed transcendent, universal truths for us to live by. And without divine revelation, each person is locked into his or her own limited, individual perspective—which is exactly what postmodernism teaches.

This direct line from naturalism to postmodernism was argued brilliantly in an article in *Humanist* magazine. The author points out that "naturalism eliminates the possibility of transcendent spiritual . . . knowledge." Hence "the logical next step for the culture that has presided over the death of God" is the death of universal truth (*Humanist,* January 1993).

The same progression can be traced in the personal life of postmodernist guru Richard Rorty. In an autobiographical essay, Rorty reveals that as a college student he was attracted to Christianity, especially to the Anglo-Catholic elements in the poetry of T. S. Eliot.

But Rorty writes that he was "incapable" of the "humility that Christianity demanded," and he turned away from God—only to discover that a world with no God is a world with no basis for universal truths or moral absolutes. None of us is capable of stepping outside our own culturally limited perspective to see how things really are in themselves. Only divine revelation can give us that kind of objectivity. So Rorty rejected transcendent truth to become a peddler of postmodernism.

When you hear teachers debunking the classics as the work of Dead White Males, remember that it all begins with Darwinism. Once you deny that the world needs God to explain its existence, the "logical next step" is to deny any transcendent truth.

Then truth becomes hostage to every race, gender, and ethnic group.

Billboards That Teach

Character Education

IN TYLER, Texas, the entire town joined forces in a new educational experiment that's as old as the classics: They decided to teach kids character.

All across Tyler, schools choose a value of the month to promote in the classroom. Local businesses join in, using billboards and signs in store windows. Police officers participate by eating lunch at school and handing out baseball-style cards featuring their favorite value. When officers in squad cars see children doing a good deed, they turn on their sirens and award the children a certificate allowing them to enter a special school raffle.

Tyler is pioneering a trend called "character education." The new approach takes aim at the educational fads of the '60s and '70s that went under labels like "values clarification" and "decision making." Those were nondirective approaches, teaching students to question their parents and churches—to be "autonomous decision makers." But they failed to teach any moral standards for making those decisions. In short, they focused on the *mechanics* of moral decision making but failed to teach the *content* of morality.

The result can be summed up in the words of one student, who described an ethics course by saying, "I learned there was no such thing as right or wrong, just good or bad arguments." No wonder surveys show more kids than ever are cheating, lying, and sleeping around. Crime is rising faster among juveniles than among any other age group.

In recent years, character education has begun to emerge as a countermovement. This approach to teaching ethics is highly directive; it's based on the conviction that virtues exist that children ought to know and ought to practice. You might fear that in a pluralistic society no one could agree on *which* virtues to teach. But communities that adopt character education find they can agree on a basic list: things like honesty, courage, and respect for others.

The results so far look promising. Since Tyler's program began four years ago, the number of kids fighting in school or being expelled has dropped significantly.

There's no doubt that in our relativistic age, character education will be a tough concept to sell. When some members of Congress suggested adding character education to the elementary and secondary education bill, several of their colleagues snickered.

"Are you serious?" they asked (*Wall Street Journal,* 10 May 1996).

Liberals are afraid that character education will mean pushing religious values down their kids' throats. Conservatives worry that values could be redefined according to standards of political correctness. These are genuine concerns. But by accepting the premise of character education, at least we are engaging each other on moral issues. At least we're participating in a communal debate over what is right and wrong instead of abandoning values to the fuzzy arena of subjective choice.

Christians have a distinctive ethic, revealed in Scripture and empowered by the Holy Spirit, but we must also support a public standard of morality, justified by prudential arguments. The fact is that societies that encourage the classic virtues are better places to live.

Which is just what the citizens of Tyler are finding out—even if it means using baseball cards and billboards.

Academic Freedom for Whom?

....

Viewpoint Discrimination

SHOULD college teachers be allowed to speak freely in the classroom about their personal beliefs? If you're a feminist professor, or a Marxist, the answer is, Of course. That's what academic freedom is all about: professors being free to teach students all viewpoints, including their own.

But when it comes to professors who are Christian, however, academic freedom is often replaced by conceptual shackles.

Consider the case of Phillip Bishop, who teaches classes in exercise physiology at the University of Alabama. Bishop makes no secret of his religious views: He tells students he believes the human body was designed by God and is not the product of naturalistic evolution. Students who want to hear more are invited to attend a voluntary, after-hours meeting to discuss what Bishop calls "evidences of God in human physiology."

Or rather, I should say these are things he *used* to do. When a handful of students complained, the university ordered Bishop to cease and desist from making any comments about his faith.

Bishop challenged the restrictions in federal court, and at first he was successful. The court noted that the restrictions were aimed only at religious speech, not any other forms of speech. Besides, several professors testified that it was common practice to share their personal views with students and that the university had never objected before. The court concluded that the university's actions toward Bishop amounted to unconstitutional "viewpoint discrimination."

57

The decision rested on a crucial distinction: The university had claimed that Bishop was introducing a new *subject* into his course: namely, religion. The court said no, he's merely discussing a new *viewpoint* on an existing subject: namely, a Christian viewpoint on human physiology. And academic freedom means a university may not discriminate against any viewpoint.

Nevertheless, the university appealed the decision, and it was overturned by a higher court. The Supreme Court declined to grant a hearing in the case, which means the university's restrictions on Bishop still stand.

The story is told in Phillip Johnson's book *Reason in the Balance,* and it shows how important it is for Christians to redefine the very terms we use in framing the debate over public education. We're not trying to get a new subject—religion—introduced into public school classrooms. Instead, we want the freedom to present a Christian perspective on subject matter *already in* the classroom—whether science classes or family living and sex education.

Debates can be won or lost by the way views are classified. If a Christian view on a subject is labelled "religion," it can be marginalized, banned from the classroom, relegated to the private sphere, where it has no power to affect our national culture. But if a Christian perspective is categorized as simply one viewpoint on an accepted subject matter, then to ban it is to practice viewpoint discrimination.

Learn how to make the case in your own children's school by reading Johnson's book *Reason in the Balance.* Christian teachers ought to enjoy the same academic freedom as feminists and Marxists.

Tantrum Tribalism

··

Are Schools Cheating Girls?

THERE'S a hidden conspiracy infecting our public school system these days. At least, that's the theme of a book by educators David and Myra Sadker. Titled *Failing at Fairness,* the book claims that American teachers are cheating girls out of a good education.

But the conspiracy is so well hidden, even people sympathetic to the cause are unable to detect it.

For instance, one chapter in the book relates that the staff at NBC's *Dateline* loved the Sadkers' work and decided to do a show on it. They hauled their cameras into a fifth-grade classroom in order to capture sexism in action. To their chagrin, the *Dateline* staff couldn't *find* any sexism.

In alarm, the producer called the Sadkers and asked, "How can we show sexism on our show when there's no gender bias in this teacher's class?"

Not to worry, said the Sadkers. By repeatedly halting and replaying the tape, they were able to pinpoint minute differences in the way the teacher related to her students, which they claimed favored the boys over the girls. The *Dateline* staff was convinced and ran the program.

But other educators remain skeptical. In the *Wall Street Journal,* education writer Rita Kramer argues that much of the extra attention little boys get in the classroom consists of discipline, not real teaching. Little girls, who are generally less active and more verbal, may actually process information more effectively than boys do.

Empirical evidence supports Kramer's argument. In general, girls get higher grades than boys. In high school, more girls than boys complete courses in chemistry, algebra, biology, and geometry. Girls also outnumber boys on college campuses, making up 55 percent of undergraduates and 59 percent of students in master's programs (*Wall Street Journal,* 1 March 1994).

These figures are impressive, and they suggest that it's the Sadkers—not schoolgirls—who need to be taking more higher math courses. The fact is that overt sexism has been virtually wiped out of American schools.

So why are some people still so eager to paint schools as hotbeds of bias?

The answer is that radical feminism is driven by a quasi-Marxist ideology that divides society into victims and oppressors. In classical Marxism, the victim group was the proletariat; today it can be any race or gender you please.

In this vision of the world, the path to social justice is to foment rage and resentment among the victims until they revolt against their oppressors. Marxist ideology virtually *compels* adherents to search for signs of oppression—even when the facts are flimsy. Grievances practically have to be manufactured in order to maintain the ideology.

Some have dubbed it "tantrum tribalism."

For Christians, this approach should ring false from top to bottom. The Bible calls for social justice as strongly as any radical activist, but it utterly rejects rage and resentment as means of getting there. We cannot use evil to create good. Justice is established through compassion and charity.

You and I have a biblical duty to help those who are genuinely subject to cruelty and oppression. But we should stand firmly against the Marxist-inspired search for manufactured grievances.

Justice was never served by throwing tantrums.

First-Amendment Camp

The Battle behind PC

IN A delightful turnaround, the doyens of political correctness are being forced to swallow their own medicine.

We've all heard stories about college campuses where students who offend the reigning liberal orthodoxy are subject to sensitivity training. Well, the tables are being turned. At the University of California in Riverside, the administration itself was required to undergo a sensitivity training course—this time a course on the First Amendment.

It seems the administration had punished members of a student fraternity for wearing T-shirts that featured a Mexican sitting on a beach. A militant Chicano group on campus protested that the T-shirt was racist. Campus officials immediately revoked the fraternity's campus recognition and required its members to perform sixteen hours of community service, while attending seminars in multicultural awareness.

In this case, however, the forces of political correctness were brought skidding to an abrupt halt. A lawyer with the Individual Rights Foundation brought suit against the university—and amazingly, campus officials backed down. They acknowledged that the school had violated the fraternity members' right of free speech and agreed to attend a training course in First Amendment principles.

The irony in all this is delightful, yet what we're seeing is not simply tit for tat. Campus speech wars are a symptom of a much deeper warfare in the world of ideas—one that Christians desperately need to understand.

The defenders of free speech are heirs of the Enlightenment, the Age of Reason. The Enlightenment ideal was that rational minds, stripped of the restraints of religion and tradition, could arrive at an objective consensus on what is true and good. The right of free speech was taken to mean that rational discourse is the path to truth.

But today the Enlightenment ideal is under severe attack by campus radicals who've adopted a philosophy called postmodernism. This philosophy says it is impossible to strip the mind of tradition and other preconceptions. It is impossible to conduct rational discourse that is objective and neutral. Every statement is inevitably colored by the speaker's class, race, and gender.

In short, postmodernists argue, it is impossible to have free speech in the Enlightenment sense. Postmodernist doyen Stanley Fish of Duke University has even written a book bluntly titled *There's No Such Thing as Free Speech.* American college campuses are caught in a face-off between modern Enlightenment rationalism and postmodern relativism.

For Christians, this is a unique opportunity: We are in a position to offer a perspective that leads the way out of the impasse. You see, Christianity rejects the Enlightenment claim that the human mind has godlike powers to find absolute truth on its own. The Bible teaches that human beings are finite and sinful.

But we also reject the postmodernist retreat into radical relativism. Human beings *can* know the truth—because God has spoken. He has given us divine revelation, and his Word guides us into truth in every area of life.

This is the good news we can bring to our fractured culture. The Bible offers a balanced perspective that brings peace to the PC wars.

The Sexual Wilderness

··

Getting Real about Sex Education

"IF WE talk about marriage, the schools won't let us in."

The speaker was Elayne Bennett, executive director of Best Friends, a program that teaches girls to delay sexual involvement until after high school. Why don't you teach girls to delay sex until marriage? she was asked. Her answer was shocking: The public schools won't even *consider* a program that holds up marriage as an ideal.

What a vivid revelation of the reigning philosophy in sex education today.

Educators argue that these programs are merely "realistic" about today's sexually active teens, but the truth is that they are hopelessly *unrealistic.* In a penetrating article in *Atlantic Monthly,* Barbara Dafoe Whitehead of the Institue for American Values argues that standard sex-education programs adopt a rose-tinted view of teenage sexuality (*Atlantic Monthly,* October 1994).

For starters, they assume that teens are rational, deliberate decision makers. Hence, the curricula stress giving teens accurate information and access to birth control, with the assumption that these things are enough for teens to make the right decisions.

Second, sex education programs assume that teen sex is basically benign, so long as kids avoid pregnancy and disease. The typical sex educator is a middle-aged woman, and many of the arguments for sex education reflect what it was like for an eighteen-year-old coming of age in her generation, during the sexual revolution of the '60s. Unfortunately, these arguments have little to do with what fifteen-year-olds face in the '90s.

The hard truth is that many teens are *not* rational

sex—they're impulsive and emotional—and far from being benign, most sexual relationships are exploitative—for girls at least. Statistics show that most sexually active fifteen-year-old girls are involved with men who are eighteen, twenty-one, or even older. A relationship between an adolescent girl and a man five to ten years older can hardly be considered consensual. The balance of power between them is sharply skewed.

No wonder one survey of one thousand sexually active teenage girls found that what they want most is to learn how to say *no.*

Not long ago adult society *helped* teens say no—by reinforcing a moral code against adolescent sex. The idea was to protect young people so they could acquire the skills of adulthood before taking on the responsibilities of marriage and parenthood.

But today an influential segment of adult society accepts adolescent sex as normal. Whitehead gives the example of Susan Wilson, a prominent sex educator, who writes, "It is *developmentally appropriate* for teenagers to learn to give and receive [sexual] pleasure" (*Atlantic Monthly,* October 1994). In this view, the role of adults is not to protect teens from sexual involvement; their role is merely to teach teens to manage their own sex lives, while giving them access to health technology, like birth control.

This is a completely novel view of adolescence: It lets adults off the hook and leaves kids to fend for themselves in today's freewheeling sexual culture.

You and I need to take a close look at the sex education our own children are receiving. Programs that refuse to give kids any moral code—that treat *marriage* as a dirty word—are not only hostile to Christian morality. They're also downright cruel to kids desperately searching for guidance in today's sexual wilderness.

Tracing Our Roots

....

Christianity and Biology

WHEN several Christians were elected to the school board in Vista, California, national groups immediately swooped down for the kill. The American Civil Liberties Union and People for the American Way relentlessly attacked the board members as bigots and religious extremists.

What is their crime? Why, the Vista board actually asked schools to teach students about the scientific evidence against evolution.

The Vista controversy is proof once again that science has grown rigidly dogmatic. To question the ruling orthodoxy of evolution is dismissed as out-of-bounds. To go further and suggest that life may be the product of design or purpose is regarded as really outrageous—as some oddball invention of the Religious Right.

But design in nature is no recent invention of religious extremists. In fact, it has a long and respectable history. As Nancy Pearcey and Charles Thaxton show in *The Soul of Science,* for nearly three centuries biology was dominated by the Christian concept of creation.

Take, for example, John Ray, in the seventeenth century. Ray is credited with offering the first biological definition of species, based not on how organisms look or behave but on reproduction: No matter how much variation an organism may exhibit, it belongs to the same species as its parents.

To modern ears, this sounds obvious. That's because reproduction—the ability to interbreed—has become the standard definition of species. But where did it originate? From Genesis 1. John Ray proposed that a species consists of all the descendants of a male-female pair created by God—just as the human race consists of all the descendants of the original human pair, Adam and Eve.

Another famous believer in creation was Georges Cuvier in the nineteenth century. It was said that Cuvier could reconstruct an extinct animal from a single bone. His stunning accomplishments flowed from his conviction that God created each organism as an integrated system—with each part adapted to its way of life. So carnivores have claws and sharp teeth for catching prey, while grazing animals have hooves instead of claws, and flat, rough teeth for grinding.

Cuvier was adamantly opposed to any notion of evolution. He argued that since an organism is an integrated system, you cannot create a *new* organism by random changes. It would be like letting a child randomly move a few wires around in your computer. Obviously, that would be much more likely to *destroy* the computer than to create a new and better one.

If these arguments sound familiar, it's because they have been revived in recent years by the creationist movement. Creationism is not a recent fabrication by religious zealots. It has a rich and respectable history.

Groups like the ACLU will continue to inflame public fears, warning that any mention of creation in the classroom will destroy science. But our response ought to be that for centuries the *majority* of biologists believed in creation—and biology survived very well indeed.

It is vitally important that we Christians recover our history and reclaim our rich heritage in science.

What Kind of Literacy?

Tools for Developing Christian Literature

SCHOOLS and businesses are constantly hyping the use of computers. It's become fashionable to think computers will inspire a new level of literacy.

Well, they will—but not in the classical sense.

Computer science is moving rapidly into the realm of visualization: the use of full-color moving images to simulate everything from brain activity to black holes. It's all very impressive, but the trend doesn't bode well for the written word. Coming on top of television, video, and Nintendo, computer visualization is sure to hasten our shift from a culture built on words to one based on images.

That may well reverse a trend started and nurtured for centuries by Christianity.

Since the Reformation, Christianity has been a powerful force for literacy, rooted in a practical need to teach people to read so they could read the Bible for themselves. Respect for the written word soon extended to all forms of literature. But this respect for literacy is being challenged today by the rise of electronic media.

What can we do to stave off the onslaught?

The first and most important step is to make sure we ourselves are literate—and our children too. Gene Edward Veith's book *Reading Between the Lines* is a useful guide to great Christian literature. The easiest place to start is with contemporary Christian authors. Read Walker Percy's book *Lost in the Cosmos* for a zany parody of self-help books. Read Annie Dillard for her stark descriptions of contemporary life from a Christian perspective. Immerse yourself in Walter Wangerin's devotions based on nature. Enjoy the richly textured prose of Frederick Buechner.

But don't stop with contemporary writers. Dip back a few decades and read the science fiction of C. S. Lewis. Sample the fantasy of J. R. R. Tolkien, the detective books of Dorothy Sayers, the romances of George Macdonald, and the supernatural novels of Charles Williams.

Going back a little further, remember that most writers up to our own century were Christians. Books by Robert Louis Stevenson, for example, clearly reflect a Christian worldview. You may have read *Kidnapped* and *Treasure Island* as a child, but try them again today and you will appreciate them all the more.

The Count of Monte Cristo, with its complex themes of revenge and forgiveness, is another book generally read by children much too young to appreciate it. And if you know *The Swiss Family Robinson* only in the Disney version, try reading the original. It is rich in Christian piety.

Once you've come this far, you'll have the tools to tackle the older Christian classics: authors like John Donne, John Milton, and Dante. The poetic language of *Paradise Lost* may be difficult at first, but stay with it, and you will be richly rewarded.

Educators may debate what children need most as they enter the twenty-first century: verbal literacy, visual literacy, or computer literacy.

But the best gift you can give yourself and your children is Christian literacy.

Politically Correct Volunteers

How Do You Define Charity?

ARIC HERNDON is a sterling example of what it means to be a community volunteer. This North Carolina teenager has devoted huge amounts of time and elbow grease to building split-log benches for a community nature trail.

But when Aric's high school initiated a public service requirement, he was surprised to learn that his long hours of volunteer work did not qualify. Why? Because Aric had received a Boy Scout merit badge for his work. School authorities said he had to start over with a completely new volunteer project.

All across the country, schools are establishing public service requirements for graduation, and I'm in favor of asking our kids to give something back to a country that has given them so much. The trouble with many of these programs is that they put strict limits on what counts as acceptable volunteerism.

It's not only Boy Scout and Girl Scout activities that are disqualified. Many young people spend much of their time helping out their own family members—baby-sitting nieces and nephews or taking aging grandparents to medical appointments. But family charity doesn't count in most public school volunteerism programs.

Neither does charity practiced through the church. If you take your turn in the church nursery or teach vacation Bible school, that often fails to qualify as an acceptable form of volunteerism in the eyes of school officials.

What does qualify is activism on behalf of politically correct causes, such as environmentalism, AIDS awareness, and helping the homeless. Even then, the emphasis is often on political activism over genuine altruism.

For example, in Maryland schools, students are encouraged to "investigate U.S. companies whose products exploit the rain forests." Since when did altruism mean investigating businesses?

Older children are invited to become "watchdogs for the Americans with Disabilities Act, and take action to remedy noncompliance with employment . . . provisions." Students are encouraged to engage in direct political advocacy, such as "writing a letter to the editor, lobbying for a cause, [or] engaging in a political campaign" (*Washington Times,* 16 August 1994).

Turning students into teenage lobbyists may not be your idea of community service, but it's all part of many schools' emphasis on activism over direct charity.

Even direct charity is allowed only if it is politically correct. In Maryland, students may volunteer at Planned Parenthood, the nation's foremost abortion provider. But they may *not* volunteer at a Christian crisis pregnancy center, helping meet the needs of women who decide to carry their babies to term.

As Christians we agree with teaching our kids that helping others is not optional; it's one of the commandments of Christ. But we should be wary of school programs that send a message that helping family members is less important than saving the rain forest, or that teaching Sunday school has less value than political activism for trendy causes.

If your kids attend a school that imposes mandatory community service, you'd better make sure they aren't learning the *wrong* lessons about charity.

Generic Gratefulness

....

What Are We Teaching Our Kids?

ONE Thanksgiving a few years ago, over turkey and dressing I decided to quiz my eight-year-old grandson, as proud grandparents often do on such occasions. I leaned over and said, "Charlie, why did the Pilgrims celebrate the first Thanksgiving?"

Charlie resorted to the obvious answer, as grandchildren often do on such occasions. He said, "They wanted to give thanks."

"And who did the Pilgrims give thanks to?"

The boy's face clouded, and he squirmed a little. "I don't know—I guess they were thanking the Indians," he said. "That's what we learned at school."

I was aghast. Here we were celebrating a major national holiday with deep Christian roots, and my own grandchildren didn't know its significance.

The real Thanksgiving story starts in 1621 in Plymouth Colony, Massachusetts. Life was hard for the Pilgrims settling in the new world, and through the first winter the tiny colony endured severe hunger and privation. Nearly all of them fell sick, and half did not survive the winter.

But spring came, the crops were planted, and the first harvest proved bountiful. Governor William Bradford called a special feast to give thanks to the Creator. They celebrated for a week, along with one hundred Indians they invited to join them.

Let me make it clear: The Pilgrims did not give thanks to the Indians; they invited the Indians to *join* them in giving thanks to *God*—the God of Abraham, Isaac, and Jacob, the God made known in Jesus Christ.

Days set apart for thanksgiving were a common feature of colonial life. In 1631 in Boston, Massachusetts, a Puritan colony faced starvation when a ship carrying food supplies was delayed. Governor Winthrop declared a day of prayer to God. On the appointed day, right as they were praying, the ship sailed into the harbor. The day of petition was turned into a day of feasting and thanksgiving.

Other thanksgiving days were held in Virginia, Florida, Maine, and Texas. One colony wrote into its charter that the day of their arrival was to be "kept holy as a day of thanksgiving to Almighty God."

Today we don't hear much about thanking God, even on Thanksgiving Day. The holiday has been secularized; we are urged to conjure up a generic gratefulness directed to nobody in particular.

When I realized my grandson had lost sight of the Christian meaning of Thanksgiving, I knew I'd better do some homework. I pulled together information about George Washington, who declared a day of national thanksgiving in 1789. I tracked down literature on Abraham Lincoln, who declared Thanksgiving an annual holiday in 1863.

And I sat down for a good, long talk with Charlie.

As Christian parents we need to make sure we are passing on our religious heritage to our children. We can't rely on the public schools; what they teach may even be a distortion of history—like the hogwash Charlie learned about Thanksgiving.

So, don't assume everyone knows why you are gathering over turkey and cranberry sauce. Make a point of teaching your children and grandchildren that generic gratefulness isn't enough—that Thanksgiving means giving thanks to the one true God.

Innocence Lost

....

The Lesbian Avengers Come to School

ON Valentine's Day a few years ago, a group of women stood inside the doorway of a Massachusetts elementary school handing out small bags of heart-shaped candy. Was it a group of parents helping out with the festivities?

No, it was the Lesbian Avengers, an aggressive gay-rights activist group. Along with the candy, they handed out leaflets that said, "Lesbians are everywhere! . . . Girls who love girls and women who love women are OK!!! Happy Valentine's Day."

Parents were outraged. And no wonder. The children who received the candy and leaflets were only seven, eight, and nine years old. They came home confused and upset. One little girl said, "Nora is my best friend, and I love her. Does that make me bad?" Parents found themselves forced to explain the difference between homosexuality and heterosexuality to children too young to be burdened with such detailed sexual information.

As one mother put it, "It's not fair for someone to rob our children of their innocence" (*Washington Times,* 28 February 1994).

The Lesbian Avengers are admittedly more flamboyant than most gay rights groups, but their stunt reveals some of the uglier truths about the movement. Most disturbing is the determination to push kids into sexual knowledge—and even sexual activity—at an ever-younger age.

Of course, introducing youngsters to sexuality is always couched in terms of defending their rights. In 1986, the International Lesbian and Gay Association adopted a position supporting what it called "the right of young people to sexual and social self-determination." In 1990, the association stated that it "supports the right of every individual, regardless of age, to explore and develop her or his sexuality."

Of course, children are too young to be capable of asserting any kind of rights. So all this talk about children's rights really means, *Let's get young people out from under their parents' protection so they can be approached by gays and other adults.*

Today gay groups are starting to admit openly that this is their real agenda. When the Lesbian Avengers came to school, they were wearing T-shirts emblazoned with a simple slogan: "We recruit!" Obviously they had no scruples about recruiting even small elementary-school children.

This is frightening—but what's really disturbing is that the language used by gay groups is exactly the same as the language used by mainstream sex-education leaders. For example, Mary Calderone, longtime president of the Sex Information and Education Council of the United States (SIECUS), has stated that children have a fundamental right "to know about sexuality and to be sexual."

Family therapist Larry Constantine is even more explicit. He says, "Children are a disenfranchised minority. They should have the right to express themselves sexually—which means that they may or may not have contact with people older than themselves" (*Time,* 7 September 1981).

This is dangerous stuff, and it shows that gays are part of the most explosive aspect of the culture war—a debate over the purpose and meaning of sexuality, of families, and of childhood. Christians need to make it absolutely clear that God gave *parents* the responsibility for bringing up and protecting their children.

And no one else should dare to take away their innocence.

Four

MODERN MYTHMAKERS

Life Is Short: Play Hard

Ads That Market Death

A FULL-PAGE ad shows a young man leaping high into the air on a Schwinn bike. The ad copy promises: "One ride will coat you in . . . goosebumps." Then suddenly the ad shifts to the macabre. At the bottom of the page, a picture shows a coffin being lowered into a grave. The ad copy taunts the reader: "What, a little death frightens you?"

Clearly, Schwinn is marketing more than bicycles. It's teaching kids that it's cool to court death. The same death-defying message is being marketed by Union Bay. In a TV commercial, two teenagers wearing Union Bay fashions play chicken by racing their cars toward the top of a cliff. One driver catches his sleeve on his gearshift and sails over the edge. As his clothing floats to the surface of the water, a tag line appears on the screen: "Union Bay. Fashion that's made to last."

This attitude of flouting death is a sign of the moral and spiritual nihilism of our times. Death is the end of life, we are told, and there's nothing after that. We live in a closed system of natural cause and effect. There is no supernatural; we have no souls. Instead, our emotions and aspirations are merely chemical reactions set off by physical experiences. In a world where everything is just matter, physical thrills like playing chicken on a cliff are the closest we'll ever get to a spiritual experience.

The problem is, when the game of chicken is over, the thrill seeker is still trapped in a world with no true spiritual dimension. The experience is a counterfeit for real purpose and meaning.

As Christians we know that our lives do have meaning and purpose through a relationship with our Savior. Christ doesn't give us a rush of danger and excitement. Instead, he gives us the real thing—which may not be as flashy but does something even more awesome: He transforms human character from the inside out.

It was Christ who gave the early Christians the strength to stand up to emperors and wild beasts. It was Christ who led medieval Christians to rebuild Europe when it had fallen to the barbarians. He inspired missionaries to bring literacy and medicine through dark jungles across the globe. Today, Christ gives his followers the courage to invade the dark corridors of prisons to ransom the broken lives of prostitutes and drug addicts.

That's real meaning, real excitement.

You and I have to teach our teens to be wary of ads that promise fulfillment through danger. We must help them understand that there's more to life than simply thrill-seeking our way into an early grave and that death-defying feats are a poor substitute for a relationship with the living God.

Batmania

Surviving Popular Culture

WHEN Hollywood released *Batman Forever,* it spurred a wave of Batmania. The film hadn't even hit the theaters before millions of dollars in Batman merchandising landed in the stores—toys,

T-shirts, and beach towels—a vivid example of America's mass-produced culture.

Modern technology has made popular culture all-pervasive. As Ken Myers warns in *All God's Children and Blue Suede Shoes,* the danger is that popular culture may blunt our taste for the higher things.

Think back to college days when most of us were required to read the famous anti-utopian novels: George Orwell's *1984* and Aldous Huxley's *Brave New World.* Orwell was predicting what the future would be like under Communism; Huxley was predicting the future in the West.

Both books have proved to be disturbingly accurate.

Orwell foresaw a Communist government that would ban books; Huxley foresaw a Western government that wouldn't *need* to ban them—because no one would read serious books anymore.

Orwell predicted a society deprived of information; Huxley predicted a society oversaturated by information from the electronic media—until people lost the ability to analyze what they saw and heard.

Orwell feared a system that concealed the truth; Huxley feared a system where people stopped caring about truth and cared only about what made them feel good.

Today, these two scenarios sound frighteningly familiar. Orwell's book describes life in a totalitarian state, most prominently the collapsed Communist regime. But Huxley's book opens a window on our own society—where the Christian message is not forcibly suppressed; instead it is swamped by triviality.

How can Christians respond? How can we safeguard our distinctive message in a mass-produced society where cartoon characters like Batman appear overnight on everything from beach towels to children's underwear?

To begin with, we can just say no: Unplug the television and the boom box. But that is only the beginning. The best way to overcome banality is to demand something better—to seek out, as Paul writes in Philippians 4:8, whatever is noble, right, pure, admirable, and to "think on these things" (KJV).

Paul is commanding us to discipline ourselves to reflect on excellence. And he doesn't limit that to spiritual things, either. The command applies to everything—the music we listen to, the books and magazines we read, the films we watch. We are to *train* ourselves to love the higher things, things that challenge our mind and deepen our character.

And we need to start early. Parents who regularly use television as a baby-sitter end up with teens hooked on boom boxes and MTV. But parents who read to their children, introduce them to enriching music, and play games together are planting a love for excellence. Children raised on good culture at home find it much easier to resist the peer group and popular culture when they are teens.

So don't let yourself be shaped by a mass-produced culture. Resist Huxley's brave new world by thinking on what is noble, right, pure, and admirable—by nurturing, in yourselves and your families, a love for excellence.

Feral Fatherhood

....

The Lion King

FOR many kids, a walk on the wild side means the wilds of the African savanna, where the warthog and the wildebeest roam.

These are some of the characters in Disney's much-loved animated film *The Lion King*.

Parents like it as much as their kids do because of its positive portrayal of fatherhood.

The story is about a lion cub named Simba and the lessons he learns from his father, the Lion King. When Simba brags about becoming the next king, his father teaches the cocky young cub that real leadership is not just about "getting your own way all the time." When Simba explores forbidden territory and is attacked by hungry hyenas, his father comes to the rescue. When Simba is nearly killed by a herd of stampeding wildebeests, the Lion King risks his own life to save him.

This is sacrificial love—strong, masculine, and protective.

Then disaster strikes. The Lion King is viciously murdered by his jealous brother, Scar, who wants to be king. Simba flees, falling in with a gang of ne'er-do-well party animals who urge him to live for pleasure. But his early moral training eventually pays off. A childhood friend begs Simba to return home and save the lion pride from his corrupt Uncle Scar. Simba remembers his father's teachings and agrees to shoulder the duties of kingship.

This is great entertainment—with a great message. What a refreshing contrast to the image of fathers that Hollywood usually dishes up: father as a bumbler, who is merely tolerated by his wife and kids—the image portrayed in programs such as *The Simpsons* or *Married with Children*.

In fact, we need look no further than another hit movie, which portrays a father as a dim-witted Neanderthal whose most articulate expression is "Yabba dabba doo." Yes, I'm talking about *The Flintstones*. Consider the contrast between that movie and *The Lion King*.

The Lion King's wisdom wins the respect of his community. Fred Flintstone, while a kindhearted guy, is constantly derided by his family and friends as being "dumber than mud," and he proves them right when he scores lower than a chimpanzee on an IQ test.

The Lion King bravely rescues his son from a pack of vicious hyenas. But Fred Flintstone is so incompetent that his angry coworkers are ready to string him up—and *he* has to be rescued by his long-suffering wife.

Both these films are clean family fun, but the messages they convey are dramatically different. One portrays fathers as wise leaders; the other portrays them as incompetent bumblers. Which message would you rather teach *your* kids?

If your children haven't already seen these films, why don't you rent *both* videos and see if your kids can pick out the hidden messages. Use the films as the basis for a lesson in the way Christians must be discerning in a secular culture.

It's not too early to teach kids that everything—including animated lions and Neanderthal dads—expresses *someone's* worldview.

Kilts, Clans, and Courage

The Heroism of Braveheart

IN THE cold morning light, hundreds of English soldiers are poised on horseback, swords and shields at the ready, the sun glinting off their helmets. Across a grassy field, a ragtag band of Scots are lined up on foot, gripping primitive homemade weapons, quaking at the sight of an army several times their size.

As their courage falters, a man on horseback rides up. His

eyes burn with an almost fanatical glow. With a few stirring words, he inspires the Scots to fight for their freedom—to fight like warrior poets. And in what became known as the Battle of Stirling, the Scots routed their English oppressors.

This dramatic scene will be familiar to readers who have seen the movie *Braveheart*. Produced by and starring Mel Gibson, the film depicts the life of William Wallace, the thirteenth-century freedom fighter, and manages to convey a deeply moral vision of the world.

Anyone who has been to the movies lately knows that's no mean feat. In fact, some filmmakers go out of their way to depict evil as good. Remember *Natural Born Killers,* the movie that glorified a couple who go on a murder spree?

By contrast, *Braveheart* depicts a Christian view of good and evil. High moral behavior appears heroic and immoral behavior, shameful.

For example, we understand the full horror of murder when William Wallace's beloved wife has her throat slashed by English soldiers. We comprehend the shame of treachery when a Scottish prince betrays Wallace to the English. We even learn how betrayal affects the perpetrator when we see the prince suffer lasting guilt *after* carrying out his act of treachery. We learn to admire courage, sacrifice, and patriotism as Wallace leads the clans into battle against incredible odds.

The movie includes positive depictions of faith as well: Before going into battle, the Scots pray for God's aid, and after his capture, Wallace prays for the strength to endure a painful death with honor.

You see, what makes a film great is not the themes it deals with—themes like war and treachery and patriotism. What's important is how a filmmaker *treats* those themes. Good films deal with deep human problems in a way that teaches right and wrong.

Few people leave the theater unmoved by the heroic exploits of freedom fighter William Wallace. *Braveheart* actually makes righteous behavior look exciting and attractive.

While the graphic depictions of battle may be too much for some, the violence in *Braveheart* takes place within a proper moral and historical context: a context that celebrates a Christian worldview of right and wrong. And for that I give *Braveheart* two thumbs-up.

The New Racism

Black America's Culture War

ROBERT TOWNSEND is a popular black filmmaker who vaulted to fame several years ago with a film called *Hollywood Shuffle*. It lampooned the insulting stereotypes of black people in entertainment: Amos 'n' Andy, Uncle Tom, Aunt Jemima.

Today, Townsend is back, fighting a new stereotype of black people, in a movie called *Meteor Man*. But this time the stereotypes he's out to destroy are perpetrated, ironically enough, by other black entertainers.

The new stereotype is nothing like Amos 'n' Andy—but it's just as distorting, says Townsend. In the past few years, movies made by black film directors have concentrated almost exclusively on ghetto life. Their characters are gang members, street criminals, drug dealers. The scenes reek of violence; the language is larded with profanity.

White film critics rave about the films, calling them daring, gritty, and honest, yet they can be deadly to young people who accept their characters as role models. Along with hard-core rap music, these films create a media environment that encourages the worst aspects of ghetto life: crime, degradation of women, and hostility toward mainstream culture.

Robert Townsend calls this "black-on-black film crime." It takes the worst, the most dysfunctional, side of black life, and projects it as the norm.

Townsend isn't out just to criticize, however. He has also created a positive alternative: *Meteor Man* is a funny, lighthearted movie with a serious message. It features a timid schoolteacher who acquires superpowers from a falling meteor. He becomes a reluctant superhero, complete with cape and tights, and organizes the community to close the crack houses, chase the gangs out, and clean up the neighborhood. All without a word of profanity.

Townsend had a clear goal in making *Meteor Man*. "When I look at what's going on right now in movies and television and music," he said, "the kids aren't getting a lot of morals, a lot of values." *Meteor Man* is intended to provide some balance to the harsh, nihilistic themes that predominate in black entertainment (*Milwaukee Journal*, 8 August 1993).

Other black Americans are rallying to the same cause. Maulana Karenga, a professor of black studies, criticizes many rap musicians for presenting a distorted public image of black culture. They have "tried to elevate street life into black life," Karenga says. But "the reality is that we are a working-class people and have held things together with religion, self-respect, creativity."

The Reverend Calvin Butts, of the Abyssinian Baptist Church in Harlem, has adopted an activist approach, launching a crusade against hard-core rap, movies, and profanity—things that, in his words, "insult our women and degrade our race" (*Milwaukee Journal*, 22 August 1993).

We often hear it said that America is in a culture war, but black Americans are fighting a culture war of their own. We ought to support and pray for people like the Reverend Calvin Butts, who are taking a stand for strong morals and strong families.

They may not be donning capes and tights, but they're fighting evil all the same. They need to know that their Christian brothers and sisters are standing alongside them.

The Jungle Book

More Civilized Than Thou?

A HUNDRED years ago, the great author Rudyard Kipling amused his friends by tacking a sign to the door of his London home reading: "To Publishers: Classics written while you wait." These days, some exasperated observers might urge the Walt Disney Company to tack a sign to *their* door reading: "Classics *ruined* while you wait."

Disney recently came out with a film entitled *Rudyard Kipling's The Jungle Book*. But Kipling himself wouldn't recognize this politically correct rendering of his jungle tale. Kipling gave us a story about an East Indian man-child named Mowgli, who is taught by animal mentors how to survive in a dangerous jungle. Disney gives us an adult Mowgli who reenters civilization at a British army post. He falls in love with a young English woman named Kitty. When dastardly British soldiers kidnap Kitty, Mowgli takes off after them on an Indiana Jones-style chase through the jungle. In their search for a fabulous treasure, the soldiers fall off cliffs, drown in quicksand, and confront what must be the scariest snake in Hollywood history.

The movie is great fun for kids who enjoy action-packed thrillers, but even Disney spokesmen admit that the film bears little resemblance to Kipling's classic. Most important, the film teaches a philosophical lesson that is profoundly unbiblical: that human beings are by nature good and uncorrupted—that they are corrupted by society.

Disney portrays a child brought up in the jungle without human parents, outside the rules of civilization, as the most civilized character in the film—a person immune to the petty hostilities that plague the rest of us. In one scene, a puzzled Mowgli asks a British officer, "What is enemy? What is hate?"

By contrast, the upper-class British soldiers Mowgli meets are vicious, greedy men who will stop at nothing to obtain the treasure they seek. The message is clear: The men reared on the playing fields of Eton are corrupt; the man raised *outside* the rules of society is morally innocent.

But this is the exact opposite of what Kipling wrote. Kipling's *The Jungle Book* gives us an animal society that closely parallels human society: wolves, tigers, panthers, and monkeys exhibit a realistic mix of goodness and evil, cleverness and stupidity, nobility and pettiness, compassion and cruelty.

When Disney screenwriters turned Mowgli into a noble savage, they were following the ideas first taught by nineteenth-century philosopher Jean-Jacques Rousseau. Rousseau believed that children are naturally innocent, that civilization is the source of all corruption—that traditions, customs, and rules hem in our natural goodness.

But the Bible teaches that we're all born with a sinful nature, and modern studies are backing the Bible up. Children raised with the *least* adult discipline are the most likely to behave in uncivilized ways—not as noble savages, but simply as savages.

So go ahead and check out Disney's *The Jungle Book* on video and watch it with your children. Then help them to understand the *true* nature of sin: There are no "noble savages," only sinful people in need of God's grace.

The Best of the West

American Moral Leadership

"PEOPLE are entitled to *political* self-determination. They must also . . . enjoy *cultural* self-determination!"

The words sounded like the defiant manifesto of a Third-World nationalist throwing off the bonds of colonialism. But, no, the person speaking was a French politician, complaining about what he called a "U.S. cultural invasion" (*Calgary Herald,* 6 October 1993).

Our military may be in Kuwait or Bosnia, but our *culture* is crossing borders all around the world.

During the Cold War, many emerging nations imitated the Soviet Union—from its top-down, centralized politics to the style of its Red Army uniforms. Today the same nations are looking to the United States. In his book *Out of Control,* Zbigniew Brzezinski says Third World nations are waging American-style political campaigns, writing American-style constitutions, and, yes, even adopting American-style military uniforms.

A few years ago, when Chinese students demonstrated for freedom in Tiananmen Square, their symbol of hope was a replica of the Statue of Liberty. When Czechoslovakians rose up against communism, a worker stood up before a factory crowd and read, with tears in his eyes, the American Declaration of Independence. The Western model of political and economic liberty has captured the imagination of the world.

But while the best parts of Western culture are being imitated around the globe, so are the worst. More than half the movies watched around the world are produced in America. Television programs like *Melrose Place* and *Beverly Hills 90210* are exported to every dusty African village, providing a distorted image of American values and American life. Not long ago the U.S. Coast Guard intercepted a boatload of refugees from southern China. Their entire knowledge of the English language consisted of a single word: "MTV." This is the "cultural invasion" the French politician was fulminating against.

We stand today at a defining moment in world history. We are witnessing the decline of totalitarian nations ruled by the iron fist of ideology. But we also face the urgent question, What will come next?

The world is looking to the West, but the West is sending a mixed message. On one hand, there is a rich heritage that has blossomed from the soil of historic Christianity, a heritage of free governments, where power flows from the consent of the governed, not the barrel of a gun. A heritage of free markets that increase standards of living. A heritage of free thought and religious belief.

But undercutting it all are newer, compelling images beaming out from movie and television screens—images that glorify the secular, the sexual, and the sensational. A U.S. cultural invasion.

We in the West bear a particular responsibility today. The nations of the world are reaching out for Western ideals. But they are also falling prey to Western materialism and moral permissiveness.

This is a unique opportunity for Christians to make a case for biblical principles as the basis of Western ideals—the very ideals the world is yearning for. Let us call on America to scrutinize what we are exporting to the watching world—to take stock of ourselves.

And to remember that the best of the West is firmly rooted in the biblical tradition.

The Anonymous Self

Cyberspace Psychology

The classified ad read, "I am the man of your dreams. I love late night walks under star-filled skies." The ad ended by asking, "Are you the woman of my dreams? E-mail me soon, and let me touch your heart!"

Welcome to classified advertising in cyberspace. But just as in the notorious singles bars of the '70s and '80s, you never know what you're really getting. In cyberspace, people are known only by their log-on names, and they often adopt a whole catalog of on-line personas: completely fabricated names and personalities.

In fact, pretending to be someone else is part of the attraction. When you're on-line, nobody knows what you look like, whether you're a man or a woman, how old you are, or where you live. You can present yourself as a beautiful blonde woman, a priest, an Olympic athlete, or a child—even if you're none of these things. On-line junkies can even pretend to be the opposite sex in so-called chat rooms, where people converse via their keyboards—sometimes in sexually graphic terms.

MIT scientist Sherry Turkle describes this proliferation of identities in her new book *Life on the Screen.* Turkle argues that technology is rendering obsolete the belief in a single, unified self. One's personality becomes whatever one chooses to make it. As Turkle puts it, cyberspace creates "a decentered self that exists in many worlds, that plays many roles at the same time."

The amazing thing is that many psychologists are *applauding* these virtual multiple personalities. It used to be that psychologists helped people find their true selves. People spoke of "getting themselves together." But postmodernism has come to psychology, just as it has permeated the rest of our culture. It is the radical rejection of everything formerly considered to be stable and unchanging—truth, morality, even human nature itself. Postmodernism teaches that all we are is a collection of the different roles we play in the changing phases of our life.

The new breed of postmodern psychologists defines the healthy personality as one that constantly reinvents itself. People who have a stable, consistent personality are not viewed as healthy but repressed. Since truth is relative, it's considered neurotic to be tied down to enduring beliefs that give order and stability to your life.

What this means is that we may soon be facing a culture where Christians are labeled, by definition, "psychologically unhealthy." Christian churches might even be considered threats to the public health. We need to be ready to argue that real mental health starts with knowing who we are and where we stand in relation to ultimate truth—which is God himself. At the core of our being is a coherent self that God addresses, a self that God calls to respond to him.

Cyberspace may give opportunities to lose ourselves in a hall of mirrors. You may never know whether the person behind the on-line ad really is the man of your dreams or a thirteen-year-old kid with acne.

The task for Christians in the electronic age is clear: to bring a message of wholeness to fragmenting souls.

Dirty Pixels

Computer Pornography

TEN-YEAR-OLD Anders Urmacher of New York City likes to hang out with other kids in the Treehouse chat room on

America Online. One day Anders received an E-mail message from a stranger. When he downloaded the file, he discovered that it contained ten pictures showing couples engaged in various sex acts. His mother was horrified: "I was not aware that this stuff was online."

Today's computer technology allows a pornographic photograph to be scanned onto a disk and distributed via modem. Disk catalogs now advertise electronic erotica. Computer games now have erotic themes as well—from Leisure Suit Larry, sold in local computer stores, to hard-core games featuring bondage and bestiality.

Even computer bulletin boards, used by thousands for legitimate information exchange, have become haunts of pornographers and pedophiles. A new counterpart to phone sex is "cybersex," erotic conversations typed back and forth on a computer screen. Police have investigated child abuse cases that began when men struck up conversations with adolescent boys via computer bulletin boards, then arranged to meet them in person.

Computers are adding a new, interactive dimension to pornography. Old-fashioned photos were effective enough in arousing lust and inciting sexual assault, as police records show. But the medium itself was passive. The active part was the user's imagination.

A computer program, on the other hand, requires interaction. You type in commands and tell your character what to do. You can give commands to a female character, and she'll do anything you want—at least, anything she's programmed to do.

With full-color screens, movement, and sound effects, computers can create the equivalent of X-rated movies . . . where *you* are a participant.

Well, the technology may be new, but the age-old moral law still applies. Jesus taught that looking at someone with lust in our hearts is sin. The images we linger over with our eyes train our appetites—and ultimately influence our behavior. In cybersex, that influence can be even stronger. The interactive format literally rehearses behavior.

How can we protect ourselves from computer pornography? Laws governing the content of the Internet are currently in a state of flux. Parents cannot count on the law to protect their kids from indecent garbage on-line. So Christian parents need to supervise their children carefully. Today many homes have a computer, often hooked into computer bulletin boards. Don't assume that everything your children encounter there will be benign.

The futurists tell us we're moving toward a global village. Let's make sure there's not an electronic smut shop on every corner.

Cross Dressing

Religion as Fashion

NOT long ago, the fashion world raved over a chic new accessory: the cross.

Top designers like Bill Blass draped crosses around models on Seventh Avenue. Jewelers offered crosses in every conceivable size and style.

To go along with the crosses, designers came up with what they called the monastic look. Ralph Lauren introduced long black dresses with demure white collars that made the models look like convent novices. Calvin Klein showed long, dark coats and tunics, reminiscent of the Amish or Orthodox Jews. Other designers offered styles based on monks' robes, sometimes with a cord at the waist, sometimes hooded, sometimes adorned with rosary beads.

What's going on here? A spiritual revival among clothing designers?

Not in the least. These religious styles had nothing to do with religion. They were purely fashion. Designers explained that the religious styles conveyed a sense of "serenity" and "simplicity." Fashion historian Caroline Rennolds said the simple lines represented "restraint." In her words, "They are almost demure in contrast to the body-baring, in-your-face" fashions of past decades (*Chicago Tribune,* 18 July 1993).

What this trend represents is religion reduced to a sort of ethnic curiosity—something chic to imitate in art and fashion but not to take seriously. It's exactly like the Southwestern fashion of wearing Indian jewelry or decorating your home with Indian rugs and pottery. No one treats these as objects of religious worship, even though many of the designs were originally used ceremonially in Indian religions. Rugs may show the Rain God casting down thunderbolts, but for most Americans the religious dimension only makes these objects more "interesting," in an anthropological sense.

This is the same attitude the fashion industry has adopted toward Christian symbols. The cross and the rosary are used for their ethnic and historical associations, not their religious meaning.

As a case in point, one jeweler boasted that many of the people buying his crosses were Jewish. For them, clearly the attraction of the cross was not religious. If there's any lingering association with Christianity, the jeweler told a reporter, "they manage to get over" it (*Dallas Morning News,* 21 July 1993).

Get over it? Fashion has become a means of draining religious symbols of their rich spiritual meaning—of reducing the sacred to an empty fad—so empty that some people no longer even remember its original meaning.

The story is told of a jeweler whose customer asked to see a cross. He replied, "Do you want an ordinary one or one with a little man on it?" The jeweler apparently had no idea of the identity of the "little man" traditionally shown hanging on the cross (*Sunday Telegraph,* 9 May 1993).

This appalling spiritual ignorance is a reminder that as our nation grows more secular, our own communities are becoming mission fields. In fact, maybe you can turn fashion fads into an advantage. If you see people wearing a cross, why not find out if they know what it means? It just might be the perfect conversation opener.

And they might learn for the first time about the Man who hung on the cross for our sins.

Holographic Souls

....

Science Fiction and Humanity

THE YEAR is 2058. A massive earthquake is toppling all of California into the ocean. Atop a Los Angeles skyscraper, a scientist is about to achieve immortality: Moments before his body plunges to the ground, the scientist downloads his mind into a computer located thousands of miles away.

In effect, the scientist has downloaded his soul.

That's the climactic conclusion to Arthur C. Clarke's popular new novel, *Richter 10.* Clarke has written more than fifty books, but *Richter 10* is the fullest expression yet of the philosophy that governs most science fiction: namely, that sheer intelligence—the ability to process information—is the essence of what makes us human.

This one-dimensional view of human nature is widespread in our culture today. Clarke's best-known work is *2001: A Space Odyssey,* featuring an incredibly complex computer named HAL. HAL is so intelligent that the computer attains human consciousness, complete with an endearing personality.

Isaac Asimov, another popular science-fiction writer, has written a novella called *I Robot,* depicting robots that exhibit human traits like emotions, conscience, and the capacity for ethical judgment. In the story, a court of law ultimately declares a technologically advanced robot to be fully human.

To make intelligence the measure of humanness is to change the concept of immortality itself. In *Richter 10,* the human soul is defined as the collected memories of an intelligent mind. If people have the foresight to store the contents of their minds on computer chips, Clarke writes, their "souls" are "held . . . within [the] electrical charges" of the computer. After their bodies die, they can live on in the form of holographic projections.

The problem with this worldview is that it reduces everything that is uniquely human to mere data: our memories, our feelings—even our morals and beliefs. It shrinks human nature to the level of computers.

Christianity teaches a completely different model. Genesis 1 says God created humans as whole beings—not only our intellect, but also our will, our emotions, our moral sense, our spiritual nature, and the unique capacities of our physical bodies. This rich and complex understanding of human nature is often lost in science-fiction literature and films.

If you're not interested in the science-fiction genre, it's easy to lose sight of the cultural importance of sci-fi books and films. We need to remember that many of our most enduring cultural symbols emerged from the minds of science-fiction writers, including films like *Independence Day, Jurassic Park, 2001,* and *Star Wars.* As I write, thousands of people—including, perhaps, your own child or grandchild—are curled up reading the latest sci-fi thriller or watching the hottest new science-fiction movie, and absorbing its philosophical message.

War of the Worldviews

The Rise of Secularism

THE FILM *Independence Day* was one of Hollywood's biggest hits in recent years, full of state-of-the-art special effects. Yet many viewers left the theater with the odd feeling that somewhere, somehow, they'd seen this film before.

In effect, they had. In many respects *Independence Day* was a remake of the 1954 science-fiction classic *War of the Worlds*— but with one significant difference. And in that difference we can trace a radical shift in our culture's dominant worldview.

In both *Independence Day* and *War of the Worlds* alien space-ships arrive on Planet Earth. In both films, the world's leaders watch helplessly as cities are destroyed, millions are killed, and the human race reaches the brink of annihilation. Both films show the president desperately ordering a nuclear strike. When that fails, the films' characters begin wondering if anything can possibly save them. The only thing left seems to be prayer and faith in God.

It's at this point the films diverge dramatically.

In *Independence Day,* characters engage in "God talk," but God himself plays no role in solving the dilemma. Despite a scene showing characters in prayer, there's no doubt that human effort will ultimately save the day. Sure enough, deliverance finally comes through advanced military technology.

By contrast, in *War of the Worlds,* the weapon that scientists come up with is destroyed, forcing people to rely upon God alone. Churches across the nation are jammed with people. At the hour of mankind's greatest need, as the Martian death rays beam down through stained-glass windows, people gather together to pray for God's intervention.

The result is a deliverance so sudden, so unrelated to any human effort, that the survivors are shocked. One character points out that after all, they *had* been praying for a miracle, hadn't they? In case viewers still don't get the point, the final voice-over explains that "all that men could do had failed" and that humanity had been saved by God.

Just as the movie ends, we see people standing on a hillside, singing praises to God.

The difference between the two films is a profound illustration of the rapid rise of secularism during the past forty years. Today, most film producers are so thoroughly secularized that they wouldn't dream of coming up with a cinematic solution that gives God the glory. They're convinced modern moviegoers would not find such a solution plausible.

Ironically, in coming up with a purely human solution, the makers of *Independence Day* have been criticized for tacking on a climax to the film that is technically impossible.

You and I have to help our children and grandchildren understand how the entire culture influences worldview. Even movies that don't directly attack our faith may ultimately denigrate the power of God.

If your kids were among the millions who have seen *Independence Day,* why not rent *War of the Worlds* and watch it with them. And then, while you're finishing off the pizza, you can discuss how the worldview of each producer influenced the outcome of the film—and how each film influences the way people think.

It's what might be called the "war of the worldviews."

Get a Myth

....

Inventing Stories to Live By

THE AGE of myth seems to be returning. Consider the theme of *Highlander,* an immensely popular film and television series: The hero everyone believed was dead has come back to life. He leads the forces of good in an apocalyptic battle against the forces of evil, promising a new age of peace and harmony. It's the outline of the classic myth of the dying god who miraculously returns to conquer.

The modern age was supposed to get rid of myth and teach us to live by the bare truths of science. But as the *Highlander* craze proves, the myths are returning with all their power over the human imagination.

The film version of *Highlander* tells the story of a sixteenth-century Scottish warrior called Connor McLeod. While fighting a rival clan, McLeod is mortally wounded in battle. But instead of dying, McLeod discovers that he's a member of a clan called "the immortals." Good immortals like McLeod are destined to spend the next several centuries fighting evil immortals.

Highlander has attracted a huge international following since the release of the film a decade ago, followed by the beginning of the television series five years later. *Highlander* fans can chat with other devotees at World Wide Web sites based in Norway,

England, Italy, and the U.S. Devotees can immerse themselves in complex role-playing games with strict rules, noble quests, and supernatural enemies.

What makes supposedly "modern," up-to-date Westerners gravitate toward retreads of ancient myths?

The answer is, in the words of cultural critic Neil Postman, we all need a narrative to make sense of life—a story that tells us where we came from, where we're going, and how to live. The scientific age didn't wipe out the deep human need for a story. All it did was undercut the traditional story embodied in Christian teaching—the drama of sin and redemption.

Deprived of the true story—the gospel—people desperately search for *any* story to make sense out of life. This explains why dramatically rich stories like *Highlander* can become obsessions, with on-line role-playing games that give people an active role in the story.

In themselves, fantasy and creativity are good things—gifts from God. The great Christian fantasy writer J. R. R. Tolkien explained that when we create imaginary worlds, we're simply copying our Maker. Tolkien called this "refracted light"—a human reflection of the creative impulse first exercised by God when he created the world.

Many Christians, including C. S. Lewis, Charles Williams, and Dorothy Sayers, have used stories—including fantasy and science fiction—to teach Christian truths.

If you see your own kids or grandkids playing on-line fantasy games, take the opportunity to discuss the right use of imagination and stories.

Then you can explain the greatest narrative of all—the one that has the great advantage of being true.

Hell on Earth?

....

Sci-Fi Scenarios

IF YOU were to watch many science-fiction movies, you'd think Americans are the most pessimistic people in the world.

Think of *Blade Runner,* the definitive futuristic film of the past two decades. It portrays Los Angeles as a decayed ruin. The glamorous movie stars are gone, replaced by swarms of wretches who speak an unintelligible street dialect. Billboards urge people to flee the wreckage of earthly civilization and join more civilized settlements on other planets.

In theological terms, the vision of the world one gets from sci-fi films is of a place devastated by human sin, and offering no hope of God's redemption.

Los Angeles seems to be the favorite setting for these grim visions because it is where the future arrives first. In another example, *Demolition Man* is a darkly shot film that shows Los Angeles as a war zone. Mass murder and arson have become commonplace, and the police resort to military tactics in an attempt to restore order.

Another futuristic film, *Strange Days,* describes Los Angeles as a chaotic, out-of-control dystopia with zombielike people escaping into drugs and virtual-reality games.

These violent and depressing movies may not appeal to many of us. But Christians need to be aware that there's more going on in these films than mere entertainment. Like other elements of pop culture, science-fiction films convey a worldview— one that is absorbed by many of the people who watch them.

The good news is that the worldview of science-fiction films includes a realistic view of human sin and evil. The people who populate the cities of the future aren't viewed as innocent victims of some malevolent force. Instead they are people who willfully engage in evil and suffer the tragic consequences. In effect, they're punished for their sins.

At this point, science fiction and Scripture part company. Christianity teaches that sinful humans are offered redemption through faith in Jesus Christ. But in most futuristic films, redemption is not an option. Naturalism—the belief that nature is all there is—permeates much of the science-fiction genre. It's a philosophy that denies the existence of a personal, loving God who can save us from our sins.

In the place of a Holy Savior, science-fiction films offer an antihero—a protagonist who is scarcely more sympathetic than the films' bad guys. Rogue cops, drug dealers, rock musicians—these are humanity's last, best hope against the forces of darkness.

But instead of leading people out of the chaos, these anti-heroes simply fight their own battles. As the credits roll, Los Angeles remains a hopeless dystopia.

This pessimism is dished out to viewers who are often just kids, easily depressed by the complexity of the adult world they are entering. If *your* kids are aficionados of science fiction, you ought to sit down with them and watch a few sci-fi films on video. Help them to grasp each film's underlying message, and contrast it with the biblical teaching on sin and redemption.

We need to remind our children that if they accept Christ's redemption, their future won't be a crime-ridden dystopia but a heavenly home—one filled with glorious hope.

Don't Make Her Mad

··

Is Mother Nature a Person?

IT WAS January 1997, but film critics were already predicting the biggest movie hit of the upcoming summer: a film called *The Lost World,* the sequel to a previous blockbuster, *Jurassic Park.*

The *Lost World* gave us more of what made *Jurassic Park* a cultural landmark: rampaging dinosaurs and spectacular special effects. The underlying message of *The Lost World* is likewise identical to that of *Jurassic Park* and many other recent disaster films: Don't mess with nature because nature is an angry god just waiting to punish humans for their misdeeds.

In *Jurassic Park,* a film based closely on the book by the same name, a team of genetic engineers brings dinosaurs back to life by extracting dinosaur DNA from fossilized amber. In one telling scene from the novel, a consultant named Ian Malcolm warns the owner of the new dinosaur theme park that he shouldn't meddle with nature. The owner reassures Malcolm: Not a chance, he says, that the dinosaurs can escape and "destroy the planet."

Destroy the planet? *That* wasn't Malcolm's concern. "This planet has survived everything," Malcolm says. "This planet lives and breathes. If we are gone tomorrow, the earth will not miss us."

Notice the language here: The planet "lives and breathes," suggesting that the earth is a living organism, with intelligence and purpose.

This same theme has popped up in other recent science-fiction disaster movies. Last summer's megahit *Twister* featured a climatologist who was convinced that tornadoes were deliberately trying to kill her. What made her think that?

Perhaps she'd seen the trailer to the film, which told viewers that periodically, nature "will, in a kind of psychotic fit, go completely, randomly mad."

And in *Twister,* that's exactly what nature did.

In this Hollywood version of science, the natural world not only has intelligence and purpose—it also makes moral judgments. A 1996 movie called *Outbreak* suggested that if humans mess with the rain forests, nature will send a nasty virus to kill us all. *Outbreak* was based on the best-selling book *The Hot Zone,* in which author Richard Preston writes: "The earth is mounting an immune response against the human species. It is beginning to react to the human parasite[s] . . . [who are] threatening to shock the biosphere with mass extinctions."

There you have it: Humans are a malignant intrusion into nature, and Mother Nature is going to get even.

These books and movies reflect an extreme form of environmentalism called the Gaia hypothesis. As Charles Krauthammer writes, "Gaia theory actually claims that Earth is a living organism." The trouble with this kind of environmentalism, Krauthammer goes on, is that it "indulges in earth worship to the point of idolatry." This is the idolatry reflected in films that feature dinosaur hit squads and tornadoes with an attitude (*Time,* 17 June 1994).

These movies are fun to watch, but you and I need to make sure our children understand that the underlying philosophical message conflicts with Christian teachings.

According to Scripture, people aren't pests who make Mother Earth sneeze. They're just a little lower than the angels, the crown of God's earthly creation.

Boldly Going Nowhere

....

The Religion of Star Trek

"SPACE . . . the final frontier."

More than thirty years ago, television launched a series called Star Trek, in which the crew of the Starship *Enterprise* promised to "boldly go where no man has gone before."

Three decades later, the fictional starship has discovered hundreds of new life-forms and civilizations. And the late Jerry Garcia of the Grateful Dead might have noted, "What a long, strange trip it's been." But in its lengthy jaunt through the galaxy, the program's philosophical message has remained constant: that there is no personal God—at least, not the God of biblical revelation.

Today, Star Trek is nothing less than a cultural icon. The Star Trek franchise has churned out seven movies and three spin-off TV series, all of which are still on the air. According to the *New York Times,* thirteen Star Trek novels are sold every minute. Tens of millions of Star Trek fans around the world have been exposed to this thirty-one-year-long outer-space philosophy lesson.

And what *is* that philosophy lesson?

Gene Roddenberry, the creator of Star Trek, grew up in the Baptist church. But eventually, he decided that "the concept of God was too great and too encompassing to be explained and appreciated by any single system of belief" (quoted in David Alexander, *Star Trek Creator,* 1994). Late in life, Roddenberry came to believe that "relation to God as a person is a petty, superstitious approach to the All, the Infinite" (Quoted in Terrence Sweeney, *God and I,* 1985).

Roddenberry's personal religious philosophy is fleshed out in the programs he created. For example, Roddenberry filled the flight deck of the *Enterprise* with crew members from alien cultures, each possessing a fully developed alien religion—and all presented as equally valid.

Another example is the 1989 Star Trek movie, *The Final Frontier.* In this film, the *Enterprise* travels to a planet described as the "place where all the questions of existence can be answered." Here, the crew believes, they will finally find the real God.

But after a long and difficult trip, what the crew discovers is not God but a malevolent being imprisoned in a globe of energy. After the crew escapes, one character asks Captain Kirk, "So is God really out there?" The captain answers by tapping his chest and saying, "Maybe he's not out there. Maybe he's right *here* in the human heart."

By the time we reach the second Star Trek series, The Next Generation, the program reflects a postmodern mind-set—one that has "given up the Enlightenment quest for one universal, supracultural, timeless truth." So says theologian Stanley Grenz in his book *A Primer on Postmodernism*. In other words, since no one can know anything for sure about God, we might as well *create* our own belief systems.

Of course, as Christians, we know we don't have to settle for this subjective postmodern mush. When our kids sit down to watch the latest Star Trek spin-off, we need to remind them that our God is both transcendent and immanent—that Jesus is sitting at the right hand of the Father and also living within us.

Roddenberry's Captain Kirk character had it wrong. There *is* a God, "right here in the human heart," but he is also the God "out there," who is objectively real.

Knowing *this* God is one adventure the crew of the *Enterprise* has missed.

Going to the Dogs

Our Cultural Heritage

SUSAN HELLAUER, a singer with the vocal ensemble Anonymous 4, was walking in New York's Riverside Park recently when she was stopped by a fan. The woman told Hellauer that Anonymous 4's recordings had helped calm down a dog who was struggling to give birth to a litter of puppies.

Hellauer was taken aback. "I didn't know what to say," the singer recalls. So "I said, 'How wonderful.'"

The story is amusing, but I suggest that it's ironic that a pregnant pooch would appreciate what most evangelicals have lost sight of—our Christian musical heritage.

Anonymous 4 was founded in New York City in 1986 and consists of four singers. In addition to Hellauer, there's Ruth Cunningham, Marsha Genensky, and Johanna Maria Rose. The quartet specializes in the music of the high Middle Ages—what historians call the Age of Faith.

Anonymous 4's recordings and performances of medieval chant have been an unqualified success both commercially and critically—and with good reason. As music critic Antoinette Rainone explained in *The Record,* "Unison singing may seem straightforward, but the tiniest error is instantly audible. Anonymous 4, whose voices consist of strong altos and plaintive sopranos, [succeed] in creating uncanny blends, faultless intonations, and an unmatched purity of sound" (*Record,* 17 December 1996).

As *The American Record Guide* put it, "Surely, this is the sound of Heaven."

Why this recent interest in what is, after all, the music of the church? Publicists for Anonymous 4's label, Harmonia Mundi

USA, say that "our age is searching for its identity in the earlier age." The result is an unprecedented interest in early music.

Anonymous 4's 1993 recording, *On Yoolis Night,* is a medieval music celebration of Christmas. "Alleluya: A Nywe Werke" is sung in Middle English. The song tells us that "a new work has come on hand, through the might and grace of God's messenger, to save the lost of every land."

Anonymous 4's newest release, *A Star in the East,* surveys Hungarian medieval Christmas music. As Hellauer explains, Christianity replaced Hungary's pagan gods and hymns to the earth but kept sacred song at the heart of Hungarian spiritual life.

Close your eyes and imagine yourself in a cathedral in thirteenth-century Hungary at Christmastime. You would hear, in song, the words of the prophet Isaiah foretelling the coming of God's Messiah and the promise that "the people that walked in darkness have seen a great light."

Unfortunately, music that once communicated the gospel is now frequently marketed as "mood music," used to calm everyone from pregnant dogs to dental patients undergoing root canals.

While happy for any sales, members of Anonymous 4 hasten to add, "You're supposed to really *listen* to this stuff."

Good advice—especially for Christians. You see, much of today's Christian music is simply watered-down versions of popular music. Musically speaking, we've inherited a collection of gourmet recipes but insist on eating fast food every night.

But if our cultural heritage has fallen into misuse, the fault lies in part with Christians themselves. For example, if Christians want to sample music from the Age of Faith, they'll have to search for it at secular music stores. Few Christian bookstores carry Anonymous 4 or any other early music ensemble.

As you prepare for the holidays this year, why not take a

medieval musical tour, one that will help you understand how the worship of our God led to the creation of a culture envied by the world.

If we lose that understanding, we shouldn't be surprised if more than our musical heritage eventually goes to the dogs.

Five

DISCERNING DISTORTIONS

Petri-Dish Papas

The Ethics of Sperm Banks

A 1995 television program showed a young woman named Melody leafing through old medical-school yearbooks, searching the faces of male students to see if anyone looked like her. Melody is trying to find her biological father: She was conceived through artificial insemination.

"I find [it] maddening," Melody says, that intelligent people "fooled themselves" into thinking my biological background would be "inconsequential to me" (*Washington Post*, 29 January 1995).

The fact is that our entire legal system treats artificial insemination of single women as inconsequential. The federal government does not regulate sperm banks, and all but two states allow a completely open consumer market for buying and selling sperm.

This laissez-faire approach is part of an increasingly common idea that children don't really need fathers anymore. As David Blankenhorn writes in his book *Fatherless America*, "Sperm-bank fatherhood is essentially a commercial product, something bought and sold in the marketplace." After his date with the petri dish, the father—if we can call him that—simply takes his cash and leaves.

But human life is never that simple. The children of donor insemination are growing up—and, like Melody, many are pursuing their biological roots. Andrew Kimbrell, in his book *The Human Body Shop*, says these children "often become curious, even obsessed, with discovering their genetic background." Many are angry, "deeply disturbed that their births were part of a business transaction," Kimbrell writes. They have "feelings of being rejected and sold by their biological fathers."

Many say things like "My father sold me for twenty-five dollars."

Perhaps the most puzzling thing is that there is virtually no moral debate on the subject—a magazine article here, a television program there, but very little serious discussion. The predominant attitude seems to be that artificial insemination of a single woman is a private matter, beyond the proper reach of moral judgment or legal restraint. The politically correct view today is that a single woman can raise a child just as well as a married couple can. To imply otherwise is said to insult the woman.

Ironically, at the same time, social experts are admitting that children raised without fathers are statistically more likely to drop out of school, have teen pregnancies, and be in trouble with the law. This is especially clear in the inner cities, where crime correlates with fatherlessness more closely than with race or economic status.

If fatherlessness is generally a bad thing, then I say it's time to rethink America's wide-open sperm market that allows women to purposely produce fatherless children. Most European countries outlaw the sale of sperm to single women. They understand that it amounts to official sanction of male irresponsibility.

Human fathers are meant to mirror the fatherhood of God himself. We should no longer tolerate official policies sending a message that children don't really need fathers anymore.

The Hite Hype

....

Fathers: Who Needs Them?

YOU CAN forget all you've ever heard about the importance of family values. So says sexuality researcher Shere Hite. In a provocative *Washington Post* article, Hite announced that "the breakdown of the family is a good thing" (10 July 1994).

But the way she describes it, the real problem is not families, it's fathers.

In Hite's view, the increase in single-parent families merely shows that women are tired of the old "repressive" father-headed household. Family breakdown is a "clear signal," Hite says, "that more and more women cannot be bribed into traditional, Mom-as-servant families."

Besides, Hite goes on, look at the wonderful freedoms it offers for men. In her words, the single-parent family caters to "men's desire to be free of the traditional roles of breadwinner and family disciplinarian." Her dream is a Brave New World of "female child-rearing partnerships" and "networks of friends." Hite seems to have come down with a severe case of romantic nostalgia for the communes of the '60s (*Washington Post,* 10 July 1994).

Ironically, the very same issue of the *Washington Post* carried another article that ought to cure anyone of '60s romanticism. A report by Patrick Fagan of the Heritage Foundation found that family breakdown is the primary predictor of crime. Fagan discovered that high crime rates are less a function of race, poverty, or bad neighborhoods than of having children outside marriage.

The numbers are staggering: Sixty percent of rapists grew up in fatherless homes, as did 72 percent of adolescent murderers and 70 percent of long-term prison inmates. The solution to crime,

Fagan concludes, is not more cops or more prisons. The solution is more fathers marrying the mother of their children—and staying married (*The Heritage Foundation,* 29 June 1994).

This ought to be common sense. It's obvious that two parents can invest more love and time in a child's life than one parent can. Besides, a father's love has a different nature from a mother's love; children benefit most when they have both kinds. It's no wonder that the two-parent household has been the universal ideal across both time and geography.

But our culture seems to have lost sight of this commonsense ideal. In the words of David Blankenhorn, of the Institute for American Values, our cultural elites have embraced the idea of the "superfluous father"—the idea that fathers don't offer children any special relationship, that the only drawback to single parenthood is lack of economic support. We hear little about the unique and irreplaceable kind of love fathers give their children.

Christians need to learn how to defend the biblical teaching on family and fatherhood in a hostile culture—a culture where radicals like Shere Hite are actually celebrating the breakdown of the family.

Mothers at Work

Is It a Real Job?

WHEN Zoe Lofgren filed papers to run for Congress, she listed her occupation as "mother." But California election officials told her to cross it out. Listing motherhood as an occupation is against state law, they said.

"They're telling me motherhood is not a job," Lofgren said in disbelief. "As any mother will tell you," she added, "it *is* a job—twenty-four hours a day" (*Los Angeles Times,* 8 April 1994).

Lofgren is right, of course. But her experience illustrates just how confused Americans have become over the value of motherhood. Is motherhood in the '90s a real job—or just a lifestyle option for the privileged few?

The dismissive attitude Zoe Lofgren encountered is a common one. Consider the annual Take Your Daughter to Work Day, sponsored by the Ms. Foundation. By inventing a holiday that celebrates mothers who have outside careers—but *not* mothers who are homemakers—the Ms. Foundation is clearly promoting feminist values. The message is that real women are in the corporate world pursuing profit margins, not at home chasing preschoolers.

In fact, on Take Your Daughter to Work Day last year, one Cincinnati school principal announced that homemakers could not participate. "Being a housewife is not an occupation," the principal said. Later, under pressure, she backed down.

The problem is that since the Industrial Revolution, work once performed in family industries is now performed outside the home by professionals—everything from food production to clothing manufacturing to care of the sick.

An attitude has set in that anything not done professionally—anything not done for pay—has less value.

But there are some things best done for love, not for gain. Child rearing is one of the most obvious examples. Children need to know that their parents love them unconditionally. By sacrificing a second income so one parent can be home, parents boost their children's self-esteem much more than by taking them to work once a year.

Bill Mattox, of the Family Research Council, tells the story of taking his eight-year-old daughter, Allison, to work. He introduced her to women who were lawyers, accountants, and policy analysts. On the way home, Mattox told Allison that her *own* mother used to do many of the same exciting tasks that she had witnessed that day. Then he said: "Allison, your mother could be using her talents . . . in all sorts of jobs in the workplace. But she has chosen instead to use them at home teaching you. She must love you very, very much and think you are very, very important" (*Wall Street Journal,* 28 April 1994).

I suspect that one conversation raised Allison's self-esteem in a way the Ms. Foundation never dreamed of.

Parents sacrifice in many ways to affirm the value of raising children—and not working outside the home is one way many mothers sacrifice. This is the message we ought to be teaching our own daughters on Take Your Daughter to Work Day. When prominent folks like election officials and school principals deny that motherhood is a real job, you and I need to stand firm for the value of a loving home—where parents are committed to biblical principles for raising their children.

Marital Contracts

Not Worth the Paper They're Written On

SHOULD husbands and wives be granted a "no-fault" divorce— even if their marital faults are legion?

Phyllis Witcher of Pennsylvania says an emphatic *no.* When her own husband deserted her after twenty-five years of marriage, he wanted a no-fault divorce—even though Phyllis claims he committed adultery and physically abused her.

Phyllis filed a counterclaim on fault grounds. She believes it's a violation of her due-process rights for Pennsylvania law to force her to accept a no-fault divorce giving her husband the right to demand half the family's assets. Why should he receive an equal share of their assets when it was he alone who flouted the terms of their marriage agreement? Why shouldn't he suffer some penalty for breaking his marital contract—just as he would if he broke any other legal contract?

Only a few years ago, a man knew that if he abandoned his wife, he'd have to leave his home to his family and pay child support and alimony. Wives faced grave consequences if they ran off with another man. But that changed in the '70s, when states began passing no-fault divorce laws. As Larry Huff of the Family Research Council puts it, no-fault divorce has turned the marriage "covenant" into a "testament"—a one-sided transaction whose terms serve the wishes of only *one* of the parties (*Perspective,* October 1994).

The result is that today the marriage covenant, with its honorable clauses about sticking together "for better or for worse, in sickness and in health," is not worth the paper it's written on. No other contract can be broken so easily. Yet innocent spouses and children suffer when the offending spouse forces the sale of the family home and takes off with half the proceeds.

Bryce Christensen, director of the Rockford Institute's Center on the Family in America, says it's become harder to get rid of an unwanted employee than an unwanted spouse. Why? Because an employer has to live up to the terms of the contract with the employee or face legal consequences. But the same man can walk away from his marital contract with almost no repercussions (Chapman, *Chicago Tribune,* 30 April 1992).

That's unjust, and people like Phyllis Witcher deserve credit for attempting to force the state to put the moral dimension back into family law.

You and I ought to get behind changes in the law that would force couples to take the marriage covenant seriously. Changes that would assign the same serious consequences to broken marriage vows that apply to any other broken contract.

Rearing Children

....

A Luxury Few Can Afford?

A FEW years ago Great Britain's Princess Diana was photo-graphed wearing a pink-and-white sweater bearing the slogan: "I'm a luxury few can afford." Given the Princess of Wales's jet-setting lifestyle, it was an appropriate fashion statement.

Today, that slogan can be applied not just to well-heeled British princesses but also to middle-class American children. Thanks to the rising tide of federal taxes, *families* are becoming a luxury few can afford.

Stephen Moore, a tax analyst at the CATO Institute, says most families have no idea how much they really pay in taxes. For example, the National Taxpayer's Union found that in 1991 a family of four making $52,895 paid almost $27,680 in taxes, including federal, state, local, and indirect taxes. That's 50.4 percent of their earnings.

In other words, Moore says, "the government [took] home a larger share than the worker."

It didn't used to be this way. The first federal income tax in 1913 demanded what sounds like pocket change today—about fifty dollars per family in 1990 dollars. The same family today pays more than five thousand dollars. Robert Rector of the

Heritage Foundation says that after taxes, families with children are now the lowest income group in America.

Some families sacrifice the mother's paycheck so she can stay home with the kids. But they discover on tax day that the federal child-care credit gives a tax break only to parents who *pay* for child care. There's no break for parents who raise their own children—even though they may pay just as much indirectly through the loss of a second income.

Families who care for their own children are in effect subsidizing wealthier, dual-career families who place their children in hired care.

But when families send Mom back into the workplace, they're in for another shock. In the '50s a typical middle-income family man paid only about 4 percent of his income in federal taxes. Today, a dual-career couple sacrifices about 24 percent of their combined income to federal taxes alone.

That ought to make us angry, because these taxes aren't just making it harder for parents to provide for their kids, they're undermining the family itself. Parents spend 40 percent less time with their kids than they did in 1965. Why? Because, Moore says, "parents have to be out working more, in large part because taxes on families with children are so much higher" (*Washington Times*, 13 March 1995).

And that's a problem with repercussions through *all* of society. Decreased parental supervision is linked to problems in language skills, school performance, and internalization of moral values.

On April 15, when we drop our returns in the mailbox, we need to remember that tax codes express a society's values. The government raises taxes on behavior it wants to *discourage,* and lowers taxes on behavior it wants to *encourage.*

What values does our current tax policy express?

It penalizes couples for *having* children, and it penalizes them again if they leave the workforce to *raise* their children. Our government is acting as though its goal is to destroy the family itself.

You and I ought to ask our lawmakers to support changes in our tax codes—changes that take the tax burden off the backs of America's middle-class families.

Because bearing and rearing children shouldn't be a luxury that only the rich can afford.

Marie's Story

Why Women Choose Abortion

MARIE was the mother of two children when she discovered she was pregnant with a third. When she told her husband, he scowled: "Only ignorant people have more than two kids. You *have* to have an abortion."

Marie kept hoping her husband would change his mind. Even as she climbed onto the abortion table, she prayed he would rush in and stop her, but he didn't.

Marie's story is told in a book by Frederica Mathewes-Green called *Real Choices.* The author spent a year researching the reasons women have abortions. She proposed that if we could learn *why* women get abortions, we could more easily reduce what amounts to consumer demand for a deadly product. So Mathewes-Green contacted hundreds of crisis pregnancy centers. She studied case histories, and she talked to women across the country about their decisions to have abortions.

What she discovered stunned her.

Mathewes-Green found out that many women aren't having

abortions because they're poor or because a child would interfere with school or career plans. No, many are aborting their babies because *the men in their lives tell them to.* The abortion lobby tries to convince us that women are unfettered, empowered, and free—that when it comes to terminating a pregnancy, women are boldly making a choice all by themselves. But many of the women Mathewes-Green interviewed didn't talk about *choice,* they talked about *coercion.* They spoke of being threatened with loss of affection and support by the most important people in their lives—boyfriends, husbands, parents.

In fact, fully 88 percent of the women interviewed said their trip to the abortion clinic was a capitulation, not a choice at all. They didn't feel empowered; they felt isolated, overwhelmed, and sad. Like Marie, many women submitted to an abortion to please someone else.

French feminist Simone de Beauvoir recognized this phenomenon as long ago as 1952 when she wrote: "It is often the seducer himself who convinces the woman that she must rid herself of the child." But it's a tragic truth that feminists hope to suppress. After all, as Mathewes-Green asks, how would it look if pro-choice marchers carried a banner that read: "I'm proud I killed my baby to keep the man in my life"?

As Christians, we know that God intends for husbands and wives to love and support one another. That's why Mathewes-Green found that even a poor woman is likely to continue her pregnancy *if* the baby's father loves and supports her. But even a financially secure woman is likely to abort if her husband demands it of her.

Pick up a copy of *Real Choices* to learn more about why women abort. If we know *why* women are aborting 4,400 babies every day, we'll be better equipped to help them make not only *real* choices but also the *right* choice.

Can Men Have It All?

....

New Priorities

ROGER HORTON, a computer-firm manager, came to work at seven o'clock one morning so he could put in a ten-hour day and still leave in time to coach his son's Little League team. Yet when Roger packed his briefcase that evening, his boss reproached him for leaving early.

If this sounds like your own life, you're not alone. American culture often defines men by their jobs. In her "Work & Family" column, Sue Shellenbarger notes that "a growing body of research suggests many male professionals wish for a better balance between work and family," but employers are slow to acknowledge the importance of life outside the workplace (*Wall Street Journal,* 16 March 1994).

It was not always this way. In his book *American Manhood,* historian E. Anthony Rotundo says Americans once held a very different ideal of manhood. In colonial times people lived in economically independent households—either family farms or family industries. The husband and father was regarded as the head of this small commonwealth. Headship was not considered a personal privilege but an "office": It imposed on men a duty to represent not their own interests but those of the entire household in all their actions.

In this setting the dominant definition of masculinity was what Rotundo describes as "communal manhood." That is, a man fulfilled himself not through economic success but through what was termed "public usefulness" or service. Men were urged to subordinate personal ambition to the common good.

These cultural values were turned upside down by the

Industrial Revolution. Productive work was removed from the homestead to the factory, and men had to follow. Being gone from home all day sharply reduced their role as fathers while highlighting their role as breadwinners.

At the same time, women lost their traditional productive tasks: From weaving cloth to preserving food, production was transferred from the home to the factory. Women at home became economic dependents, living on their husband's wages.

These economic changes shifted the male role, redefining it in almost purely financial terms. Masculine character ideals likewise shifted. Whereas men were once exhorted to promote the common good, the new market economy fostered competition and individual ambition. The old ideal of "public usefulness" crumbled, and men began to base their identity mostly on individual achievement.

Does this sound familiar? Today economic achievement has become a virtual idol for many men. I know. Before I became a Christian, I fell into this pattern myself, which I deeply regret.

Christians ought to challenge this one-dimensional standard of success. God calls us to a richer vision of our purpose in life: to a deep communion with himself that spills over into love for our families, service to the community, involvement in Christian ministries, and cultivation of the arts and culture. Whether we are employers or workers, this is the vision we should be promoting: not merely economic success but the older virtue of public responsibility.

The Roger Hortons of this world should not be made to feel guilty when they leave work in the evening to coach their son's baseball team.

Taming Men

....

Is It Women's Work?

WILLIAM RASPBERRY, well-known columnist, has come up with a novel solution to crime: The answer, he says, is women.

Most criminals are male, Raspberry points out; therefore, women must not be fulfilling their traditional task of civilizing men. In his words, "Men have always jumped through all sorts of hoops . . . to make themselves attractive to women." Men have bowed to women's demand for commitment and stability in marriage, and stable families are turning out to be the key to preventing crime. So the problem today, Raspberry concludes, is that women are simply not making enough demands of men (*Washington Post,* 24 November 1993).

But before we start blaming women for the crime crisis, we need to ask some tough questions. Is Raspberry giving a biblical view of the relation between the sexes? Does Scripture hold women responsible for holding men in check?

Of course not. God holds men accountable directly to himself for their behavior as husbands and fathers. Yet the idea that women are responsible for "taming" men has a long history. It took root with the Industrial Revolution, when household production was replaced by factory production.

As men followed their work out into the new industrial work culture, they developed a new set of attitudes. The industrial world promoted individualism over community, treating workers as interchangeable units in the production process. It rewarded ambition and competitiveness. Men began to equate being masculine with being tough, aggressive, independent.

Over against the dog-eat-dog world of commerce and industry stood the home. Here the gentler virtues still reigned: love, altruism, self-sacrifice. It became women's job to protect these virtues and teach them to their husbands and children. Nineteenth-century clergymen and social reformers pleaded with women to curb male aggression—to "civilize" men.

Did it work? Clearly not. Today more than ever the media purveys images of men as violent loners: James Bond, Clint Eastwood, and Arnold Schwarzenegger. In real life, men are deserting their families in record numbers; male violent crime is rising faster than ever.

What went wrong? The problem is that the nineteenth-century strategy of defining family virtues as "women's work" guaranteed that men would eventually reject them. After all, no self-respecting man will submit to standards he regards as unmanly. So when William Raspberry urges women to "tame" men, he's promoting an old and defeated strategy.

The only real solution to male crime and other social pathologies is a return to the biblical teaching on the sexes. The Bible admonishes *husbands* to be responsible for the family's moral and spiritual health. We cannot allow them to pass the buck to their wives by defining family responsibilities as women's work.

Christians need to make it clear that nurturing family virtues is a *man's* job—that commitment and stability in marriage are *God's* standard for men, not a female standard that women must cajole men into accepting.

We ought to encourage every father to face up to his family responsibilities—like a man.

Men in the Shadows

....

Welfare Fathers

OFFICIALS know they are there: At a Chicago housing project, men can be seen coming and going, playing with the kids, or hanging around beat-up Chevys in the parking lot. Yet hardly any men are listed on the leases.

"They live in the shadows," says a tenant legal adviser. Since getting married can cost a woman her welfare benefits and her public housing, men lurk around the edges, refusing to become "a legitimate part of their own families" (*The Plain Dealer,* 29 November 1993).

The result is that welfare has become one of the most potent destroyers of family life today. As social-work professor Anthony King puts it, "Our entire social welfare system is set up to de-emphasize the father . . . to exclude the father . . . to discourage the father." Most social programs are aimed at women, whether it's job training, parenting classes, or Aid to Families with Dependent Children.

Charles Ballard, a Christian who ministers to inner-city men, says these social programs send a harsh message to fathers. In essence, they say, "What role could *you* play? You've got no job. You're no good to anybody. Just get out of the way."

The result is a system that robs communities of committed husbands and fathers, and communities without fathers are inherently unstable. Criminals prey on women and children. Schools flounder. Businesses leave. Fatherless neighborhoods quickly deteriorate into ghettos.

Why did our government institute welfare policies with such destructive effects? One explanation is that social-service professionals bought into the idea that fathers are superfluous to family life and can be safely shunted aside.

In a book called *Fatherhood in America,* Robert Griswold says a low view of fatherhood took root in the early twentieth century, when social work, education, and psychology first became professionalized. There appeared a host of advice columns, books, and child-development classes—all pressuring parents to adopt the latest theories expounded by the experts.

Soon the cult of the expert was replacing the authority of the father. Since most books and classes were addressed to mothers, they were the first to absorb the new theories of child rearing. By contrast, fathers were made to feel old-fashioned, uninformed, incompetent.

The incompetent father eventually became a stock figure in entertainment media. In the 1962 film *Mr. Hobbs Takes a Vacation,* a young couple argues fiercely over their children—with the wife repeatedly quoting the dictates of a professional psychologist to override her "unenlightened" husband. Today the same negative stereotype is reinforced in comic strip and TV characters, such as Dagwood Bumstead, Homer Simpson, and Al Bundy.

The assumption of the superfluous father has also helped shape welfare policies that discourage fathers—policies that push men into the shadows.

As Christians we need to fight against this low view of fatherhood. We need to teach men that the Bible calls them to a high position within the family as its leader and head, its provider and protector. American society is suffering gravely for listening to the word of the social experts—instead of the Word of God.

Tears and Roses

....

A Father's Remorse

BY THE time Greg reached the front of the room, he was crying. The two roses he carried in his hand trembled. Greg turned to face the crowd and explained in a soft voice that the roses were in memory of his two sons—who were dead.

Greg wasn't the only one in tears that day. A hundred men and women had gathered, most of them to mourn the deaths of their own children—children who had died through abortion.

Abortion is touted as the safe, easy, efficient solution to a problem pregnancy. But today the evidence is mounting that abortion is often traumatic and distressing. A survey conducted by the *Los Angeles Times* found that more than half the women who have had an abortion feel "a sense of guilt." More than one-fourth say they "mostly regret the abortion."

Amazingly, the survey found that *fathers* of aborted children felt even worse. Two-thirds of the fathers said they felt guilt over the abortion; more than a third reported feelings of regret.

Abortion has been exclusively defined as a women's issue, and we often forget that every abortion involves a man as well. In his book *Men and Abortion,* Wayne Brauning describes a survey finding that fathers experience the same negative reactions after an abortion that women do: anger, depression, guilt, and broken relationships. Even a man who pressured the woman into abortion, who drove her to the clinic, can wake up months or years later and suddenly realize he has delivered his own child over to death.

It can be a terrible blow. One of the men interviewed for the book—we'll call him George—says he now realizes he was just "too insecure and wimpy" to stand against his girlfriend's abortion.

Another interviewee, Jack, says men who stand by while their own children are aborted are "spineless and gutless." Jack knows. He did the same thing himself.

These days when one of his friends considers abortion, Jack tells him to stop and think: "Imagine saying to your child, 'I'm footloose and fancy-free and I know they're going to kill you but, hey, don't slow me down.' What kind of father would say that?" Jack demands. "Not a real man. Being a man means you assume responsibility."

The men we meet in *Men and Abortion* are troubled not only by their dead children but also by a crumbling sense of their own manhood. Is a father a noble protector and provider? Is he courageous and strong—unafraid of self-sacrifice? Is he fulfilling his duty toward those who depend on him?

No matter how you look at it, a man who pushes a woman into an abortion *knows* he's taking the coward's way out.

As Christians we ought to be on the front line not only fighting against abortion but also fighting *for* a rich, vibrant commitment to fatherhood. Let's remind each other that human fathers caring for their children are God's best object lesson for teaching the next generation about the fatherhood of God.

Keeping Promises

How the Church Nurtures Men

DURING the summer of 1994 in cities across America, nearly 2 million men joined hands to pray and sing. Attorneys in suits stood alongside bikers with tattooed arms and ranchers with cowboy hats and pointed boots.

The occasion was an annual series of conferences held by Promise Keepers, the largest Christian men's group in the country. Prodded by the secular men's movement, churches are beginning to minister more aggressively to men.

I say it's about time. Policy analysts today agree that most of the social pathologies plaguing America are linked directly to family breakdown: school failure, drug use, teen pregnancy, and crime. And family breakdown is primarily a matter of male desertion. In the words of Randy Phillips, executive director of Promise Keepers, "The men of this nation are leaving a trail of broken promises to their wives and children" (*Albuquerque Tribune*, 27 November 1993).

The only surprising thing is that the church has taken so long to respond. For a long time we've known that fewer men than women attend church. For a long time we've known that many men dismiss religion as something for women and children.

In fact, this negative stereotype is rooted back in the Enlightenment, when Christianity first came under attack from the forces of atheism. At the time, many churchmen responded by circling the wagons. Instead of developing a robust intellectual defense of Christianity that could stand up in the public square, many theologians retreated to the private realm of experience and emotions. They redefined faith as religious feelings.

Since men thought of themselves as less emotional than women, they began to withdraw from the faith.

The tragedy is that churches did little to *halt* the male flight. Instead, they started pitching their appeals to women. In the nineteenth century, for the first time women began to outnumber men in many evangelical churches, often by two to one. Pastors began to speak of women as having a special gift for religion and morality. They began to preach that mothers were more important than fathers in raising godly children. They urged pious wives to convert their worldly husbands.

Ironically, the ministers who preached this message seemed oblivious to the fact that it undermined the biblical teaching that the *father* is responsible for teaching his children and exercising spiritual leadership. In fact, by focusing on women, churches helped let men off the hook in moral and spiritual matters.

What this means is that Christians today must stand against a host of negative stereotypes—both inside and outside the church. We need to recapture the biblical vision that being a real man means being a man of God. That being committed to Jesus Christ is a manly challenge. And that being a good husband and father is a profoundly masculine virtue.

The key to restoring American society is to restore the family, and the key to restoring the family is to restore fathers.

Prodigal Dads

....

Tough Love for Fathers

CHARLES BALLARD faces a group of young, inner-city men. "How many of you have children?" he asks. All the men grin and raise their hands.

"Let me rephrase that," Ballard says. "How many of you are *fathers?*" The grins fade away to stony frowns.

Charles Ballard is founder of the National Institute for Responsible Fatherhood. How do you teach a boy to be a father—a boy who perhaps never even knew his own father's name? As Ballard explains, the first step is teaching a sense of the future. "We think about living in poverty as living in deprivation, and it is," Ballard says. "But what people may not see is that . . . poverty offers young men one thing in abundance: absolute freedom." They can stay out all night, get up whenever they want, even disappear for days. In their world, planning is measured in hours, or even minutes (*Policy Review,* winter 1995).

How can these young men be taught to plan over a five- or ten-year period? The key, Ballard discovered, is their children. Your daughter is two years old now, he might tell a young man. Where do you want to be when she's twelve? When her teacher asks the class about their families, what do you want your daughter to say?

No father can bear the thought of his daughter saying, "My dad's in prison" or "I don't know where he is." Even the aimless, impoverished young men in Ballard's program know that, at the heart of their being, they want their daughters to be able to say, "My dad's responsible; he takes care of me."

The way to help men become responsible, Ballard discovered, is by refusing to spoon-feed them. His ministry encourages fathers to claim paternity for their children, finish school, and get a job. But the organization never does anything a young man can do for himself. "We don't bundle them into a bus to take them down to the county courthouse to find the clerk in charge of birth certificates," Ballard says. "We don't take them to the board of education for copies of their school transcripts. We don't even hand them a slip of paper with phone numbers. Instead, we talk them through the necessary steps, and *they* take those steps—on their own."

This is "tough love," and it works. According to one study, eight years after going through the program at the Institute for Responsible Fathers, 70 percent of the men had finished high school, 75 percent had no additional children out of wedlock, and 97 percent were providing financial support for their children.

The heart of Ballard's ministry, however, is introducing young men to their heavenly Father—to the one who loves them as a father loves his children. It is God who put fathers at the head of families. And Ballard's ministry shows that in poor inner-city neighborhoods, what children really need is not food stamps and subsidized housing; they need their fathers back.

God's strategy is still the best—for family renewal *and* for urban renewal.

The Third Wave

Parents in the Information Age

FINANCIAL consultant Michael Fey was fed up with having too little time with his kids—so fed up that he decided to do something drastic: He set up an office in his home.

Immediately his relationship with his children began to improve. "Helping the kids get off to school, being involved in their squabbles . . . I'm being a real parent," Fey says. "It's changing their image of what a father is" (Quoted in Paul and Sarah Edwards, *Working from Home*).

Michael Fey is on the cutting edge of a new trend—men who want to be real fathers and not just a meal ticket—and he's had the courage to challenge an industrial work structure that requires fathers to be absent from their children most of the day.

What Fey is doing is re-creating an older, more humane work structure. In colonial days, most men worked in the home and its outbuildings, in family industries or on family farms. They trained their children in the diverse skills needed in a preindustrial society, from tracking game to planting crops.

In this setting, fathers—not mothers—were considered the primary parent. They were held responsible for their children's spiritual and intellectual education.

But with the Industrial Revolution, the role of fathers changed dramatically. When productive work was removed from the home, fathers began going out to work in factories and offices. No longer did they spend the day supervising their own children. In fact, today it's not unusual to hear of fathers who leave the house before their children are awake and come home after they're tucked back into bed.

The good news is that many men are rebelling against a work structure that doesn't allow them to be real fathers. James Levine, director of the Fatherhood Project, reports that the number of men who complain that work conflicts with their family responsibilities rose from 12 percent in 1977 to a staggering 72 percent in 1989. Another survey found that 74 percent of men prefer a "daddy track" job to a "fast track" job. A *Washington Post*/ABC News poll found that nearly half of fathers have cut back on their work hours for more time with their children.

Some fathers are even experimenting with flexible work schedules, telecommuting, and home-based work. According to a study by Ameritech, the number of workers working at least partly at home is growing nearly five times as fast as the overall workforce.

Alvin Toffler, in his book *The Third Wave*, predicted the coming of the "electronic cottage"—the use of telecommunications technology to bring work back into the home. Toffler hoped that home-based family businesses could recreate the strong family bonds of preindustrial times, as whole families once again work together in a common economic enterprise.

That day may be in the future, but Christians ought to be

pressing toward it today. We worship a God who is our *heavenly* Father—and who commands fathers to be the leader and head of their families.

Christian fathers ought to be living demonstrations that real success cannot be reduced to being a meal ticket. Real success, like charity, begins right at home.

The War on Adoption

Feminists Draw a Battle Line

WHEN you hear the word *adoption,* what's the first thing that comes to mind? Warmhearted couples taking in a needy child? Noble-minded single mothers giving their child the best chance in life?

These are the positive images traditionally associated with adoption. But today pro-choice forces are painting a far different picture: a dark, foreboding picture that shows adoption as heartless and traumatic.

If you think I'm exaggerating, consider what happened not long ago in a California school. One teacher told his class, "Adoption is the worst thing you can do to a child." Better to abort the child, he said, than to give it up for adoption (*Time,* 9 October 1988).

Traditionally, women who gave up a child were comforted by the confidence that they were choosing the best course, but today that confidence is often shattered. One pamphlet called *Adoption? Abortion?* warns women that if they select adoption, they will "live a life filled with pain, worry, anger, wonder, and mourning without end."

A book called *The Dark Side of Abortion*, by Marsha Riben, insists that mothers who choose adoption are "seldom at peace"—that they suffer "a limbo loss," never knowing "if the children they bore are dead or alive."

An article in *Mirabella* magazine portrays private adoptions as the exploitation of poor birth mothers by greedy middle-class couples, who shop for newborns in a "shadowy and competitive adoption bazaar" (Quoted in *National Review,* 7 June 1993).

Why is adoption suddenly receiving such bad press? The answer has nothing to do with the facts. Statistics show that most adoptions work out well for everyone involved. Instead, the answer has to do with the politics of abortion.

In a *National Review* article called "The War on Adoption," Marvin Olasky points out that for abortion to be widely accepted, it must become a guilt-free operation. That means women must be convinced that they had no choice, that under the circumstances they *had* to have an abortion. But adoption is a reminder that every woman *does* have a choice, that there are two different roads before her.

For abortion to be guilt free, a woman must be convinced that the fetus is her own property, entirely subject to her needs and interests. Adoption is a reminder that some women have the strength of character to put aside their personal needs for nine months and consider the needs of their baby instead.

For abortion to be guilt free, women must be convinced that there are no viable alternatives open to them. But every adoption is a reminder that there is an alternative, that there are loving couples on waiting lists for children of every race, color, and physical condition.

In *Real Choices,* Frederica Mathewes-Green describes efforts by the Pro-Life Adoption Network and by Bethany Christian Services to help women overcome both the emotional and practical obstacles to adoption. For example, women are encouraged to imagine their child cradled in the arms of loving adoptive parents—instead of dead by abortion. One study found that unmarried teenage women are seven times more likely to choose adoption when they understand the benefits of it.

Scripture exhorts us to remember that even we, who are evil, know to give bread, not stones, to our children. As *Real Choices* shows, just a little extra effort can make it possible for thousands of pregnant women to choose the "bread" of life, instead of the "stone" of death, for their unborn children.

A World without Children

P. D. James Gives a Warning

THE YEAR is 2021, and the entire male population of the world has mysteriously become sterile. For twenty-five years, not a single baby has been born.

This is the imaginary scenario painted in P. D. James's recent book, *The Children of Men*. James built her reputation as a mystery writer, but this is in a very different genre. *The Children of Men* is an anti-utopian novel, an allegory of the culture of death spreading today through abortion, infanticide, and euthanasia. James imagines a world where all adults are free to pursue careers and personal interests without the responsibility of caring for children. Through a policy of euthanasia, the government also relieves them of the responsibility of caring for the elderly.

You might think this would be an adult heaven—a world of freedom and individual self-fulfillment. But with no future to build toward, people drift into apathy. Schools close, libraries decay, scientific research stops. With no hope of creating a better world for our children, no one cares about justice, charity, or even democracy. Instead, all they want is guaranteed "freedom from fear, freedom from want, freedom from boredom."

In Britain, where the story takes place, a benevolent dictator takes power, promising to deliver the mindless security that citizens demand. To keep them entertained, the dictator opens pornography shops. To keep them safe, he sets up a penal colony on an island, where all criminals are dumped for life—even minor offenders. Churches merely imitate the spirit of the age. Instead of preaching a message of sin and redemption, they offer a feel-good gospel to comfort a dying civilization.

Yet there are some who refuse to be comforted. The unfulfilled nurturing instinct pushes some people over the edge. Unbalanced women cuddle dolls as though they were children. Deranged couples wrap dogs and cats in lacy blankets and demand christening services. In some cases, the elderly resist the government's euthanasia program, but they are drugged into compliance. In a parody of a religious ritual, they are dressed in white gowns, paraded onto barges, and then drowned.

The story climaxes when a young Christian woman finds herself pregnant. The British dictator—like a modern King Herod—wants to claim her baby, so she flees and gives birth in a wooden shed in a forest. P. D. James seems to be making an allusion to Bethlehem—pointing back to the birth of the Child so long ago as the only antidote to the culture of death.

You may want to read *The Children of Men* for a vivid picture of the direction our own society may be heading. But don't expect the book to entertain you; it's more likely to disturb you with its ominous vision of the future. People often wonder if the human race will be destroyed by some external threat: by nuclear war or ecological disaster. But P. D. James is a churchgoing Anglican, and she seems to be warning us that we just might destroy ourselves from *within*—if we continue to embrace a culture of death.

As Christians, we need to tell the world that the only sure antidote is a return to Bethlehem and to the Child born there.

Six

CRIME
AND
CULTURE

The Glamour of Evil

Why the Literati Love Criminals

KODY SCOTT is a prisoner in a California prison. Covered with tattoos, scarred by bullets, Scott is nicknamed "Monster." He is a former gang member and a remorseless killer.

He also became the darling of the publishing world. Scott published his life's story in a book titled *Monster*. Larded with four-letter words and crude rap speech, the book tells a lurid tale of drugs, murder, and gang warfare.

Literary types immediately swooned over it. At an international trade show, Scott overshadowed even proven winners like Tom Clancy and Stephen King, netting an advance of $250,000.

The literary world, it seems, has a fascination with criminals. The best-known case was in 1981, when novelist Norman Mailer pressed for the release of a criminal named Jack Abbott, who had become a writer. Within a month of his release, Abbott was back in prison for murder.

Why do the literati find criminals so fascinating? The answer is that they romanticize criminals as rebels against established society.

Listen to the way Mailer glamorized the ghetto. In his book *The White Negro,* Mailer urged that middle-class folks have a lot to learn from ghetto culture. Learn to give up "the sophisticated inhibitions of civilization." Learn to live for the moment, to "follow the rebellious imperative of the self." Forget "the single mate, the solid family, and the respectable love life," Mailer went on. The real life is one of "Saturday night kicks"—of sex and drugs.

These words were written in 1957, and they express the ideas that drove the '60s. Ultimately, they derive from the philosophy of existentialism.

In fact, the first writer to work for the release of a convicted criminal was the French existentialist philosopher Jean-Paul Sartre. Existentialism teaches that there are no moral absolutes, that all law and morality is man-made. Hence moral rules are by definition oppressive—imposed on us by whoever has the most power.

If that's the case, existentialism says, then conforming to society's moral code means giving in to an oppressive system. The only healthy response is to rebel—to prove one's autonomy.

And so, unbelievable though it may sound, the existentialists actually celebrated crime as a regenerative rebellion against oppression. In his book *The Dream and the Nightmare,* Myron Magnet explains how the young hoodlum became a symbol of courage and authenticity. Today the literary world is still glamorizing evil, and Kody Scott—the "Monster"—is held up as a rebel hero.

The worst part of all this is that the ideas of the elites eventually filter down to the streets. The glamourization of crime is now commonplace among untutored ghetto youth.

Laws will never be enough to stop crime. We must first address ourselves to culture: the ideas and attitudes of the elites who shape the way people think. The philosophy of existentialism is simply false: Real morality is not man-made, nor is it imposed on us merely by society. The source of true moral standards is God himself.

And when we bow before him, we do not lose our freedom. We discover what true freedom really is.

Getting Away with Murder

....

Juvenile Justice

IN THE classic 1938 film *Boys Town,* Father Flanagan says, "There's no such thing as a bad boy."

But Father Flanagan never met Billy.

Billy is a twelve-year-old boy who raped and beat up a bag lady in New York's Central Park. When Billy was arrested, an investigation revealed that weeks earlier Billy had raped and murdered another bag lady. After serving a short, one-year sentence in an unlocked rehabilitation program, he was immediately involved in another case of rape and beating.

It seems some kids never learn.

Billy's story is told in Rita Kramer's book *At a Tender Age.* The blind spot in our juvenile-justice system, Kramer says, is that it cannot handle youngsters like Billy who are already hardened criminals.

The American juvenile-justice system was designed for the kids portrayed in *Boys Town,* whose most serious transgression was telling a fib or sneaking a smoke. The juvenile courts were founded at the turn of the century by progressive reformers steeped in the philosophy of Jean-Jacques Rousseau, who taught that children are innocent unless corrupted by society. And if society was the problem, then society could also be the solution. Many juvenile-justice professionals decided that the way to treat delinquent kids was not with punishment but with therapy.

This explains why our juvenile-justice system lets kids off for a first or second offense with nothing more than a judge's scolding.

It explains why records are sealed, so that kids who murder at age seventeen have a clean record by age eighteen.

It explains why kids in detention for serious crimes like aggravated assault are locked up for only a year or two. When they hit eighteen, they go free—no matter how heinous their crime.

The entire system is toothless, and it inspires nothing but contempt in many young offenders. In family court, young thugs who rob and murder will taunt the judge: "You can't do anything to me, I ain't eighteen yet."

It's these hardened young criminals who commit most juvenile crimes. A University of Pennsylvania study found that a majority of serious juvenile crime is committed by only 6 percent of the juvenile population.

But our criminal justice system fails to draw a distinction between minor offenders and the 6 percent who are violent repeat offenders—like twelve-year-old Billy, who had already raped and killed more than once. Some states are beginning to require juveniles to be tried as adults if charged with certain violent crimes. In Colorado, juveniles are tried as adults but are housed in separate prisons designed just for juveniles.

As Christians, we want to minister to kids who get into trouble with the law. But we are also realistic about the evil that can corrupt the human heart—even a child's heart.

Father Flanagan was wrong: There *is* such a thing as a "bad boy." And our juvenile system needs to stop pretending it can be Boys Town.

The Toughest Day in Prison

··

Reconciling Criminals and Their Victims

CRAIG has spent fourteen years of a life sentence behind bars for murder. But if you ask him what was the hardest thing he's faced so far, it wasn't a prison riot or an attack by a fellow inmate.

What really hurt, Craig says, was sitting down face-to-face with the family of the man he murdered—and hearing first-hand how his act of rage shattered their lives.

Craig met the family through a program designed to reconcile criminals and their victims. Programs like these are catching on across the United States, and often they do more than years in prison to change a criminal's outlook.

In the American criminal-justice system, most criminals never talk with the person they have wronged. At best, the two might catch a glimpse of each other across a crowded court-room. The crime is prosecuted as an offense against the state, not against the victim.

In this impersonal system, the offender rarely confronts the personal pain and trauma he has inflicted. That's where Victim-Offender Reconciliation programs can make all the difference. As Craig puts it, meeting with the victim's family "brought me to grips with my own culpability and personal feelings of guilt." And an awakened sense of personal responsibility is much tougher to deal with than any punishment meted out in a prison yard.

Reconciliation programs can benefit everyone involved in a crime. For victims, it gives a chance to express their deep pain and anger over the trauma they have suffered. For offenders, it gives a chance to face the consequences of their actions—and to set things right again as much as possible. Often the meetings end with the criminal apologizing and offering to pay restitution.

Finally, reconciliation is good criminal-justice policy. A scandal of our current system is the high number of criminals who return to prison—again and again. Clearly, we need to look for programs that go beyond simply locking criminals up—programs that change them from the inside. Reconciliation programs can offer just such a life-changing experience.

A prison inmate named Julius says he used to feel real sorry for his crime. Sorry he got caught, that is. Then he attended a Victim-Offender Reconciliation meeting—and for the first time, he said, he saw his victims as real people. As he put it, "I realized this could have been my mother, father, brother, sister." By the end of the meeting, Julius says, he felt "genuine remorse and empathy."

That remorse often translates into real reform. A 1992 study by the Minnesota Citizens Council on Crime and Justice found that juvenile offenders who participated in reconciliation programs were less likely to commit crimes after their release from prison.

Why don't you find out whether your local court system is using reconciliation programs. Biblical teachings on justice aim not only at punishment for crime but also at restoration of the community. Crime tears a jagged hole in the fabric of our social life, but reconciliation and forgiveness mend that hole.

They can help restore the civil peace that the Bible calls *shalom*.

Deep-Freeze Criminals

Can We Thaw Them Out?

KIRBY was a prison inmate who just wanted to start over. But when he was released from prison, the state put a mere one hundred dollars in his pocket. With that hundred dollars, Kirby had to buy food, find an apartment, and get a job.

"Needless to say, I failed," Kirby said in a letter to Prison Fellowship, "and I turned back to crime."

Few of us realize how difficult it is for ex-prisoners to reenter the outside world. During their prison tenure, they lose marketable skills, break off with friends, and are often deserted by their families. No wonder many end up right back in jail. And no wonder most crimes are committed by repeat criminals. Crime is the only way of life they know, the only skill they have.

Across America today, public fear about crime is epidemic. Lawmakers are clamoring for tougher laws, stiffer sentences. But if we really want to get tough on crime, there are strategies politicians never talk about. One of the most effective is helping ex-prisoners break the cycle of crime.

Here at Prison Fellowship we hold Life Plan Seminars behind bars. Aimed at prisoners about to be released, Life Plan Seminars teach them how to set realistic goals for getting a job, finding a place to live, and building a support network.

When prisoners are released, Life Plan tries to match each one with a volunteer mentor, often an ex-convict himself. The mentor offers support during the first six months in the outside world—the time when the risk is highest for falling back into crime.

For long-term support, Prison Fellowship volunteers organize Philemon Fellowships, groups of former prisoners who meet to encourage one another. Even such elementary tasks as getting a driver's license can be a hurdle to someone who for years has had no responsibility for his own life.

Philemon Fellowships are named after the book in the Bible, a letter from Paul to a man named Philemon, urging him to restore a runaway slave. The slave had converted and was now eager to reform his life. In essence, Paul used his personal influence to reinstate the slave to his former job.

This is the kind of practical support all ex-prisoners need if they're going to make it in the outside world. If you manage a business, you might even consider hiring reliable ex-convicts.

An inmate named Donald says his prison experience reminds him of a movie he once saw: a fantasy film about a Rip Van Winkle character who was frozen in ice for several years and was then thawed out to face a world he no longer understood. "That is what they are doing to most convicts," Donald said bitterly. "They arrest us, freeze us, and thaw us out"—without giving us a clue how to start over.

If Americans are serious about fighting crime, we need to stop putting prisoners in deep freeze. Read Prison Fellowship's book *Staying Safe* to find out how you can help an ex-convict go straight.

Let's stand beside them as they walk the often precarious line from crime to freedom.

Hateful Crimes

....

Censoring Unpopular Ideas

WHEN the U.S. Senate debated an omnibus crime bill in 1993, there was one provision that passed with hardly a murmur of debate: A measure to enhance the penalties for certain hate crimes passed overwhelmingly, 95 to 4.

Such massive support reflects society's dismay over hate crimes. And we *should* be dismayed. But there's mischief lurking in hate-crime legislation that few people have noted.

Certainly we should not tolerate physical attacks on people for their race or religion—any more than we tolerate attacks on people for their money or their watches. Every reasonable person agrees on that. But hate-crime laws go one step further. They punish hate crimes *more* harshly than attacks on people for their money or their watches. In essence, they send a message that crimes motivated by prejudice are more serious than crimes motivated by simple greed or cruelty.

But is this a message society really wants to send? By elevating victims of hate crimes, we are *devaluing* other victims. We're in essence telling people that if they're attacked for their money instead of their race or sexual orientation, then their suffering doesn't count as much.

The mischief doesn't end here. Even more pernicious, hate-crime laws come dangerously close to criminalizing attitudes instead of behavior. The offender is punished once for the crime itself, then punished again for the same crime if a judge rules that the motivation was racist or sexist or some other prohibited kind of thought.

For example, in a Wisconsin case, a group of black teens were charged with beating up a white teenager. The ringleader, Todd Mitchell, was sentenced to two years for assault. But it turned out that Todd had egged his friends on with the words, "There goes a white boy. Go get him!" As a result, Todd was given an additional two years for his racist attitude.

The Supreme Court upheld the ruling, and now the Senate has jumped on the hate-crime bandwagon. But no one is facing the issue squarely: Should a free society punish not only the violence of the crime but also the thought behind it? Once we allow our laws to get into the business of punishing thoughts, then our lawmakers face a truly totalitarian task: deciding which thoughts should be permitted and which should be punished.

Think how easily this could be politicized. Recent court rulings have decreed that protesting at abortion clinics can be classified as a hate crime against women. We're standing at the top of a slippery slope that could end with any opinions being outlawed—*except* those of so-called enlightened liberal legislators.

In a free society, no one should be punished twice for the same crime.

Abortion by Bullet

The Death of Baby Brittany

IN A Florida hospital a young mother watched in agony as her tiny baby struggled to live. Born three months premature, the two-pound girl bristled with tubes. But despite the high-tech medical care, the baby's undeveloped organs failed, and two weeks after birth, she died. "I've never had nothing hurt so bad," her grieving mother said (*St. Petersburg Times,* 8 September 1994).

But perhaps what hurt most was the knowledge that she herself had caused her baby's death.

You see, the mother's name is Kawana Ashley, and many read about her in the news as the teenager who shot herself in the stomach in a desperate attempt to abort her baby. Kawana had tried to abort her baby by conventional means. But she was already in her fifth month of pregnancy, when abortions cost

$1,300 to $1,800, a sum she could not afford. The father of the child had abandoned her, and finally—just twelve weeks before the baby's anticipated birth—Kawana picked up a gun and shot herself in the side, hoping to kill her baby.

Well, she succeeded. But not right away. The baby was wounded, Kawana went into premature labor, and it took two weeks for the baby to die. Kawana was charged with the manslaughter of her child.

The incident sparked a storm of political debate. Pro-choice forces used Kawana's story to argue for more government funding of abortion for poor women. Pro-life leaders replied that the abortion clinics that turned Kawana away should have pointed her toward the nearest crisis pregnancy center; there she would have received financial and emotional support through the remainder of her pregnancy.

In legal terms, it is an excruciating irony that if an *abortionist* had killed the baby in the womb, it would all have been perfectly legal, and no one would be facing murder charges.

But what almost no one has picked up is the other side to this story: the change in Kawana herself. Once she actually saw her tiny baby and held her in her arms, Kawana was overwhelmed with a deep love. She gave her baby a name—Brittany—and reportedly told her family that she hoped desperately the baby would survive. At the baby's funeral, she wept openly, expressing her deep sense of grief and loss.

In other words, the story *behind* the headlines is that once Kawana knew what her baby was really like, she fell in love with her. In fact, it's possible that this entire tragedy could have been avoided if someone had taken the time to paint a picture of her baby for Kawana in the first place: if she had seen a photo of a baby in the womb with its perfectly formed arms and legs, sucking its tiny thumb.

The lesson for Christians is that we need to be certain we're not only making the case against abortion intellectually—using ethical arguments—but also engaging the whole person. When abortion becomes a reality—and not just an abstraction—then we all know deep in our hearts that it is wrong.

It's up to you and me to make sure the Kawana Ashleys of this world know that—before it's too late.

Adding Death to Injury

When Pregnancy Follows Rape

JULIE MAKIMAA is a completely ordinary young woman, with a loving husband and family. But some abortion rhetoric would suggest that people like Julie should never have been born.

Julie was the result of what we might call a "problem pregnancy." According to a new federal directive, all women who experience this problem ought to get an abortion. And for poor women, taxpayers should even pay for it.

The problem I'm talking about is rape. Thirty-one years ago, Julie's mother was sexually assaulted and became pregnant as a result. Instead of having an abortion, she carried the baby to term and gave her up for adoption. Today mother and daughter have been reunited; they travel across the country speaking against abortion.

A directive from the national Medicaid Bureau has decreed that in rape cases, abortion should be considered "medically necessary in the light of both medical and psychological health factors" (Quoted in *National Right to Life News*, January 1994). The assumption here is that having a child after rape endangers a woman's psychological health—that it prolongs the trauma of the assault. But pro-life advocates need to assert that this assumption has already been tested—and it has been proved false.

Julie Makimaa is the founder of a group called Fortress International, which polled hundreds of rape victims. The survey found that women who have had an abortion actually reported *more* pain, guilt, and anger. As one rape victim wrote, "The rape was a violent crime against me—but the abortion was the violent murder of my child, and I was a willing participant." Far from assuaging the pain of the assault, abortion made it worse (*Washington Times,* 22 August 1996).

By contrast, the rape victims who carried their babies to term told a completely different story. For them, having a baby meant that the horror of being assaulted had at least one positive outcome: a child to love. These women view their children as innocent victims of the crime, just as they themselves were. Having an abortion, they say, would only have compounded the crime.

Julie's own mother puts it starkly: Having an abortion, she said, would have meant giving Julie "the death sentence for the sexual-assault crime her *father* committed."

That would be neither justice nor mercy.

Tragically, the federal government seems to be paying no attention to the empirical facts—like the results of this survey. Instead, in a display of raw power, the administration has simply announced that henceforth all states must pay for Medicaid abortions in cases of rape or incest. States that prohibit or limit Medicaid coverage of abortion are seeing their laws simply bulldozed by the federal government.

Rape is a horrible crime, but abortion doesn't reverse it. It only adds death to injury.

NYPD Blues

Changing Our Outlook on Crime

PRECINCT 75 in Brooklyn used to be one of the most dangerous places to live in America. Young men turned the streets into open-air drug markets. The sound of gunshots frequently shattered the peace. Parents were afraid to let their children play outside—with good reason: Just three years ago, the neighborhood experienced 126 homicides.

But last year, homicides were down by an astonishing 65 percent.

What's behind this phenomenal decline?

For years the New York Police Department had relied on traditional anticrime measures: more arrests, longer prison terms. But instead of getting better, the neighborhood's crime problem got worse. In 1993, more people were murdered in this one *precinct* than in many of America's largest cities.

But then the NYPD adopted a new philosophy of crime. Instead of treating crime as an assault on the individual victim, the New York Police Department began treating it as an assault on the public order. Solving crime then meant looking for ways to rebuild the social order. The NYPD decided to show zero tolerance not only for crime itself but also for *any* social disorder.

In high-crime neighborhoods, police often turn a blind eye to such minor violations as running a red light. But the NYPD began cracking down on all traffic violators, looking for guns and drugs. They chased away loiterers, who often turned out to be drug dealers looking for a sale. They hired more cops to walk the beat.

These measures don't attack any major crimes directly. Yet they had an enormous effect on the neighborhood's overall crime rate. Why? Because small violations of the public order send a signal that nobody cares about the neighborhood.

Criminologists James Q. Wilson and George Kelling call this the "broken window syndrome." If authorities overlook petty offenses like vandalism and graffiti, they invite more serious offenses, such as assault and murder.

That's why cracking down on trivial offenses can discourage far more serious crime. Wilson and Kelling are echoing a classic Christian understanding of crime. Augustine wrote that peace should be thought of as "right order." If the right order of the community is disturbed and that disturbance is not addressed immediately, more chaos inevitably follows.

When the cops in Precinct 75 began going after loiterers and traffic violators, they were reestablishing the "right order" of their community. Today, kids in the seventy-fifth precinct play in the streets again. Adults sit on their stoops and visit with one another.

Helping Americans change the way they think about crime and punishment is the reason my colleague Dan Van Ness and I founded Justice Fellowship as an arm of Prison Fellowship in 1983. We had both spent many years working in prison ministry, and we had come to the same conclusion: Current solutions just weren't working.

We realized we needed to reintroduce basic biblical concepts about crime into America's criminal-justice system. Like the people of New York's Precinct 75, we can work together to find real solutions to crime.

Volunteer Power

....

The Revival of Civic Associations

THE HOUSTON park was once an inviting place for children to play. But tots on trikes were replaced by drug dealers who turned it into a "needle park" littered with hypodermic syringes. Then a citizen group called the Little League Squad arrived on the scene—and they turned a "needle park" into a ballpark.

The Little League Squad was made up of volunteer cops trained by law-enforcement officers in Houston's tough Precinct 6. The volunteers ran the drug dealers out of the park and cleaned it up. Then they invited neighborhood kids to form Little League teams. Churches, businessmen, and civic groups helped pay for bats and uniforms. Little League Squad members volunteered as coaches and patrolled the park for drug and alcohol abuse. Before long, enough kids had signed up to form several Little League teams—the neighborhood's first in twenty-five years.

One hundred fifty years ago, French statesman Alexis de Tocqueville wrote that America's greatest strength was her voluntary associations. And until a couple of decades ago, it was volunteers who took care of most neighborhood problems. Whether it was rowdy boys, abandoned children, a teenage girl in trouble, dilemmas were dealt with by churches and civic groups *before* they became matters for police or political platforms.

But many of the old voluntary associations have gone the way of poodle skirts and Packards—and the sobering consequences now litter our streets. Instead of actively solving neighborhood breakdown, citizens now peer nervously from behind barred windows.

What's behind this rapid decline in a sense of community? Part of the problem is that people today are more transient and put down shallower roots. But much of the problem also lies with government programs that have elbowed out local private and religious charities. Far-off bureaucrats simply can't compete in effectiveness with volunteers who live right in the community. Local problems should be solved by local people because they're most competent to handle them. For example, Houston's Precinct 6 doesn't just have a Little League Squad. In addition, the streets are patrolled by two hundred volunteer cops. A Graffiti Squad prevents vandalism. A Church Patrol stops criminals from robbing cars while their owners are worshiping.

This active community involvement has led to a decrease in homicides by nearly 50 percent. Robberies have dropped by 34 percent. Auto thefts are down 48 percent.

The success of voluntary groups over government programs really shouldn't surprise Christians. Seven centuries ago, Thomas Aquinas taught that the state's role in promoting the common good is limited. Aquinus warned that the state must recognize and uphold the rights of the family and of so-called intermediate institutions, such as the church, school, and voluntary associations.

Only citizens can really rebuild civil society, one city block at a time.

Citizens on Patrol

New Forms of Crime Prevention

IN ONE Baltimore neighborhood, thieves and burglars have all but given up. The streets are simply too well patrolled for anyone to make a dishonest buck. But the men driving the patrol cars don't wear badges, as you might expect.

Instead they wear yarmulkes.

These men are members of a large citizen patrol consisting solely of Orthodox Jews. The group formed in 1983, when local crime rates skyrocketed. Since then, according to the *Wall Street Journal,* street robberies have dropped 50 percent. A local police agent estimates that assaults on people have dropped from roughly one every three days to one a month (*Wall Street Journal,* 23 May 1994).

What makes this citizen patrol unique, however, is the religious motivation that keeps them on the streets day after day. These volunteers are out there because their rabbis insist on it. Keeping watch over their neighbors is not considered optional; it's a *mitzvah*—a religious duty.

On a typical evening, a dozen patrollers gather in a synagogue basement. A Baltimore police agent briefs the men on neighborhood crime patterns, then doles out flashlights, radios, and magnetic signs to attach to their cars.

Then the patrol cars hit the streets. One patroller stops at a local pizzeria and stands guard while the owner locks up. Another keeps watch while a young couple unloads their car from a late-night shopping trip. If patrollers spot anything suspicious, they radio the police at once.

Baltimore citizens love the patrol. "It's a pleasure having [them] come in and check on us," says a local businessman. "It's like the olden days, having the cop on the beat come in and see if things are OK."

This patrol doesn't stop at watching the streets, either. They lobby judges for strict and fair sentences for anyone arrested on their beat. And they show up at parole hearings, working with parole boards for the best balance in the needs of the neighborhood and the offender.

Police tend to be skeptical of citizen patrols; many collapse as the novelty wears off. But the Baltimore patrol is one of the largest and longest lasting in the country. The secret to its success is its religious motivation.

Their motto is "We Are Our Brothers' Keepers."

When citizens take their religion into the social arena, critics often paint them as intolerant and divisive. But this group of Orthodox Jews, patrolling the streets in their yarmulkes, demonstrate the *positive* social effects of biblical religion. When they put their faith into action, the entire community benefits.

Americans have developed a tendency to look to the government to solve the problem of crime. But the solutions government offers—building new prisons and passing tougher sentences—just don't work. The only real solution to crime is for every American to become his brother's keeper. Your local police department can tell you how to set up a citizen patrol in your own neighborhood.

Christians ought to be the first to put our faith into action. We should be the first to realize that taking care of our neighbors is not optional. It's what Orthodox Jews call a *mitzvah*—a religious duty.

Sentenced to Church

Crime and Moral Reform

EMMA JEAN OLIVER, a single mother of four, stood before a Texas judge awaiting sentence for a first-time drug offense. By law, she could get three years in prison, with fines up to $250,000. But when the judge banged his gavel and pronounced the sentence, Emma Jean gasped. Her punishment, the judge ruled, would be five years in the big house—the one down the street with the steeple on top. In other words, Emma Jean wasn't going to prison after all; instead, she was sentenced to five years' probation. As a condition of probation, Emma Jean and her four children would have to attend church every Sunday.

Whoever heard of anyone sentenced to church?

The ACLU and liberal members of the press muttered grimly over possible violations of the First Amendment. But Emma Jean was elated. She's a Baptist and felt that more consistent church attendance might be just what she and her family needed.

Besides, consider the alternatives. Would the ACLU prefer to see Emma Jean locked up? Emma Jean wasn't personally involved in any drug deals; she merely allowed a friend to store illegal drugs in her home. It would be ludicrous to throw her behind bars alongside hardened criminals.

What's more, if Emma Jean went to jail, her four children would be placed in foster care. In essence, the judge would be imposing a sentence on the children as well as their mother, tearing them away from their family and neighborhood. For minor offenses, it makes much more sense to use community-based alternatives to prison.

And, yes, even *church*-based alternatives. In sentencing Emma Jean to church, the judge was giving expression to a growing conviction among Americans that our society is being destroyed by moral decay. America has tried just about every known solution to crime. We've passed tougher laws. We've built more prisons, doubling our prison population since 1980. Conservatives have used prisons for deterrence, and liberals have used them for rehabilitation. Yet violent crime continues to rise. Our streets are no safer.

Out of desperation, people are beginning to realize that crime is not a malady that can be cured by public policy; it's a sickness of the soul. And the cure has to be sought in the deep wells of spiritual and moral tradition. When we see news items like a judge sentencing a lawbreaker to church, it's a sign that the American people are finally turning to spiritual answers to our social disorders. Only faith gives people the motivation to change their lives from the inside out.

That's why people like Emma Jean don't belong in a building surrounded by barbed wire. Instead, they belong in a building with a steeple on top.

Like a Good Neighbor

Taking the Offensive on Crime

IF YOU had visited the Graves Manor housing project in Memphis, Tennessee, a few years ago, you would have seen kids fighting, selling drugs, or roaming the neighborhood in gangs.

Today you would see the same kids quietly doing homework, acting out skits, or heading out on a field trip.

What transformed this neighborhood was a committed Neighborhood Watch organization. You may know Neighborhood Watch as a group that organizes in the suburbs, with citizens taking turns patrolling the streets to keep criminals out. But in crime-ridden places like Graves Manor, Neighborhood Watch has started innovative programs to reach kids *before* they turn to crime.

The Memphis Area Neighborhood Watch has been running a special Violence Reduction Program for children between the ages of five and seventeen. They provide tutoring and a quiet place for homework. They bring in a local theater group to teach the kids to write and act out skits. They organize a

Saturday school to teach leadership skills. And for special occasions they organize cultural programs and field trips.

Parents love it. Not only do they see their children's behavior improve, but the programs also bring parents together and create a sense of community. The program is so successful that it was showcased by the National Crime Prevention Council.

What the residents of Graves Manor discovered is something we all need to learn: that preventing crime is not someone else's job. It's not something we can slough off onto the government or the police or the social-service agencies. Preventing crime is your job and mine.

If you have any doubts, listen to the experts—to criminals themselves. In a recent survey Prison Fellowship asked prison inmates what could have prevented *their* crimes. One inmate wrote back: "My main job was breaking and entering into houses and offices. . . . I noticed that none of my victims lived in a crime-watch district."

Criminals do take notice when people care about their neighborhood, when they look out for one another.

Taking care of your neighbors isn't exactly a new idea. Two thousand years ago Jesus told a parable about a Samaritan who saw a man lying beside the road, beaten by criminals, desperately ill. The Samaritan didn't turn aside; he stepped in to help.

The Memphis Neighborhood Watch saw not one man but an entire housing complex reeling from the effects of drugs and violence. They didn't turn aside; they responded as neighbors.

The people of Graves Manor did not wait for the government to act; they acted on their own to breathe new life into a crime-ridden housing project. You and I should follow their example. We can take the offensive in fighting crime—not by buying guns and becoming vigilantes . . . but simply by following Jesus' command to be good neighbors.

God with Us

....

Emmanuel's Good News

"O COME, O come, Emmanuel"—every Advent we sing the song. But for me it evokes especially poignant memories ever since last Christmas, when Patty and I participated in Angel Tree—a Prison Fellowship ministry for distributing gifts to the children of prison inmates.

As we drove into the housing project to deliver our gifts, we saw broken windows and grim-faced gang members lounging in doorways. When we found the apartment, a boy about nine years old cautiously opened the door.

"Merry Christmas," I said, holding out the presents. "These are from your daddy."

Immediately, the door swung wide open to let us in. The boy's mother was working late, and as we waited, we saw that the apartment inside was as bleak as the courtyard outside: The furniture was torn, the stuffing falling out. A straggly Christmas tree leaned against the wall, bare of any presents.

"What's your name?" I asked the boy.

"Emmanuel," he replied.

"Emmanuel! Do you know what your name means?" I opened my Bible and read from Matthew: "And they shall call him Emmanuel—which means 'God with us.'"

When his mother came home, Emmanuel threw his arms around her, crying, "Mama, Mama, guess what my name means: God is with us!"

At that moment, in that clear, childish voice rising above the squalor of neglected hallways and crime-filled courtyards, I heard the message of Christmas proclaimed afresh: that God is indeed with us at all times—and in a special way at Christmas, when he entered history through Jesus Christ.

This is the message that Angel Tree volunteers bring to the children of prison inmates every Christmas. Even more exciting, many volunteers are beginning to keep contact with Angel Tree kids all year round. When they do, they're helping to hold back a wave of violent crime looming on the horizon.

The children of the baby-boom generation will soon be teenagers, the age most prone to violent crime. By the turn of the century, there will be one million more teens. *U.S. News & World Report* warns, "America should brace itself for a new surge of youthful violence" (*U.S. News & World Report*, 29 August 1994). Yet the most serious crimes are committed by a small percentage of teens: Only 6 percent of boys produce about half of all serious crime for each age group. According to criminologists, these boys tend to have parents who are themselves criminal; they tend to do poorly in school, to abuse alcohol and drugs, to live in poor, disorderly neighborhoods. What's more, they tend to begin their misconduct at an early age, often by the time they're in third grade.

In other words, these are the very kids Angel Tree volunteers are reaching out to.

The coming crime wave will swamp our criminal-justice system, no matter how many prisons we build or police officers we hire. But through Angel Tree, we can reach the children most at risk for a life of crime.

The government can't do it. The only people who can are Christians willing to take young children by the hand and tell them the message of Emmanuel—that God is with them.

Seven

THE FIRMAMENT PROCLAIMS HIS HANDIWORK

How Scientists Are Changing Their Spots

....

New Theories in Evolution

IF YOU pulled a book off the library shelf titled *How the Leopard Changed His Spots,* you might expect to find a children's story. But a recent book by that name is clearly aimed at adults. It's written by a well-known British biologist named Brian Goodwin, and it promotes a surprising theme: that Darwinism has failed to explain living things.

Goodwin is not a professing Christian, but he is one of a growing number of biologists who are questioning Darwinist orthodoxy. Darwin attributed evolution to small-scale changes taking place over vast periods of time. He studied the work of farmers and breeders who produced colorful varieties of domesticated animals, like pigeons, horses, and dogs. If the same small changes were to accumulate over long periods of time, Darwin theorized, they might add up to produce large changes—the kind that separate fish and reptiles, birds and mammals.

This assumption is the essence of Darwinism: that small-scale change, like the differences between breeds of dogs, is the source of large-scale change, like the difference between a dog and a horse. To use biological lingo, *micro*evolution—small, gradual change—is the mechanism for *macro*evolution—from molecules to man.

But it is precisely this link that biologists like Goodwin say is broken. "Look at all the variety of dogs," Goodwin writes in an essay. "But they're still dogs. You never go beyond canine characteristics" (In *The Third Culture,* ed. John Brockman). No breed of dog ever leads gradually to another kind of animal.

Nature gives us variations on a theme, not a ladder to new and different life-forms.

"Clearly something is missing from biology," Goodwin concludes. He urges biologists to drop Darwinism and adopt a theory based on what he calls laws of form in biology. Now, most biologists are skeptical of Goodwin's proposals, and some have even called him a New Age mystic. But the important message for Christians is that serious scientists are indeed questioning Darwinist dogma.

The scientific establishment would have us believe that the only dissenters from Darwinism are creationists and religious fundamentalists. A myth is perpetrated that all sensible scientists are Darwinists. Christians who question evolution are admonished in no uncertain terms to enter the modern world and reconcile their faith with the dictates of science.

But biologists like Brian Goodwin are exploding that myth. They show that the case against Darwinism is not simply a matter of religious prejudice. Good scientific arguments can be raised against Darwinism: As Goodwin puts it, Darwinism is simply "inconsistent with the evidence."

Ironically, Darwin's revolutionary book was titled *On the Origin of Species,* yet, as Goodwin points out, that is exactly what Darwin failed to explain. "The large-scale aspects of evolution remain unexplained," Goodwin writes, "including the origin of species."

So don't be intimidated by sweeping claims that "all scientists" accept Darwinian evolution. Biology has never demonstrated that all the wonderful variety of life can develop on its own, by purely natural causes, without a Creator.

And today some scientists—even non-Christian ones—are honest enough to admit it.

Take Me to Your Leader

....

Was There Life on Mars?

"TAKE me to your leader." Remember those words from the corny science-fiction films of the '50s? They featured bald, ET-like Martians who plotted to take over the world.

But the *real* Martian invasion turned out to be a lot less dramatic. In 1996, NASA scientists announced that they may have found evidence of life from Mars: organic molecules embedded in a meteorite found in Antarctica. The press instantly went into orbit, and even the president hailed the discovery as significant.

The reason for all the hoopla is that life on other planets has been long considered potential confirmation of the naturalistic worldview—the theory that life arose by purely natural forces. Science journalist Timothy Ferris argues that if organisms existed on Mars, then "life, far from being a singular miracle" on Earth, may in fact be the predictable consequence of certain planetary conditions. Life on Mars, Ferris argues, would prove that life starts "routinely," whenever conditions are right—on Earth, Mars, or anywhere else (*New Yorker,* 19 August 1996).

In other words, if Martian life *did* exist, some interpret that as tipping the balance in favor of naturalism instead of a Creator.

But would life on other planets really prove there is no God? Not at all. No matter where life is found, it is more complex than anything produced by known natural forces. Finding new forms of life in strange places doesn't change that fact.

Imagine you were from a Stone Age culture and saw a computer for the first time. You would have no idea where such a complex structure came from. If someone handed you a second computer, would that tell you where computers come from? Of course not. No mystery was ever solved by adding a second mystery.

In the same way, if the origin of life on Earth is a mystery, then finding life somewhere else does nothing to *solve* the mystery. The simplest living things are astonishing in their complexity. If life existed on Mars, even as tiny bacteria, it would still be far beyond anything purely natural laws can explain.

Christians believe that wherever life occurs, it was created by a personal God. As biologist and philosopher Paul Nelson puts it, "The intelligent design claim is not that life is restricted to earth. It's that wherever life occurs, it's created by intelligence."

The Scriptures say nothing about whether life-forms exist anywhere else in the universe. Historically, many Christians have found it perfectly possible that life existed on other planets. In *God in the Dock* C. S. Lewis wrote that the universe "may be quite full of life" and argued that we humans have no right to prescribe limits to God's interests. Of course, the molecules in the rock found in Antarctica may or may not really indicate traces of life. Many scientists remain skeptical, and this side of heaven, we may never know for sure whether life exists on other planets.

But wherever life exists, we can be sure of one thing: It was not the product of natural forces but of an intelligent Creator.

Is Everything Relative?

What Einstein Really Meant

"THE MODERN world began on May 29, 1919." With this statement historian Paul Johnson begins his book *Modern Times*. On that historic day, photographs of a solar eclipse showed that starlight bends when passing close to the sun. The photos confirmed Albert Einstein's concept of curved space—thereby confirming his revolutionary theory of relativity.

The news hit the world like a thunderclap. Einstein rejected Isaac Newton's concept of absolute time and space. To the general public he seemed to be rejecting *all* absolute truth— including the truths of morality and religion.

"Rela*tivity* became confused with rela*tivism*," Johnson writes. "It formed a knife . . . to help cut society adrift from its traditional moorings in the faith and morals of Judeo-Christian culture."

Even today people think Einstein proved the maxim "Everything is relative." Yet Einstein himself said his theory had nothing to do with relativism. In fact, he preferred to call it "invariance theory" because it showed that physical laws do not vary across reference frames.

As Nancy Pearcey and Charles Thaxton explain in *The Soul of Science,* an easy way to understand Einstein is to consider a simpler form of relativity proposed centuries earlier by Galileo. Imagine a ship traveling ten miles per hour, with the captain strolling along the deck in the same direction. Relative to a person sitting in a deck chair, the captain is walking, say, three miles per hour. But relative to someone sitting on the shore, the captain is moving thirteen miles per hour, because you add in the speed of the ship.

So how fast is the captain *really* moving—three miles per hour or thirteen? It all depends on your frame of reference. For a measurement from the shore, you add in the speed of the ship. For a measurement from the deck, you *subtract* the speed of the ship.

This was Galileo's theory of relativity. It shows how the laws of motion apply across different reference frames. Einstein's relativity theory merely updated Galileo's to take into account the laws of electromagnetism—such as the speed of light. Einstein demonstrated that these laws likewise remain valid across all reference frames.

It's true that in the process he discarded Newton's concepts of absolute space and time, ending up with bizarre notions like curved space and time slowing down. We've all heard about the Twin Paradox, where a baby goes up in a space ship and seventy years later is still a child, while his twin brother back on Earth has become an old man. Yet these bizarre notions are all simply mathematical deductions from the assumption that the laws of electromagnetism remain constant across all reference frames.

It's all perfectly mathematical. There is nothing in rela*tivity* to support rela*tivism*.

Einstein's theory is a vivid example of the way scientific theories are often misused to assault Christian faith and morals. You and I need to learn how to respond to these assaults.

Everything is *not* relative. And we need to stand against the hijacking of science to promote a destructive philosophical agenda.

Are You "Anti-Science"?

The Christian Origins of Science

VERY soon, "the practice of religion must be regarded as anti-science."

With these words, another salvo was launched in the war between religion and science. The writer was John Maddox, editor of *Nature,* the world's most prestigious science journal—the journal that practically defines what counts as science today. And now it has defined religion as "anti-science" (*Nature,* 17 March 1994).

That would be a big surprise to the people who *founded* modern science. Most of the early scientists—Copernicus, Isaac Newton, Carl Linnaeus—were Christians. In fact, historians tell us that Christianity actually helped inspire the scientific revolution.

Consider a few examples. In pagan cultures, the world seemed alive with river goddesses, sun gods, astral deities. But Genesis 1 stands in stark contrast to all that. Nature is not divine; it is God's handiwork. The sun and moon are not gods; they are merely lights placed in the sky to serve God's purposes.

This teaching provided a crucial assumption for science: As long as nature commanded religious worship, digging too closely into her secrets was deemed irreverent. But in Christianity nature was no longer an object of fear and worship. Then—and only then—could nature become an object of scientific study.

Another crucial assumption for science is that nature is orderly. This, too, was provided by Christianity The belief that God is rational and trustworthy implies that his creation is rational and ordered. The early scientists described that order as "natural law." Today this phrase is so common, we may not realize how unique it once was. Yet as historian A. R. Hall points out, no other culture used the word *law* in relation to nature.

The idea of laws in nature came from the biblical teaching that God is both Creator and Lawgiver.

Even the experimental method of science has roots in Christianity. Since it is *God's* rationality that orders nature and not our own, we cannot sit in an ivory tower and do science by sheer rational deduction. Instead, we must do experiments and see what happens.

For example, when Galileo wanted to find out whether a ten-pound weight falls to the ground more quickly than a one-pound weight, he didn't argue about the "nature" of weight, as was typical among philosophers of his day. Instead, he dropped cannon-balls off the Leaning Tower of Pisa and watched what happened.

Some historians believe the story of Galileo is apocryphal, but the point still stands: In their writings, Galileo and other early scientists explicitly argued that God's ways are not necessarily our ways—that God's ways in nature have to be discovered by experiment and observation.

The fact is that people like John Maddox who portray religion as "anti-science" simply don't know their history. It's up to you and me to make sure we *do* know our history.

Christians need to learn how to defend their faith against irresponsible attacks launched in the name of science.

Quantum Mysteries

The New Age Comes to Science

PICTURE this for a movie idea: Two men visit a medieval abbey in France, where a physics professor lectures them for hours on the meaning of life.

Sounds deadly dull, doesn't it? Surprise: It's the theme of a trendy art film called *Mindwalk,* which has attracted a loyal band of devotees. The film is based on a book by physicist Fritjof Capra. In fact, it's little more than a series of lectures expounding Capra's view that quantum physics supports Eastern mysticism. As one reviewer put it, the movie is a "New Age seminar."

But what does quantum physics have to do with New Age mysticism?

Quantum mechanics has discovered that the parts of an atom—such as electrons—behave sometimes as particles, sometimes as waves. The reason this is so disturbing is that waves and particles have properties that are flat-out contradictory. For example, a wave is spread out in space, whereas a particle is confined to a tiny region.

Scientists resolve the contradiction by saying an electron merely *appears* as a particle or wave—depending on the kind of experiment we run. But if *we* determine what properties an electron has, some scientists say, then we are not merely passive observers; instead, we actively *create* something whenever we make an observation.

For New Agers, this rings of Eastern mysticism, which teaches that the universe is a creation of our minds. As Capra puts it in *The Turning Point,* "The electron does not have objective properties independent of my mind." In *Mysticism and the New Physics,* Michael Talbot says, "There *is* no physical world 'out there.' Consciousness creates all."

This mystical interpretation of the new physics is repeated in countless New Age books, but real physicists consider it totally bogus. After all, scientists don't affect experiments through their *minds* but through their *instruments.* Atomic particles are tracked using photographic screens and Geiger counters, and no scientist needs to be there for black marks to appear on a photographic screen or for a Geiger counter to click.

No, whatever New Agers say, quantum mechanics does not deny that an objective world exists independent of our minds. And that means that it is not really compatible with Eastern mysticism at all. The religion it actually favors is Christianity—for the Bible teaches that God created a real world, not just a dream of human consciousness.

As Nancy Pearcey and Charles Thaxton show in *The Soul of Science,* one reason modern science emerged in the West and *not* the East is that the early scientists were Christians. They accepted the biblical teaching that the world is real and can be investigated by rational methods.

You may have thought of quantum physics as an abstract theory far removed from our lives. But its impact is terribly near to all of us since a misguided interpretation is opening the door to the New Age movement.

Christians ought to be the ones teaching our children, writing books, and, yes, even producing trendy films to explain what the new physics really means. Otherwise we will continue to leave the field wide open to New Agers.

Forbidden Science

Spiritual Evolution and Other Mysticisms

SCIENTISTS are getting religion. At least that's the way it appears, based on several books now on the market. But the religion is not Christianity; instead, it's a revival of age-old pantheism.

Take *In the Beginning,* by astrophysicist John Gribbin. Gribbin starts with a theory known as the Gaia hypothesis, which proposes that Earth is alive—that Earth itself is a living, self-regulating system. But Gribbin takes that idea a step further: He claims that the entire universe is alive. He suggests that black holes are baby universes that grow up and give birth to *other* baby universes in an endless process of evolution.

Where will the process end? In another book, *Equations of Eternity,* astrophysicist David Darling gives a startling answer: The universe is evolving into a cosmic mind. As Darling puts it, the universe is becoming its own god.

All this talk about "god" doesn't mean scientists are turning to Christianity. Gribbin states quite clearly that he rejects the idea of a transcendent Creator. In his words, "As for God, cosmology . . . has no need of that hypothesis."

Instead, what we're seeing is a revival of an earlier science that many people *thought* was discredited. The idea that the universe is evolving up to godhood has roots in eighteenth-century Romanticism. Many biologists of that period believed that matter is made up of living molecules and that the entire universe is evolving up a great Chain of Being to divinity. Romantic biologists believed in a universal Life Force unfolding from simple to complex forms under a cosmic Law of Development.

Today the leaders of scientific orthodoxy would prefer to forget that period of history. They insist that "true" science must be completely materialistic. They're the authors of your children's textbooks, which often dismiss any spiritual beliefs.

But we ought to teach our kids to call their bluff. Real science has never stayed within the narrow bounds of philosophical materialism—neither during its historical development nor today, judging by the titles now on bookstore shelves.

The truth is that science has always encompassed widely diverse philosophies of nature—from the Christian teaching of creation (which most of the early scientists held) to Romantic pantheism to modern scientific materialism.

What this means is that Christians need to get busy developing apologetics for the whole range of beliefs permeating our culture—from scientific materialism to pantheistic spiritualism.

Scientists may be getting religion, but you and I need to ask what *kind* of religion. Holding a *false* religion is just as dangerous as holding *no* religion at all.

Galileo Was Right

Debunking Old Myths

GALILEO was right after all, headlines blared in 1995.

The news reports announced that the Roman Catholic Church officially revoked its condemnation of Galileo, imposed more than three centuries ago. Pope John Paul II admitted that the church made a tragic mistake in forcing Galileo to recant his conviction that the earth goes around the sun.

The story of Galileo has always provided rich fodder for critics of religion. They love to cite it as the textbook case of Christian hostility to science.

But the real story is not a simple tale of good guys versus bad guys. The pope who condemned Galileo was not opposed to his *scientific* ideas. In fact, he was once a member of a group of Galileo's supporters. What actually concerned the pope was not Galileo's *science* but the way he *used* science to attack the philosophy taught by the Catholic Church, which it had adapted from Aristotle.

You see, Aristotle offered a comprehensive philosophy covering not only metaphysics and ethics but also biology, physics, and astronomy. When Galileo built the first telescope and aimed it at the heavens, he discovered that Aristotle was dreadfully mistaken in his astronomy. For example, Aristotle taught that the sun was perfect, but Galileo discovered sunspots and other "imperfections."

Soon Galileo was attacking *all* of Aristotle's philosophy. He hoped to replace it with a new mechanistic philosophy that treated the world as a vast machine operating solely by mathematical laws, with God as the Great Mechanic.

That's when Catholic authorities got worried. They saw clearly that Galileo was not just addressing scientific questions—that instead he was attacking Aristotelianism as an entire system. But Aristotle taught a classical view of ethics that many theologians appealed to in defending biblical ethics. They were afraid that Galileo's scathing attacks could destroy the moral basis for the social order.

It was this concern for morality and social order, not any hostility to science, that motivated the Catholic hierarchy to oppose Galileo. The conflict was not between religion and science per se but between Christians holding different worldviews: the Aristotelian worldview adopted by the Catholic Church and the competing mechanistic worldview proposed by Galileo.

The fact is that Christianity itself is not inherently hostile to science. If it were, we would be hard pressed to explain why so many founders of modern science were Christians. Copernicus, Kepler, Boyle, and Newton studied creation in order to glorify the Creator. Galileo himself insisted that his target was Aristotle only, not the Bible, which he clearly accepted.

It's time for Christians to stop being defensive about our history. Don't sit passively when you hear those old charges that Christianity is an enemy of science. Debunk that myth with a true account of history.

The history of science is largely a story of *Christians* debating how to understand God's relationship to the world. Whether it's Galileo on the Leaning Tower of Pisa or Newton with his apple, Western science has a rich history of Christians putting their faith into action.

God versus Darwin

What Darwinism Really Means

WHY can't creationists just be reasonable?

Eugenie Scott, of the National Center for Science Education, raised this question in a recent debate with Phillip Johnson, author of a book debunking Darwin. I have friends who believe God created life, Scott went on, "people of deep faith," yet they accept Darwinism as the mechanism God used. Why are creationists still holding out?

That's a fair question. Many Christians *do* accept both the Bible and Darwinism. What's wrong with that?

To answer that question, we need to look closely at what Darwin really said. Even in Darwin's own day, many Christians tried to combine his theory with divine purpose and design. For example, the botanist Asa Gray tried to find a divine plan in natural selection.

But Darwin protested that this was not what he meant at all. If God was behind evolution, he said, then each variation in living things would be predetermined by divine purpose. But in that case, there would be no need for natural selection.

The whole point of natural selection is to demonstrate how limbs and organs that *appear* to be designed might actually result from random changes—by sifting out the harmful changes from those that are beneficial. But if the changes were not random—if God preselected only beneficial changes in the first place—then obviously nature would not need any sifting. In Darwin's own words, if God ensured that "the right variations occurred, and no others, natural selection would be 'superfluous' "—unnecessary, redundant.

Christians need to understand that the two central elements of Darwin's theory—random changes and the blind sifting of natural selection—were both proposed expressly to get rid of design and purpose in biology. In *Darwin, Marx, Wagner: Critique of a Heritage,* historian Jacques Barzun writes, "The sum total of accidents of life acting upon the sum total of the accidents of variation . . . provided a completely mechanical and material system to account for adaptations in living things." What this means is that Darwinism is not merely a biological theory. Instead, it smuggles in a philosophy of naturalism that is implacably opposed to any idea of purpose or design.

In *The Soul of Science,* Nancy Pearcey and Charles Thaxton show that science is always driven by philosophical and religious motivations. Throughout history many biologists, from Ray to Linnaeus to Cuvier, were Christians. They studied the finely engineered structures in living things—eyes and ears, fins and feathers—in order to reveal the wisdom of the Creator.

But Darwin's motivations were equally religious: He wanted to get *rid* of the Creator. He took direct aim at the idea of design and purpose, hoping to replace it with a completely naturalistic mechanism.

When Darwinists urge Christians to "just be reasonable," they're papering over the radically opposed religious motivations behind scientific theories. You and I ought to tear the paper off; we ought to demand that Darwinists be honest about the naturalistic philosophy implicit in their theory.

The evolution controversy shows just how strongly science is driven by deep religious commitments.

Mind Your Math

....

Uncovering the Structure of Creation

PHYSICIST Paul Davies has written a book titled *The Mind of God*—yet Davies doesn't even believe in God. So why would he choose that title? Davies's point is that modern science started out with the belief that it was uncovering the very thoughts of God.

Many of us grew up with the conception that science and Christianity are bitter enemies, but that's actually a *mis*conception. Davies is dead right when he says science started with the conviction that by studying the mathematical structure of creation, scientists could catch a glimpse of the Creator's mind.

In fact, the very idea that creation *has* a mathematical structure emerged from Christianity. The ancient Greeks, who shaped much of Western thought, relegated mathematics to a realm of abstract ideals. They thought the material world was too formless, too unpredictable to be described mathematically.

But Christianity teaches that the material world is *God's* handiwork—and therefore it is *not* formless; it is exactly what God wants it to be. The early scientists expected to find precise order in the dust and dirt of the physical world itself.

Take Copernicus. When he proposed that the planets go around the sun instead of the earth, he had no empirical evidence. Without telescopes, observations of the planets fit equally well with an earth-centered system. The sole factor favoring a sun-centered system was that it was simpler mathematically. And since Copernicus was convinced that God had made the world mathematically, that was good enough for him. Later, of course, he was proved right.

Then there was Kepler, famous for discovering that the orbits of the planets are not circles, as people thought at the time, but ellipses. It started when Kepler noticed a slight mismatch between mathematical calculations of Mars's orbit and actual observations. The difference was so tiny that other scientists had overlooked it.

But Kepler was convinced that everything in creation is precisely what God wants it to be. If God wanted the orbits to be circular, they would be *exactly* circular. And if they were not exactly circular, they must be exactly something else. Inspired by his Christian faith, Kepler struggled for years to reconcile the slight mismatch in Mars's orbit—finally hitting upon the discovery that the orbits are actually ellipses.

The same conviction inspired Galileo. The book of nature, Galileo said, is "written by the hand of God in the language of mathematics." The same conviction likewise inspired Isaac Newton, who put classical physics on a mathematical basis.

Anyone who studies the history of science is forced to acknowledge that from the beginning, science and Christianity have been allies, not enemies. Science was founded on the assumption that God created the world with a mathematical structure and that human beings can discover that structure.

The early scientists were not hostile to religion. On the contrary, they firmly believed they were discovering, as Paul Davies puts it, the mind of God.

Aping the Image of God

....

Are Great Apes Nonhuman Persons?

WHEN Thomas Jefferson penned the words "all men are created equal," was he thinking of gorillas, too?

He should have been, according to the authors of a recent book.

Titled *The Great Ape Project: Equality beyond Humanity,* the book is a collection of essays by thirty-nine ethicists, biologists, and philosophers, edited by animal-rights activists Peter Singer and Paola Cavalieri. The authors propose an audacious conclusion: that primates should be recognized as "nonhuman persons" with the same moral and legal rights as human beings.

The argument for primate "personhood" runs along several lines. First, human DNA differs from the DNA of chimpanzees by only 2 percent. Apes also show a certain capacity for language, problem solving, and self-reflection. They even seem to feel emotions—just as humans do.

Based on these facts, the notion that people are entitled to any rights denied to apes is dismissed as "human arrogance." The editors write: "We demand the extension of the community of equals to include all great apes: human beings, chimpanzees, gorillas, and orangutans." Laws should prohibit killing or detaining "without due legal process" any member of that community "who (has) not been convicted of any crime."

Due process? Does this mean cops will have to give Miranda warnings to gorillas?

The argument for primate personhood may sound silly. But some scientists have been so inspired by *The Great Ape Project* that they're lobbying to get the United Nations to pass a

Declaration on Great Apes to guarantee apes the right to life, liberty, and freedom from torture.

How would "gorilla rights" translate into law? Well, it would no longer be legal to use "nonconsenting" great apes for medical research (although how we'd know if they consented or not is anyone's guess). Zoos and circuses would be forced to free their great apes.

Giving apes personhood status is only the beginning. Singer says the next step is to declare dolphins and whales to be "persons," too. Some animal liberationists want to put *all* animals on the same moral plane as humans. As chimpanzee researcher Jane Goodall writes, "the line dividing 'man' from 'beast' has become increasingly blurred."

Well, the line may be blurry to animal-rights activists, but to Christians it ought to be crystal clear. Scripture teaches that God created humans in his own image and conferred on them a unique moral status. He then placed them in a harmonious but hierarchical creation, giving them responsibility to tend and care for the Garden.

Animal-rights activists are not just softhearted people who love cuddly animals. Instead, they're promoting a nonbiblical, naturalistic worldview that threatens to denigrate the unique moral status of human beings. The truth is that the moral chasm that divides us is big enough for King Kong to swing through.

Scientific Blinders

Overlooking the Obvious

"SCIENCE and Christianity Are Compatible," announced the title of a recent article in *The Scientist*. At least, the subtitle went on, they're compatible *if* we're willing to make "some compromises."

But when you read the article, you discover that all the "compromises" have to be made on the side of Christianity.

The author is Eugenie Scott, of the National Center for Science Education. Scott insists that science and Christianity will get along just fine, so long as each stays in its proper domain. That may sound fair enough—but it turns out that everything that matters falls in the domain of science.

In Scott's view, Christians are limited to the subjective world of faith and feelings. They're out-of-bounds if they try to explain the objective world of nature from a religious perspective. Only science is permitted to describe nature, and in her definition, science is committed to naturalism—which means, to put it bluntly, that science has to "leave God out." Her organization is dedicated to promoting Darwinian evolution as the only scientific theory of life's origin.

Now, Scott is a philosophical naturalist, so perhaps it's not surprising that her so-called "compromise" favors science. What *is* surprising is that many Christians agree. For example, Francis Collins, director of the National Center for Human Genome Research, is an evangelical Christian. Yet in a recent speech he agreed that science and religion "operate in different spheres." "Science [explores] the natural," Collins said, "faith explores the supernatural" (address given at University of North Carolina, Chapel Hill).

But reality simply doesn't fit so neatly into separate categories.

As professor Phillip Johnson argues in *Reason in the Balance,* if a supernatural Creator really exists, he just might have chosen to do some creating. It's silly to speak as though the almighty God is forbidden to affect nature.

In fact, nature offers evidence of divine purpose at every turn: Eyes are clearly designed for seeing and ears for hearing; feathers are designed for flying and fins for swimming. Even dyed-in-the-wool atheists, like biologist Richard Dawkins, admit that the evidence speaks strongly in favor of design. In *The Blind Watchman* Dawkins defines biology as "the study of complicated things that give the appearance of having been designed for a purpose."

But biologists have it drilled into them that science is by definition naturalistic—and as a result, they're forced to close their eyes to the obvious design in living things. They're forced to come up with theories explaining how living things "really" evolved by chance variations and natural laws—even though they appear to be designed. In other words, the entire evolution debate hangs on the way we define science. As Johnson puts it, "If the atheists make the rules, the atheists are surely going to win the game regardless of what is true."

But why should Christians let atheists make the rules? If God exists, there's no reason to accept a naturalistic definition of science, which assumes he does *not* exist. If Christianity is true, then it is true across the board—in science as well as religion.

Science and Christianity *are* compatible—but only if we keep our eyes open to the all-pervasive evidence for design.

Night of the Living Dead

....

Why We're Not Zombies

NIGHT *of the Living Dead.* The title alone sends chills up one's back. In the classic horror film, the "living dead" were zombies—corpses come to life. What made them so repulsive was that their bodies worked like clockwork but they had no minds, no consciousness. They were living machines.

The notion of zombies is fiction, of course, but it illustrates a fact that has puzzled scientists for centuries: namely, why aren't human beings like zombies? Why aren't we merely living machines? Why do we have minds and consciousness?

The question of consciousness was explored by a host of scientists and psychologists during a conference at the University of Arizona. It became obvious that for scientists who accept evolution, attempts to explain human consciousness have reached a dead end. The problem with consciousness is that we don't seem to need it. For the success of Darwinian evolution, all essential biological functions could be entirely automatic.

Think of it this way: If you put your hand on a hot stove, sheer reflex pulls it away—*before* you feel any pain. Biologically speaking, that's all that matters. Conscious awareness of pain—thinking, *Ouch, I burned myself*—is completely unnecessary.

So why are humans conscious of things like pain and flavors, smells and colors? Why would evolution select for something that is biologically useless?

The puzzle is put well by David Chalmers, of the University of California, in *The Conscious Mind.* The only thing natural selection requires is that every creature reproduce, Chalmers writes. Evolutionary success is defined as leaving the most offspring, and leaving offspring doesn't take mental awareness.

Even tiny bacteria reproduce quite effectively, without a hint of conscious awareness.

The upshot is that we could all just as well be zombies—creatures that act and respond to stimuli, without any subjective awareness of what we're doing. As Chalmers writes, "evolution alone cannot explain why conscious creatures rather than zombies evolved."

In a similar vein, biologist John Maynard Smith admits that the problem of consciousness has him "stumped." A confirmed atheist, Smith says that on this issue he's almost tempted to believe in God. As he puts it, "I've never had a particular wish to find a refuge in God, but if I did it would be because of the philosophical issue of consciousness" (*London Times,* 5 May 1996).

My advice to people like Smith is simple: Give in to the temptation. Where evolutionary biology fails to explain consciousness, Christian faith gives a clear and reasonable answer. The Bible begins with a personal God who thinks, feels, and responds—a God who created human beings in his image, which means we are also personal beings who think, feel, and respond. As the Westminster Confession puts it, we were created to glorify God and enjoy him forever.

If you have friends or family who are atheists, press them to reconsider. Evolution might be adequate to produce zombies, but it cannot explain the most basic facts of human experience—why we feel joy and sorrow, appreciate a sunset, or enjoy the pungent taste of an orange.

Those are things no zombie will ever be able to do.

Science Myths

....

Can Physics Explain Everything?

NEXT time you're in a bookstore, browse through the science section for some startling titles: *The Mind of God, Theories of Everything,* and *Dreams of a Final Theory.* These books promise that physics is on the brink of finding a super-theory capable of explaining everything in the universe.

In other words, while most people find ultimate truth in religion, many scientists are urging us to find it in physics.

Consider Stephen Hawking's runaway best-seller, *A Brief History of Time.* Hawking promises that science will eventually give us "a complete understanding of . . . existence." A big step toward that goal is finding a unified theory of the four fundamental forces of nature—the electromagnetic force, the weak nuclear force, the strong nuclear force, and gravity. In Hawking's words, a unified theory "would be the ultimate triumph of human reason—for then we would know the mind of God." Hawking doesn't believe in God, so what he really means is that humans would attain godlike omniscience.

Do you hear echoes of the Temptation in the Garden of Eden? It turns out that supplanting God is often precisely the motivation in the search for a unified theory. In *Reason in the Balance,* Phillip Johnson points out that such a theory would be so highly theoretical, it would be impossible to confirm by experiment. Which is to say, it would not be strictly speaking scientific at all: Its appeal would be philosophical or religious.

You see, many physicists believe that the four fundamental forces were unified in the earliest moments of the big bang, when the universe began. If you assume that the universe is a closed system of natural causes and effects, then those initial conditions determined everything else that has happened in the history of the cosmos. A theory explaining those initial conditions would thus be the key to explaining the entire cosmos by purely natural causes.

Then physics could finally dispense with *supernatural* causes—such as a divine Creator.

The question at the core of science today is whether God exists or whether nature is all there is. It's put bluntly by British physicist Paul Davies in his book *The Mind of God*. There, Davies says Hawking's theories could well "be quite wrong." But so what? The real issue, Davies explains, "is whether or not some sort of supernatural act is necessary to start the universe off. If a plausible scientific theory can be constructed that will explain the origin of the entire physical universe, then at least we know a scientific explanation is possible, whether or not the current theory is right."

Did you get that? It's an amazing admission. Davies is frankly admitting that for him *it doesn't matter* whether a scientific theory is right or wrong; it matters only whether the theory gets rid of the supernatural. This amounts to admitting that even a myth is acceptable, so long as it's a *naturalistic* myth—so long as it reassures scientists they don't have to worry about a Creator.

You and I need to teach our children how to discern real science from naturalistic philosophy. The Temptation in the Garden still echoes through the halls of human history—and in the scientist's laboratory.

Watches and Widgets

....

Does Nature Have a Purpose?

IT'S HARD to be an atheist in America.

Even our language is permeated with Christian overtones. I'm not talking only about figures of speech, like "God only knows." Even science cannot get rid of references to God.

Take the field of biology. No matter how hard they try, biologists cannot avoid talking about purpose. Philosophy professor Lowell Nissen, writing in a journal called *Studies in the History and Philosophy of Science,* says biology cannot get rid of the language of purpose.

Think of some simple examples. Why do animals have eyes? In order to see. Why do they have ears? In order to hear. In fact, biological structures are strikingly similar to man-made tools, where the purpose is its defining feature: A camera is made to take pictures; a watch is made to tell time.

But if you're an atheist, this commonsense way of talking poses a serious problem. If eyes and ears have a purpose, that implies someone *made* them for a purpose. It implies that there's a Creator—an idea that atheists want to banish from science. Professor Nissen says the language of purpose threatens to take biology right outside the boundary of natural science.

That's not true, of course. Great figures in the history of biology, such as Carl Linnaeus, John Ray, and Georges Cuvier, believed that God created living structures for a purpose—and that belief did not make these men any less scientific.

The fact is that the notion of purpose is no threat to *natural* science; it's a threat only to *naturalistic* science. There's a big difference. Natural science merely means the study of nature.

But *naturalistic* science means the acceptance of a philosophy that nature is all that exists.

Naturalism is simply atheism in scientific garb. Scientists who adhere to it are forced to deny purpose in the world—because that would imply a Creator.

Ironically, biologists keep using the word *purpose* because there's no other way to talk about things like eyes and ears. But they redefine the word. We're not talking about divine purpose, they say; we're just talking about functions. When we ask why animals have eyes, we may *say* it's for the purpose of seeing—but all we really *mean* is that seeing is the function of eyes.

But that redefinition just won't wash. The function of seeing can't explain why eyes exist. Seeing happens only when eyes already exist. Redefining purpose as function puts the cause *after* the effect; it puts the horse after the cart.

There is simply no way to get rid of purpose in biology. It would be a lot smarter to get rid of the dogma of naturalism. If we accept that God designed the world, then the language of purpose makes perfect sense. Eyes really were made for seeing— made by God.

As Christians we should be eager to talk about divine purpose in the world. The fact that biology cannot get along without the notion is a great argument we can use with our skeptical friends.

Contrary to what philosophical naturalists tell us, real science acknowledges the Creator—who made the world for a purpose.

From Junk to Jewels

....

Hidden Messages in DNA

SCIENTISTS are having to crack the genetic code all over again.

Since the '60s, scientists have known that the DNA molecule is like a written message—that it contains instructions for every living structure, from fish to flowers. But in higher organisms, the DNA code is broken up by sections of what looks like sheer nonsense—long DNA sequences that don't code for anything at all.

Scientists have dubbed these sequences "junk" DNA.

Kenneth Miller, a biologist at Brown University, even uses junk DNA to criticize the idea of divine creation. How can we believe God directly created us, Miller argues, if the human genome is littered with genetic trash? An intelligent Creator wouldn't write nonsense into our genes (*Technology Review,* February 1994).

But one researcher's junk can be another's jewels. Other scientists have discovered that junk DNA does important work after all. It functions to correct errors and regulate genes, turning them on and off at appropriate times. In short, what once appeared to be *non*sense DNA actually makes very *good* sense.

It seems that the foes of creation spoke too soon—and put their feet squarely in their mouths. DNA actually provides remarkable evidence for creation, giving a new twist to the classic design argument.

The classic argument goes like this: Suppose you discover a watch lying on the beach. Would you say, "Oh, look what the wind and waves have created"? Of course not. The ordered structure of a watch is clearly the product of human intelligence, and since living things have a similar structure, they too require an intelligent origin.

The design argument was presented nearly two hundred years ago by the English clergyman William Paley, and it rests on an analogy between the order found in man-made gadgets and living things. Later Charles Darwin attacked the design argument, countering that natural selection could create the same kind of order. There the issue rested for more than a century.

But today science offers a much more striking analogy than any William Paley could give—namely, the identical structure in written messages and the DNA molecule. Suddenly the design argument has become much more compelling. Suppose you discover not a watch but a book or computer disk on the beach. Are there any natural forces that create written messages?

None that we know of.

Evolutionists say that the DNA molecule originated by purely physical-chemical forces, but that's like saying a book is written by chemical reactions in the paper and ink. Or that a computer program is created by the magnetic forces in a computer disk. Nonsense.

The truth is that the DNA code is powerful scientific evidence that life is the product of intelligent design—evidence that is simple, easy to explain, and based solidly on ordinary experience. Whether written on paper, flashing on a computer screen, or scratched in the sand, messages are written only by intelligent agents.

That's why it's good news that "junk" DNA is not junk after all. Instead, it's bursting with information—which is striking evidence that its message was "written" by an intelligent Being.

Doubting Darwin

....

The Real Debate

FOR an eight-year-old boy, it was a startling comment: "Mama," he said, "sometimes I wonder what we're here for."

Does life have a purpose? Is there meaning to existence? These are among the most significant questions human beings face over their lifetime—questions that often drive us to God for answers.

Today many scientists urge us to turn to science instead. Science is not just about forecasting the weather or mapping our genes, we're told. It's also the basis for an entire worldview—a naturalistic worldview that tells us there *is* no ultimate purpose or meaning to life.

Cornell professor William Provine is an evangelist for the naturalistic worldview. Provine travels to college campuses giving a lecture entitled "The Unfinished Darwinian Revolution." His message is that Darwinism is not just about biology, it also entails an entire philosophy of life: It implies that the appearance of life on the earth can be explained by natural causes alone—that the history of the universe is a product of random events and impersonal natural laws.

In a word, Darwinism entails the philosophy of naturalism. The upshot is that there is no God and therefore no ultimate purpose in life. As Provine puts it, evolution operates by mindless, mechanistic principles: It is "a totally purposeless, uncaring process."

But if you ask about the evidence for the Darwinist worldview, it is surprisingly meager. For example, in a *New York Times* article, Jonathan Weiner claims he saw evolution in progress in the Galapagos Islands, home of Darwin's famous finches. Weiner observed that the finches' beaks grew larger in dry seasons, when the seeds they eat are tough and hard, but after a rainy season, when tiny seeds became available once more, the finches' beaks grew smaller again. I witnessed "evolution in action," Weiner writes (*New York Times,* 8 May 1994).

But what he really witnessed was the exact *opposite* of evolution. As Phillip Johnson explains in *Reason in the Balance,* a change in beak size is a minor adaptation that allows the finches to adapt and survive: In other words, it allows them to *stay finches.* It does not prove that they're capable of evolving into a different species of bird, and it certainly does not prove that finches evolved from some other organism in the first place.

When Darwinists claim that evolution is an observed fact, invariably they're referring to minor adaptations like the finch beaks. And on this flimsy basis they urge us to abandon belief in a Creator and take a leap of faith to a grand metaphysical story called naturalism. They insist that we accept a grim vision of a universe with no ultimate meaning or purpose.

If Darwinism were true scientifically, then we'd all have to accept its dark implications. But Darwinism is not even good science. You and I need to fight the hold it has on our culture, not only in the science classroom, but in every area of life.

Otherwise our children may come to believe their *own* lives are nothing but a cosmic accident.

It's for the Birds

What Was Archaeopteryx?

JURASSIC tales are haunting the headlines again, but this time it has nothing to do with *Jurassic Park.* This time it's about a fossil bird called *archaeopteryx* that supposedly lived during the Jurassic period. *Archaeopteryx* is typically portrayed as an evolutionary link between dinosaurs and birds.

But new scientific findings suggest it was nothing of the sort.

The standard theory is that a species of small dinosaur developed frayed scales, which eventually evolved into feathers. The result was *archaeopteryx,* a feathered reptile that clambered up trees and learned to glide—a link in the evolution of birds.

But according to *Science* magazine, the standard story has it backward. Alan Feduccia, an ornithologist (a specialist on birds), writes that birds can be compared by the shape of their claws. Ground-dwelling birds have straighter claws while perching birds have curved claws (*Science,* 5 February 1993).

Feduccia compared *archaeopteryx* to modern birds and found that its claws match exactly the curved claws of perching birds. In other words, *archaeopteryx* was not a half reptile that usually staggered around on the ground. It was a full-fledged bird that perched high in the trees.

This new finding is just the latest in a series of challenges to evolutionary dogma about *archaeopteryx.* Evolutionists used to say the bird couldn't fly. But then scientists examined imprints of *archaeopteryx* feathers and found that they had the same aerodynamic shape used by living birds to achieve lift. In short, the ancient bird was an excellent flyer.

Evolutionists once said *archaeopteryx* must be part reptile because it had teeth in its beak and claws on its wings. But then scientists discovered that several fossil birds had teeth. They also found modern birds with claws on their wings, like the hoatzin in South America. Obviously there are more types of birds than were dreamed of in evolutionary theory.

Evolutionists once said *archaeopteryx* lived too early to be a bird. But then scientists discovered fossils of true birds that lived even earlier, which means that *archaeopteryx* could not be an evolutionary link after all.

When all the facts are in, *archaeopteryx* doesn't look like a transitional form after all. Unfortunately, you won't find all the facts in most science textbooks or museum displays. There *archaeopteryx* is still proudly displayed as the showcase example of evolution.

In reality, it's a showcase of scientific bias. The first *archaeopteryx* fossil was discovered only two years after Charles Darwin published his book *On the Origin of Species*—when his followers were frantically searching for evidence to support the theory and discredit divine creation. The fossil bird was pounced on as just the evidence they needed.

Today the facts have shot it down. And the story of *archaeopteryx* has become a story of scientists who latched on to something before it was really proved—just because it fit their preconceived ideas.

But it's one theory that just doesn't fly.

Astronauts Who Found God

A Spiritual View of Space

THE BLOCKBUSTER movie *Apollo 13* tells a riveting tale of three astronauts who were flung into space and almost didn't make it back. But there's one aspect of real-life space travel that the filmmakers missed: a sense of awe before God's creation.

Just look at the number of astronauts who discovered or renewed their religious faith. Neil Armstrong and Buzz Aldrin were the first astronauts to land on the moon and take that "giant leap for mankind." But before they emerged from the spaceship, Aldrin pulled out a Bible, a silver chalice, and sacramental bread and wine. There on the moon, his first act was to celebrate Communion.

Frank Borman was commander of the first space crew to travel beyond the earth's orbit. Looking down on the earth from 250,000 miles away, Borman radioed back a message, quoting Genesis 1: "In the beginning, God created the heavens and the earth." As he later explained, "I had an enormous feeling that there had to be a power greater than any of us—that there was a God, that there was indeed a beginning" (*Miami Herald,* 20 July 1994).

The late James Irwin walked on the moon in 1971 and afterward became an evangelical minister. He often described the lunar mission as a revelation. In his words, "I felt the power of God as I'd never felt it before." Charles Duke, who followed Irwin to the moon, later became active in missionary work. As he explains, "I make speeches about walking *on* the moon and walking *with* the Son." A member of my own congregation, Guy Gardner, is a veteran astronaut who speaks in churches on the reality of God (*Miami Herald,* 20 July 1994).

What is it about being in space that seems to spark our innate religious sense? Two centuries ago the philosopher Immanuel Kant said there are two things that "fill the mind with ever new and increasing admiration and awe: the starry heavens above me and the moral law within me." Reflection upon these things, Kant wrote, leads our minds to contemplate God himself—the moral law revealing his goodness, the heavens revealing his power.

As the psalmist put it, "The heavens declare the glory of God" (Ps. 19:1).

Many of us may think science is antagonistic to faith. Yet most of the great figures who shaped the scientific enterprise from the beginning have been devout believers—people like Blaise

Pascal, who invented the first calculator; Isaac Newton, who discovered the law of gravity; and James Maxwell, who formulated the laws of electromagnetism. All were Christians who felt that the study of nature did not challenge their faith but, rather, strengthened it.

That's exactly what space exploration can do in the lives of those who are privileged to take part in it—or those of us who experience it vicariously through a movie like *Apollo 13*. Space travel has provided an unexpected spin-off: a vivid sense of the God who created the heavens and the earth.

Eight

WHAT ARE
ARTISTS
UP TO NOW?

The Naked Baby

A Postal Service Controversy

FOR the U.S. Postal Service, it was the biggest controversy since the postmaster tried to cancel a stamp featuring the baby Jesus two years before. In 1996, the question was not whether to show the baby Jesus at all but whether it was OK to show him without a diaper!

This year's Christmas stamp features part of a 1712 painting by Italian artist Paolo de Matteis. The stamp features a blue-robed Madonna gazing down at the Christ child kicking his heels on her lap.

But while St. Luke tells us Mary dressed the baby in swaddling clothes, de Matteis didn't dress him at all—and that's what threw postal authorities into a tizzy.

As columnist Peter Rexford explained, "Someone at the Postal Service thought the Christ child, [minus his] swaddling clothes, was too anatomically explicit." And so, Rexford writes, "with a few strokes of an airbrush," a postal service "artist transformed the child into an asexual being" (*St. Louis Post Dispatch,* 3 November 1996).

Fortunately, postal authorities reconsidered the matter and "came to their artistic senses" as Rexford put it. When the stamp was released a few weeks ago, the baby's manhood, so to speak, had been restored.

The controversy is more than a modern tempest in a teapot.

Since the time of the early church, artists have struggled to depict both the humanity and divinity of Jesus.

Medieval artists tended to focus on Christ's deity. In many Byzantine churches we see mosaics of a stern, majestic Christ coming in judgment. During the Victorian era, artists emphasized Christ's humanity through paintings of the "gentle Jesus."

The greatest religious artists manage to portray both Christ's deity and humanity—and that's what Paolo de Matteis does. The artist shows Jesus as a real, human child, squirming in his mother's arms. The artistic purpose of showing the baby naked was to emphasize his full humanity. The Madonna looks lovingly down on her infant, as mothers throughout the ages have always done. This is a very human scene.

Yet the scene also is charged with symbols of Christ's divinity. The baby's head is surrounded by a halo of light—a symbol of grace. The halo illuminates the face of his mother, symbolizing the fact that Mary herself is transformed through her Son's grace. The baby's expression is exalted as he gazes not at his mother but heavenward. His tiny arms are outstretched in the position of the crucifixion. Mary is wrapping him in a cloth, an image that anticipates the *Pietà,* when Mary would wrap the body of her crucified Son for burial.

The message of the painting is clear: This baby is God in the flesh . . . a divine child destined one day to die for our sins.

When you mail your Christmas cards this year, do something that will annoy the ACLU: Use this government-issued stamp to help your unsaved friends understand what the painting really communicates—how it symbolizes the entire gospel, which began with the birth of this baby.

The one who was truly God and truly human.

Art World Enemy No. 1

No, It's Not Jesse Helms

ACCORDING to the *Washington Post,* the art world has a new Enemy No. 1 (*Washington Post,* 24 October 1993).

Is it Jesse Helms, who compared contemporary art to a skunk's spray? No, it's not Jesse Helms. Is it Donald Wildman, who uses boycotts to go after lewd art and pornography? No, not him either. The *Washington Post* identified the art world's No. 1 enemy as Morley Safer, reporter for *60 Minutes.*

On one segment of the program, Safer offered a blistering critique of contemporary art, titled "Yes, But Is It Art?" He featured the work of Robert Gober, who creates sculptures shaped as urinals. He zoomed in on Robert Ryman, who paints entire canvases plain white. He showed works by Jeff Koons—such as two basketballs floating in a fish tank. And he asked, Is *this* art?

How do we define art in the first place? The ancient philosophers defined art as that which appeals to our aesthetic sense—our sense of beauty. They believed that beauty is an objective standard. In fact, the ancients listed three absolutes by which we judge things: the true, the good, and the beautiful.

But today the art world rejects any standards, in any area. The philosophy of existentialism has taken over, teaching that without God there *are* no absolute standards. Many works of art—like Andy Warhol's famous paintings of soup cans—were intended to debunk the very idea of objective standards for art.

But without standards, how do we decide what qualifies as art? If the definition is not objective, then it is subjective—rooted in the artist himself. As Christian art professor Gene Edward Veith explains, today art is defined as anything an artist does.

That's why someone can get away with dropping basketballs in a fish tank and calling it art. If you tried that, you'd be laughed out of the gallery. But if Jeff Koons does it, well, he's an artist, isn't he? So it must be art. The director of the Whitney Museum in New York has actually stated that "a work of art is whatever an artist *says* is a work of art" (*Washington Post*, 24 October 1993).

With this philosophy, no wonder artists have grown arrogant. When Morley Safer ran his *60 Minutes* segment, he was savaged for weeks. Artists who feel they have an unchallenged right to define art take offense when they *are* challenged.

Christian activists are trying to curb the worst excesses of contemporary art by limiting government funding, and that's a good start. But by itself it's a little like trying to stop a pot from boiling over by putting the lid on while leaving the burner turned up. We also need to turn the burner down by addressing the underlying cause—the rejection of standards, which makes it impossible to distinguish art from junk.

In the book of Romans, Paul says we can avoid being conformed to this world only by being transformed in our minds—our thinking, our worldview. If we want to renew art and culture in America, we have to reach out to artists and challenge their worldview, their embrace of subjectivism.

Because the No. 1 enemy of the art world isn't Morley Safer, or even Jesse Helms. The No. 1 enemy of the art world . . . is the art world itself.

Shock Art

....

Invading the Human Body

IMAGINE you're in a major metropolitan area and you witness a man with a knife slicing into another man. Do you call the police?

Not if the place is St. Patrick's Cafe in Minneapolis during a recent art program. The Walker Art Center sponsored a controversial program that involved slicing designs into the skin of one man's back, sticking needles into another man's head, and piercing two women's cheeks with steel spikes.

All in the name of performance art.

The program notes described the mutilation as "erotic torture"—and most of the audience found it torture just to watch. Some gasped, others fled the room, and one fainted. Like many other controversial art projects, this one was paid for in part by our tax dollars, through funding from the National Endowment for the Arts.

Is this what you and I pay our taxes to support?

Artists have lined up to defend the bloodletting. Helen Brunner, executive director of the National Association of Artists Organizations, argued that shocking people is precisely what the NEA is all about. "If [the] NEA is only funding work that doesn't offend anyone," Brunner said, "then it isn't fostering art."

But is art reducible to the simplistic function of offending people?

Today's shock artists flatter themselves that they stand in the tradition of the great art innovators of the past, who broke through artistic conventions of form and composition—like the Impressionist painters who scandalized the bourgeoisie of their day. But contemporary artists are not merely violating artistic conventions. They're violating basic human decency, which is the bedrock of every culture.

As art critic Martha Bayles argues, every culture seeks ways to dignify the elemental human experiences—marriage, sex, birth, suffering, and death. Every culture surrounds these elemental experiences with myth, ritual, and tradition (*Atlantic Monthly,* February 1994).

But today's shock artists equate tradition with repression, and as they see it, challenging repression is their specially appointed task. The artists who cut and pierced their bodies in Minneapolis, for example, were taking deliberate aim at the natural human revulsion to blood and violence. "People always leave" during the performance, says Ron Athey, who did the body carving. "They can't handle the live blood and live pain" (*Washington Post,* 31 March 1994).

But the reason most people "can't handle" live blood and pain is not that they are repressed; it's that they are not voyeurs. The universal human response to pain and suffering is a desire to cloak these experiences in privacy and to find spiritual meaning for them. Today's shock artists are not merely offending a few repressed, puritanical prudes; they are offending everyone who has a sense of basic decency.

Of course, genuinely great art has always portrayed pain and suffering. Think of paintings of Jesus' crucifixion. But great art does it in a manner that is dignified and respectful. Its purpose is not to shock us but to move us to ponder the deep mysteries of life and death.

And, ultimately, to worship.

Who Knows Bezalel?

Art and the Bible

AMERICAN art lovers can now tune in to their televisions to watch an unlikely art critic: a Carmelite nun named Wendy Beckett. She's the host of an immensely popular television series called *Sister Wendy's Odyssey,* a tour of her favorite paintings.

Well, why *shouldn't* a nun be an art critic? Christians have good reason to appreciate art. Throughout history, churches were always patrons of the arts. Many of the master painters were Christian believers: Rembrandt, El Greco, Rubens, van Gogh.

But a Christian appreciation of art is rooted even deeper—in Scripture itself. In Exodus 35:31 we find the story of the great artist Bezalel. He's not as well known as Moses or David, but Scripture says something quite remarkable about Bezalel. It says the Lord "filled him with the Spirit of God, with skill, ability and knowledge in all kinds of crafts."

This is an amazing verse. Ordinarily when we read about someone being filled with the Spirit of God, he's being equipped for some great spiritual task. Why was Bezalel filled with the Spirit? To work on the tabernacle, the early Hebrew tent of worship. Or, as Exodus 35:32 puts it, "to make artistic designs for work in gold, silver and bronze . . . to engage in all kinds of artistic craftmanship."

To "make artistic designs." That's what the Spirit of God equipped Bezalel to do. In fact, from the surrounding passages we can extract several biblical principles that apply to art.

First, God cares about beauty. In Exodus 28:2 the Lord tells Moses to make garments for the priests to wear—garments "for glory and for beauty" (KJV). This ought to be the slogan of every Christian artist, musician, and writer: that we work for God's glory and for beauty.

Second, we learn that being an artist can be a vocation from God. Exodus 35 explicitly says God called Bezalel by name to his work. As Gene Edward Veith says in *State of the Arts,* we normally think of people being called to the ministry or the mission field, but the Bible teaches that every occupation can be a God-given calling—including that of an artist.

Third, artistic ability is a gift of God. Several times in Exodus, the text speaks of various craftsmen as people to whom "the Lord had given ability." Artistic talent should not be hidden under a bushel; it is a gift from God, to be cultivated for the service of God and our neighbor.

Many Christians never think much about art—unless we're being outraged at the NEA for funding some blasphemous project, like Serrano's photograph of a crucifix in a jar of urine. But the call of God is not just to run around putting out fires after the secular world has started them. God calls his people to lead the way in renewing our culture by creating "artistic designs"—things "for glory and for beauty."

Art begins, after all, when God gifts his people for his glory.

PC on PBS

Good Friday on the Air

ONE of the highlights of the Easter season for me is tuning in to the classical radio stations and listening to the great musical masterpieces of the season: the Easter portion of Handel's

Messiah, with its well-known "Hallelujah Chorus," or Bach's
St. Matthew Passion.

If Christians aren't vigilant, however, someday we may no longer
hear these great classics over the air. Listen to the story of Seth
Williamson, a classical-music programmer at a public radio station.

In a *Washington Times* op-ed piece, Williamson writes about
a typical Christmas holiday when he selected several pieces
with religious themes suitable for the season, along with the
classic Christmas carols. One day he received a cranky postcard
saying, "This music is unsuitable for a radio station that takes
tax money." The postcard was signed, "Advocate of Diversity."

Notice the irony here: Someone claiming to be in favor of
diversity wanted to ban an entire category of music from
stations that accept government funding. Nor was this the first
time Williamson had received complaints. A university professor
once called to object to hearing "The Hymn of Jesus," a
beautiful choral work by Gustav Holst. "It's inappropriate," the
professor complained.

"Why?" Williamson asked.

"Because it's too—too Christian!"

But if the Music Police set out to censor all music containing
Christian references, Williamson notes, they'll discover an incon-
venient fact: A large number of the greatest musical works of
Western civilization were composed to praise God.

There's Stravinsky's *Symphony of Psalms* and Beethoven's
Missa Solemnis, a powerful rendition of the Latin mass. Brahms's
A German Requiem is a choral meditation based on texts from
the Bible. Fauré's *Requiem* is an ethereal rendition of the Latin
liturgy. Bach signed virtually all his works *Soli Deo Gloria*: "To
God Alone Be the Glory." Under the politically correct definition of diversity, these pieces would all be off-limits for public
radio (*Washington Times,* 19 January 1995).

As Christians we ought to be diligent in protecting a genuine diversity that welcomes our religious traditions. But even more important, we need to immerse *ourselves* in that tradition. Historians tell us that when Bach was composing the sublime *St. Matthew Passion,* which pictures the suffering and death of our Savior, he was so deeply moved that he sat at his desk with tears rolling down his cheeks. The work is punctuated with devotional arias, where Bach pours out his intense sorrow and gratitude for Christ's suffering.

Why not get a recording of the *St. Matthew Passion* and let it lead you into deeper personal worship. Learn to love the great classical masterpieces that express our faith with majesty and beauty.

Faceless Masses

Unmasking the PC Movement

MOST artists make sculptures out of clay or stone, but a French artist named Orlan sculpts her own body.

Orlan has undergone plastic surgery seven times to alter her face. She vows to submit to the knife repeatedly until she has the forehead of the Mona Lisa, the chin of Botticelli's Venus, and the nose and lips found in other classical paintings.

This is not just a matter of vanity. For Orlan, it is "art." She says she is remodeling her face to throw off her own identity and take on a ready-made identity from paintings. In her own words, "I'm not doing this to improve, or rejuvenate, but to *erase* my previous image" (*Washington Post,* 2 May 1993).

Now, this is an unusual goal for an artist. Most people think of art as a means to *express* yourself, not to *erase* yourself. But in his book *Postmodern Times,* Gene Edward Veith says contemporary artists are inspired by an entirely new philosophy—called postmodernism.

Modern art celebrated the individual self. Postmodern art embraces cultural determinism—the idea that people are shaped by their culture. Modern art aimed at expressing your unique personal perspective. Postmodern art aims at erasing your uniqueness and simply reflecting cultural forces.

A postmodernist German artist named Joseph Beuys writes his signature on manufactured items taken right off the store shelf—and then sells them as art. This is art as a direct attack on the very idea of personal expression and personal uniqueness. The artist merely affixes his name to whatever his society produces.

Art becomes merely the expression of a consumerist society.

Postmodernism also explains why the great artists of the past are denounced as Dead White Males. Works of art are no longer judged by their individual insight and creativity. Instead they're treated as the expressions of class, race, and gender. Postmodernist critics diligently deconstruct works of art for signs of sexism, racism, and class prejudice.

Because of this group mind-set, postmodern art often veers off into sheer political activism. Several months ago the National Endowment for the Arts funded an art project that consisted of handing out ten-dollar bills to illegal immigrants. The purpose of this crazy stunt was to protest government policy toward illegal immigrants—to turn them into a politicized victim group.

This emphasis on group identity has been bemoaned by pundits and social commentators. But few understand where it came from. Its roots are in a postmodernism that reduces the individual to a web of cultural forces.

You and I can point to postmodern art in order to argue that Christianity alone gives an adequate base for individual worth and dignity. Francis Schaeffer used to say the death of God would mean the death of man. His words were prophetic. The Western heritage of individual dignity rested firmly on the Christian belief that God created and loves each person.

But as modern culture rejects the Christian heritage, it is losing its basis for individual rights and dignity. Today's postmodernism dissolves the individual into the social group.

And it is symbolized by artists who find ways to erase their individuality—even if it means using plastic surgery to sculpt and resculpt their faces.

Art and Idols

Are Christians Anti-Art?

RUSSIANS have been lining up, not for bread or meat, but for art. German art treasures stolen by the Red Army during World War II are being taken from behind locked doors and exhibited to the public for the first time in half a century, including paintings by the great Reformation painter Lucas Cranach.

Cranach is a name that should be familiar to many Protestants. He was a close friend of Martin Luther. In fact, all the paintings we have of Luther and his family were done by Cranach.

Yet in spite of great painters like Cranach, some historians charge that the Reformation was hostile to art. Kenneth Clark, in his massive film series *Civilization,* insists that Protestantism was "destructive" of art. In fact, Clark goes on, it was "an unmitigated disaster."

But Clark is describing only one facet of the Reformation— the iconoclast movement—extremists who rampaged through cathedrals knocking over statues of the saints and smashing stained-glass windows. And even the iconoclasts must be understood within their historical context. In *State of the Arts,* Gene Edward Veith explains that we moderns can scarcely grasp how much spiritual power the medieval mind attributed to images. Icons were honored, adored, addressed in prayer. Statues of saints were said to bleed, weep, perform miracles—and even grant indulgences, exempting sinners from the pains of purgatory.

The Reformation teaching of atonement by Christ alone stood sharply against all that. In their eagerness to fight what they saw as idolatry, the iconoclasts often overdid it. They thought the way to end the *worship* of saints was to smash the statues of saints.

But this was not the true spirit of the Reformation. The true spirit was exemplified by Martin Luther. After being condemned by the emperor, Luther came out of hiding—at the risk of his life—precisely to put a *stop* to the iconoclast movement. Luther put his life on the line to save religious artwork.

Moreover, even the iconoclasts had nothing against art per se; they were opposed only to the idolatrous *use* of art. In a similar way modern Christians may oppose sex and violence on TV without necessarily being against TV itself.

The Reformation was not inherently anti-art or anti-image. Its attitude toward art was expressed well by John Calvin: "Because sculpture and paintings are gifts of God," Calvin wrote, "I seek a pure and legitimate use of each."

And indeed, the search for a "pure and legitimate use" inspired a rich flowering of the arts. Whereas medieval art was formal and otherworldly, Reformation art was natural and down-to-earth. Whereas medieval artists painted solemn saints against gold backgrounds, Reformation art depicted farmers and shopkeepers plying their trades against real landscapes.

Today Christians are often accused of being anticultural and anti-intellectual. But that is neither our heritage nor our calling. The Reformation gave us not only Lucas Cranach but also men like Albrecht Dürer, Dutch landscape painters such as Jacob van Ruisdael, and the incomparable Rembrandt—artists who wove deep spiritual themes into their portrayals of everyday life.

So the next time you visit an art museum, look for the section on Reformation art. Claim it proudly as part of your *own* heritage of faith.

What Are Artists Up To Now?

America's Christian Art

THE NATIONAL Gallery in Washington, D.C., recently put on a display of Christian art. Oh, it wasn't *called* Christian art, but that's what it was.

The display featured paintings by the nineteenth-century artist Jasper Cropsey, who was a strong Reformed believer. The highlight was a set of two paintings that were separated in 1857 and brought together in this exhibit for the first time in nearly a century and a half.

The two paintings are titled *The Spirit of War* and *The Spirit of Peace*. In the first painting, war is symbolized by a fortress jutting up against a stormy sky. An eerie red light falls on a group of knights riding off to battle while frightened shepherds and a mother and child flee from an unseen enemy.

In the second painting, peace is symbolized by a temple under a calm, luminous sky. The shepherds are serenely leading their flock; the mother plays with her child. The words of Isaiah 11:6 are illustrated by a statue of a lion lying down with a lamb.

Together the two paintings constitute a profound statement of Cropsey's Christian faith. *The Spirit of War* portrays the violence and conflict caused by human sin. *The Spirit of Peace* pictures the solution to that conflict: the peace that comes from Jesus Christ.

Jasper Cropsey belonged to a school of American art known as the Hudson River school. Most of its members were Christians, and their paintings were either landscapes or spiritual allegories.

For example, Albert Bierstadt was a master of panoramic landscape painting—with range upon range of mountains creating a sense of grandeur. "There is something of the Gothic cathedral in Bierstadt's nature paintings," writes art professor Gene Edward Veith in *State of the Arts,* "a use of light and infinite space to induce reverence as well as awe."

Another member of the Hudson River school was Frederic Church, a Christian who combined art with scientific knowledge. His breathtaking paintings of sunsets, volcanoes, and icebergs were tributes to the glories of God's creation.

The best known of the Hudson River school was Thomas Cole, who captured the American wilderness with majestic paintings of mountains bathed in golden sunlight and forests wrapped in silvery mists. But Cole is also renowned for his paintings of Bible scenes and spiritual allegories. His series *The Voyage of Life* allegorizes the four stages of life as a man traveling down a river: from a baby in a golden boat guarded by an angel, to an overconfident youth who leaves the angel behind, through the dark and deadly rapids of middle age—which drive the hero to his knees in prayer—and finally to the peaceful harbor of old age, with the doors of heaven opening above.

These great artists are part of our *own* spiritual heritage as Christians. Why don't you pick up a good book on American art history and get to know them better.

As Christians we need to stand against bad art by standing *for* good art. Today's culture war desperately needs the healing balm of the spirit of peace.

Art Wars

A Liberal Breaks Rank

THE NEW YORK art world is up in arms these days—and the furor has nothing to do with funding for the National Endowment for the Arts. No, there's something even more serious afoot: One of their own leaders has broken ranks.

The offender is Arlene Croce, widely regarded as the best dance critic in the country. Croce published a critique in *The New Yorker* magazine of a performance piece by Bill Jones, a black choreographer who is HIV-positive. The performance included videotapes of people dying of AIDS and other deadly diseases.

Miss Croce objected to the presentation of real people in a work of art. These were not actors; they were real individuals struggling desperately with their mortality. How can an art critic evaluate their performance when there was no performance— only real pain? The appropriate response is not aesthetic critique but sorrow and pity.

And that, Miss Croce says, may be precisely the point. "By working dying people into his act," she writes, "Jones is putting himself beyond the reach of criticism" (*The New Yorker,* 26 December 1994).

Jones is part of a movement that some have called "victim art," featuring oppressed groups like abused women and disenfranchised minorities. In the words of art critic Hilton Kramer, victim art "short circuit[s] criticism by foisting off social grievances as art" (*New Criterion,* February 1995). Anyone who criticizes it is accused of being sexist or racist—labels that quickly scare off most critics.

Miss Croce identifies this tactic for what it really is: simple intimidation. Avant-garde artists, she writes, are aggressively defiant of any conventions, any standards. Many make it part of their act to heckle the art critics. Bill Jones's dance company stages performances, Miss Croce writes, that have degenerated into "a barely domesticated form of street theater" that "declared war on the critics."

The critics are now fighting back—at least Miss Croce is. And we ought to cheer them on. For two centuries, Western culture has been in the grip of scientism, the glorification of science as the only form of objective truth. Ideals of beauty and art were relegated to the subjective realm, cut off from any objective standards. Victim art is one of the results. As art critic Robert Hughes puts it, today's artists reject the very concept of "quality" as a "paternalistic fiction" and demand to be judged "on their ethnicity, gender, and medical condition rather than on the merits of their work."

This belligerent subjectivism is a poison eating away at the practice of the arts in America. As Christians we are to be salt, preserving and restoring our culture—which includes the arts. To do so, we need to go beyond simply complaining about government funding for the NEA and understand the deeper causes of the decline of the arts.

In our own churches and Christian schools, we need to counter that decline by fostering appreciation for good art, art that embodies objective standards of beauty—rooted in the beauty of God's creation.

Art as Agitprop

Our Cultural Schizophrenia

SUE COE dresses like a Viet Cong guerrilla—all in black with a black beret. She also *thinks* like a Viet Cong guerrilla, for she is an unrepentant Marxist-Leninist.

But Sue Coe is also a painter—and enjoys all the fame and honor the bourgeois world can lavish on her. Not long ago her paintings were on display in the prestigious Hirshhorn Museum located on the Mall in Washington, D.C.

And the story of her success reveals a deep contradiction running through American culture.

Sue Coe's paintings are political broadsides against America. They're populated with stereotypical images that look as though they were lifted straight from old-style Soviet propaganda posters. On Coe's canvases, capitalists are wolves with top hats; political leaders are police dogs; judges are vultures. The colors are harsh: black, white, and blood red.

This clenched-fist style of art was the only style permitted by the old Soviet regime—and it's clear that Sue Coe is a hard-line Communist at heart. She also applies leftist categories to contemporary causes, such as feminism and animal rights. In a painting called *Porkopolis,* Coe depicts pigs screaming in a slaughterhouse.

The fact that a Communist like Sue Coe has won a place of honor in highbrow American culture shows just how schizophrenic our culture has become. Her propagandistic put-downs of America are welcomed by our cultural elites as great moral insights. Her show in the Hirshhorn tops a successful career as an illustrator for such impeccably bourgeois publications as *Newsweek, The New Yorker,* and the *New York Times.*

Why are bourgeois Americans so eager to embrace art that attacks the very principles they themselves live by? This is completely contrary to the role that art has played historically. Most societies celebrate art that *reflects* their own outlook and values. Ours may be the first society ever to celebrate art that *attacks* its own values: adversary art created by an adversary culture.

And you don't have to go to museums to see adversary art. Movies, TV shows, and pop music likewise taunt mainstream views and values. These entertainers devour the hand that feeds them—yet we continue to hold out the hand.

It's time for Americans to wake up to the fact that art and entertainment have the power to support or destroy a society. As Christians, we ourselves have plenty to criticize about modern society. But the things you and I would *defend* are often the very things that hip artists *attack*—namely, Christian morality, biblical teaching on the family, and classic Western liberties.

I say it's time to turn the power of art to supporting those ideals. Christians ought to be creating art that expresses a rich, biblical worldview. Churches can play the role of museums by hosting shows for artists. Christian businesses can commission works from struggling young artists. Christian magazines ought to search out and nurture artistic talent.

After all, as Christians we worship the God of truth and beauty, and we ourselves ought to be producing works of truth and beauty. In the process, we can defend what is best in Western culture from the attacks of adversary art.

Orange Hair and Symphonies

The Music of Gorecki

WHEN punk rockers with spiked orange hair go into music stores in London asking for the CD of a classical music symphony, you know this is no ordinary symphony.

The piece I'm talking about is the *Third Symphony* by Henryk Gorecki, an obscure sixty-year-old Polish composer who has suddenly turned into a pop icon. Once a leader of the avant-garde in Europe, Gorecki has now turned to a style some call "Holy Minimalism," a tongue-in-cheek reference to the religious overtones of the music.

You see, Gorecki is a devout Catholic who has composed several pieces under commission from the pope. In fact, under the Communist regime in Poland, Gorecki once lost his job for defending the pope.

His music has a hauntingly beautiful liturgical sound, borrowing on one hand from medieval music and on the other hand from folk melodies. Every time the radio stations play the *Third Symphony,* switchboards light up with calls from listeners asking, "What *is* that music?"

Gorecki's sudden fame has astonished everyone—no one more so than the composer himself. He once asked an interviewer, in a tone of self-deprecating humor, "How can young people become so interested in a piece so slow and boring?" (*Ethnic News Watch,* 1 October 1993).

Well, the piece *is* slow, with sounds drifting and piling like clouds before a storm. But young people don't find it boring in the least. For many listeners, the appeal of the symphony is precisely its sense of spirituality. As one reviewer puts it, people want music that "addresses the soul" (*Toronto Star,* 3 April 1993).

Gorecki's symphony consists of three songs, all on the theme of suffering. The first is a fifteenth-century lament representing Mary at the foot of the cross. The second is from Nazi Germany—the words of a prayer scratched on a cell wall by a prisoner. The third is a Polish folk song, the lament of a mother searching the battlefield for her dead son.

Though the music is melancholy, with themes of sorrow and suffering, the symphony ends on a gentle note of hope—the tonality changing from minor to major in the final chords. The underlying message is that through faith, all our suffering can be redeemed, just as Mary's sorrow at the cross was followed by the joy of the Resurrection.

So why don't you join the spikey-haired punk rockers and discover Gorecki's *Third Symphony* for yourself. If you were brought up on rock and pop music, give yourself a chance to feel the power of classical music—its power to communicate deep streams of religious feeling and religious truth.

Everyday Art

Living the Full Image of God

WHEN you walk into the office of Prison Fellowship president Tom Pratt, immediately you sense that this is no ordinary office. There's no imposing, executive-style desk. Instead the room is centered on a round table, small enough for easy conversation. On one side is a reading stand with a high perch; on the other, a reclining chaise.

If you ask Tom about the unusual design, you discover that everything is carefully thought out. The round table sends a message that there is no hierarchy in the world of ideas. The perch and the chaise give opportunities for altering one's physical position, which refreshes the mind and stimulates creativity.

It's rare to find an executive who has such a sensitive eye for artistic design. And office decor *is* a form of art, for art is any expression of form and beauty that elevates and inspires.

Some people say they're not interested in art. What they mean is they don't like to visit art museums and gaze at paintings. But the same people may sew their own clothes, cook gourmet meals, or renovate their homes—all of which are forms of art and creativity. Throughout history, most cultures never had museums. For the ancient Hebrews or the South American Indians, art was embedded in the staples of ordinary life—in the pottery they made, the blankets they wove, the beads they strung.

This is actually the biblical view of art, says Gene Edward Veith in *State of the Arts.* A sense of beauty ought to be expressed in everything we do. After all, the first artist was God himself. It was God who created the silvery beauty of the moon, the delicate netting of a grasshopper wing, the golden brown of a friend's eyes. When God made the world, he cared enough to make it beautiful. If God cared, so should we. We are made in his image, and a sense of beauty is part of our nature.

It's also part of the message we preach—whether we mean to or not. In *Pollution and the Death of Man,* Francis Schaeffer says he was once invited to lecture at a Christian school. The building was ugly and stark, staked out on bare ground. In sharp contrast, a nearby bohemian community was surrounded by a rich profusion of trees and lush flowers. What message were these Christians conveying about the God they worshiped? There are times, Schaeffer concludes, when planting a tree can be a form of evangelism.

The Christian life is meant to be a visible representation of the invisible God. If our schools or offices are dull and ugly—if they are filled with impersonal, mass-produced products—what an impoverished image of God we project.

When Christians hear words like *duty,* we think of going to church, reading the Bible, giving money to Christian ministries. But a biblical concept of duty is much broader: We are called to do nothing less than live out the full image of God—so that the world might come to know the God who made the roses and the sunsets.

A God of beauty.

"News of the Heart"

....

Poetic Imagery and the Gospel

MILLIONS of people have been "celebrating language in its most exalted, wrenching, delighted, and concentrated form."

In other words, they were reading a best-selling book on poetry, called *The Language of Life.* Bill Moyers, who authored the book and hosted the *Language of Life* television series, calls poetry "news of the heart." That's an intriguing phrase, and it helps Christians understand how poetry can be used to spread biblical truth.

According to Moyers, poetry is on the upswing in America because people are crying out for language that brings truth home to the heart and soul. Poets use metaphors—pictures and images—in order to engage our deepest emotions.

For example, suppose I said, "People who follow God's law have strong inner resources and live productive lives." That's true enough—but abstract and dry. Listen to the way a biblical poet expresses the same truth: The man who delights in God's law is "a tree planted by the rivers of water, that brings forth its fruit in its season." Now, *that's* an image that sticks in the mind and the heart.

We live in a technological society that rejects anything that can't be measured and quantified. The fact that millions of Americans were willing to buy a book and tune in to a television series on poetry tells us that people are hungry for something more.

This is an opportune time for Christians who are gifted in writing to make a powerful statement about their faith. *The Language of Life* profiles two Christian poets, Donald Hall and the late Jane Kenyon. Both have used the power of poetic metaphor to express the truth of the gospel.

Consider the lines of Jane Kenyon, whose bout with cancer led her to a deeper understanding of both the fear of death and the "great goodness" of God. In a poem she said was given to her by the Holy Spirit, Kenyon wrote, "Let it come, as it will, and don't be afraid. God does not leave us comfortless, so let evening come."

Kenyon's words may remind you of another powerful, poetic assurance of God's comfort: "Even though I walk through the valley of the shadow of death, I will fear no evil, for you are with me; your rod and your staff, they comfort me" (Ps. 23:4).

You and I should reacquaint ourselves with poetry, especially poetry written by believers down through the centuries—from John Donne to George Herbert to T. S. Elliot. We can allow poetry's rich, evocative words to speak to our own souls. Then we can pass these poems on as a comfort and a witness to unsaved friends—friends who may be unwilling to crack open a Bible.

As Bill Moyers puts it, poetic language is the "news of the

heart." That's something Christians need to understand—and use to the glory of God.

Leaving It to Chants

....

New Fashion in Old Music

VIRTUALLY every American today recognizes music that would have been unfamiliar to him just a few years ago: Gregorian chant. Recordings of chant music have reached top slots on the charts for both classical and pop music.

Why are twentieth-century Americans rushing out to buy music composed by sixth-century monks?

The appeal of chant music grows out of its historical purpose. Around A.D. 500, the Roman Empire fell to barbarians, and Europe entered what some call the Dark Ages: a time of social and political chaos. The only thing standing between Europe and complete barbarism was the Christian church. Its monasteries became outposts of culture, preserving education, learning, and the arts.

To hold steadfast against the pressures of disintegration, the church had to adopt a wartime mentality and impose iron discipline—even on its music. The result was the chant. Chants were intended to support the life of the church—to create an atmosphere of prayer and contemplation, focusing the mind on the spiritual meaning of the text.

To accomplish that, the monks got rid of any steady rhythm or beat; since a beat invites a physical response to the music, it was rejected as a distraction from the text. Musical harmony was likewise rejected as a distraction since it gives music its intellectual complexity.

Even the melody line was stripped of any sudden leaps and skips that create a sense of musical drama and excitement; instead, the melody moves by small, smooth steps, creating an almost atmospheric sense of peace. In short, the music was pared down to nothing but pure spirituality.

In the words of one historian, this is music that "makes no attempt to thrill our senses or entangle our emotions." Which brings me back to my original question: Why are chants such a hot commodity in the contemporary musical marketplace?

The answer may be that modern culture bears a haunting resemblance to the time when chants were first composed. As I argue in my book *Against the Night,* the West stands on the brink of moral and cultural disintegration, just as the Roman Empire did in its decline. Once again, the barbarians are at the gates, threatening a new Dark Ages. Once again, Christians must band together into communities of light to preserve the truth.

Instinctively, perhaps, we are reaching out for the same music that sustained the church in the first Dark Ages—music that is highly concentrated and focused, pared of distracting elements.

Philosopher Alisdair MacIntyre once wrote that as our culture decays, what we need is another St. Benedict. Perhaps we also need the chants that are being revived by the Benedictine monks: music that lifts us out of the chaos and noise of the surrounding culture, to the contemplation of divine beauty.

A Little Child Shall Lead Them

Who's to Judge?

A FEW years ago an unknown artist was showcased by the Manchester Academy of Fine Arts. Judges selected a watercolor entitled "Rhythm of Trees," which displayed, they opined, "a certain quality of color balance, composition, and technical skill" (*Sunday Telegraph,* 14 February 1993).

The artist, it turned out, was a four-year-old child.

How have we come to this point—where art critics cannot tell the difference between the work of a trained artist and the dabbling of a four-year-old child? To answer that question, we must understand that art expresses a view of the world, a philosophy. Through the history of art we can trace the way people's philosophy has changed.

Join me for an imaginary tour of an art museum. Beginning in the medieval section, we see figures that are stiff and formal, set against gold backgrounds. This is art expressing an other-worldly philosophy of life.

Next in our museum tour is the Reformation. Figures begin to look like real individuals instead of symbols. Reformation artists believed God could be represented not just by icons but by paintings of real human beings, who are made in his image. They also began to paint real landscapes, expressing their belief that the world has great value as God's creation.

Around the same time came the Renaissance, which revived classical culture and inspired modern humanism. Renaissance paintings often show scenes from ancient Greek and Roman mythology.

Next we come to the Enlightenment, the Age of Reason. Paintings show respectable figures in fashionable dress. Landscapes consist of neat, orderly fields. This is nature under the dominion of reason.

In the next room, the plowed fields give way to craggy mountains. Romanticism in art celebrates wild, untamed nature, the noble savage, ancient legends.

Finally we come to the room housing modern art, beginning with Impressionism. During this period, art was taken over by subjectivist philosophies: Definitions of art shifted from the subject matter being portrayed to the way light strikes the artist's eye; from great themes of human drama to daubs of paint on canvas; from the objective standards of beauty to the artist's psyche.

Expressionism and Surrealism probed still deeper into subjective experience. Eventually art lost sight of any objective standards of form and beauty. Art became defined as whatever an artist does.

Today art has become so subjective that many people sincerely cannot tell the difference between works that have aesthetic merit and works that don't. Modern art museums might display a stack of bricks beside a masterpiece by van Gogh, literally unable to say why one is art and the other is not.

This historical development explains why today the Manchester Academy of Fine Arts could be fooled into giving an art award to daubs of paint by a four-year-old child. Without objective standards of form and beauty, even unformed, random marks on canvas can be regarded as art.

Modern art seemed to make a promise: *Free yourself from restrictive standards, and you will be truly creative.* But the loss of standards has not liberated art; it has destroyed art. The artistic vision will be revived when we recover a commitment to the biblical truth that God himself is the first artist, who created a world of beauty.

Vermeer Mania

Dutch Reformed Art

IN 1996, Washingtonians suffered through the worst blizzard in fifty years. The snow piled up, the government shut down, and commuters abandoned cars all over town. Yet close to five thousand people dug their way out every day and headed downtown. Were they stocking up on bread and milk? No, they trudged through up to seventeen inches of snow and ice to see . . . an art exhibit.

For three freezing months, the hottest ticket in town was to a small exhibition of paintings by seventeenth-century Dutch master Johannes Vermeer. Some art lovers even camped out in front of the National Gallery all night in the cold to be sure of getting a ticket. Inside the museum, according to one reviewer, the crowds walked past Vermeer's light-filled portraits with an almost religious hush. Yet these paintings were mostly depictions of Dutch housewives going about their ordinary daily duties—preparing meals, writing letters, and making lace. Why would paintings of such ordinary subject matter create such a sensation?

The answer has to do with Vermeer's ability to infuse the ordinary with a sense of spiritual significance.

Although Vermeer converted to Catholicism as an adult, he grew up surrounded by the Dutch Reformed tradition. Reformation theologians believed in the sacramental view of everyday life: that God reveals himself to us in the course of our ordinary duties. As a result, artists stopped limiting their work to spiritual realms and began to paint scenes from ordinary life. In addition, the Protestant work ethic insisted that all vocations can be spheres of Christian service. This, too, inspired artists to paint people laboring away at their work, from merchants in their shops to servant girls toiling in the kitchen.

Vermeer is one of the greatest exemplars of this tradition. His paintings have an almost photographic realism. Cracks in the wall, the texture of cloth, the play of light on a pitcher of milk—all serve to illustrate the beauty of the everyday world of work.

Vermeer's Christian sensibility can be seen clearly in one of his most famous paintings, "Woman Holding a Balance." It features a young woman weighing her jewelry to assess its value. Behind her on the wall is a painting within a painting: a rendition of Christ's Last Judgment, in which souls are being weighed in the balance.

The point is dramatic: The young woman's choices and values are literally under the judgment of God. And yet, flowing through the window, illuminating her life, is an ethereal light— a symbol of God's grace. An ordinary scene becomes transfused with supernatural presence and truth.

Many historians accuse Reformation theologians of being anti-art because of their cautious attitude toward religious imagery, their fear that religious images could be used for idolatry. But the truth is that they were very much in favor of art in principle as a human reflection of God's own creativity.

Christians actually have a rich artistic heritage—one that so nourishes the soul that art lovers in Washington were willing to camp out all night in freezing weather just to see a handful of paintings inspired by a Reformation worldview.

Nine

REVIVING
THE
VIRTUES

Late on Taxes?

Call Your Therapist

PSYCHIATRISTS have diagnosed a mysterious new mental disease, and it strikes the most unlikely people: highly educated white males.

It's called failure-to-file syndrome, and the diagnostic symptom is failing to file income tax returns. The disorder came to light recently when more than fifty of the nation's most respected law partners were identified by the Internal Revenue Service in a computer sweep to pick up nonfilers.

Immediately a tax lawyer and a psychiatrist teamed up to write an article describing this mysterious malady. The authors claim that the lawyers who failed to file their taxes suffer from a psychiatric disorder giving them "an aversion to filling out forms." These folks need sympathy, not condemnation, the article said. They should not be indicted, like other tax cheaters, but given treatment with psychotherapy and Prozac.

Well, it's been said that America is becoming a therapeutic culture, but this is the most outrageous example yet. Are we really expected to believe that competent lawyers, who spend their working lives filing briefs, are psychologically incapable of filing tax returns? We're not talking here about a few psychotic or mentally incompetent people who are truly unable to manage their finances. We're talking about attorneys who are fully functional and in command of all their faculties.

Finding psychological disorders to excuse criminal behavior

has become a cottage industry in America today. When one teenager kills another over a leather jacket, we're told that the murderer suffers from "urban psychosis." When two brothers in Beverly Hills pump sixteen bullets into their parents, their lawyers plead the "abuse excuse." When a man bashes in another man's head with a brick during the Los Angeles riots, it's explained away as a product of "mob mentality."

What we're seeing here is nothing but pseudoscientific blame shifting. Liberal social theory starts with the premise that people are basically good. To explain why good people sometimes go bad, it blames environmental conditions.

The result is an extreme form of determinism that reduces people to pawns of their environment. We're building a legal system that refuses to assign personal responsibility to anyone, no matter how heinous their crime. The cause of their behavior is always something beyond their control—the way they were raised, their economic plight, or even some mysterious malady affecting their brain.

Virtually all of us can find *some* unhappy circumstance in our lives to blame.

As Christians, however, we know that someday we will all stand before the divine tribunal, where there will be no defense attorneys to get us off the hook with designer excuses. As a result, we ought to stand firmly for the principle of personal responsibility in every area of life.

Not long ago the state of New York prosecuted several prominent attorneys for tax evasion. Suddenly, many other lawyers recovered from failure-to-file syndrome long enough to get their own tax returns in the mail. This is the law functioning the way it *ought* to: holding people responsible to meet their obligations.

When it comes to tax evasion, the solution is not psychotherapy or Prozac. It's using the law to hold citizens accountable for their behavior.

Teaching Virtues through Stories

The Instructive Power of Literature

IT WAS the eleventh time Jeffrey Bob Nelson had appeared before the bench in Angelina County, Texas. This time, Judge Joe Martin decided to throw the book at him. Several books, in fact.

The twenty-nine-year-old used-car salesman was convicted of driving without a license—a misdemeanor offense. As part of his punishment, Judge Martin ordered Nelson to spend six months reading classics like Bunyan's *Pilgrim's Progress,* Milton's *Paradise Lost,* and Dostoyevsky's *Crime and Punishment.* "I've tried everything," Judge Martin explained. The innovative sentence was designed to expose the offender to "things that can teach him the virtue of morality" (*Dallas Morning News,* 23 March 1995).

Well, the judge has stumbled onto a great idea. Reading the great classics of literature can be a good way to learn virtue.

In *Books That Build Character,* authors William Kilpatrick and Gregory and Suzanne Wolfe describe how great stories help build great character. "Through the power of imagination, we become vicarious participants in the story, sharing the hero's choices and challenges." We "identify ourselves with our favorite characters, and thus *their* actions become *our* actions." In this way, the stories become a dress rehearsal for our own life choices.

By giving us good characters to admire, stories help educate the moral imagination. Virtue isn't just about knowing how to be good. To change behavior, we need to love the good. As Kilpatrick and the Wolfes explain, "stories can create an emotional attachment to goodness, a desire to do the right thing."

Stories also provide a wealth of good examples—the kind often missing from our environment. They "familiarize children with the codes of conduct they need to know," and they flesh out what these codes mean in lifelike situations.

There's a reason that Jesus himself delivered his most profound teachings in the form of stories—parables about farmers planting seeds, women finding coins, sons going bad and then repenting. These were characters his listeners could identify with.

Legal strictures prevented Judge Martin from requiring Jeffrey Bob Nelson to read the parables of Jesus, but he's made an excellent alternative choice by assigning classic literature. By reading *Paradise Lost,* Nelson will learn about sin and the Fall. In *The Pilgrim's Progress,* he'll discover how John Bunyan personalized virtues like prudence and forbearance through the colorful use of allegory.

These are stories we should be reading to our own children. As Kilpatrick and the Wolfes write, in times of real-life pressure or temptation, "the half-forgotten memory of a story can rise to our aid."

Clearly that's what Judge Martin had in mind when he sentenced eleven-time offender Jeffrey Bob Nelson to spend six months in the library, reading classics. If it works, the phrase "book him" just might take on a whole new meaning.

Selling Ourselves

....

The Body as Commodity

MORE and more Americans are selling themselves—piecemeal. Tissue, semen, eggs, and even children are all part of a fast-growing market in human "products." So says Andrew Kimbrell in his book *The Human Body Shop*.

And the trend could change the very definition of what it means to be human.

Some of the most commonly sold body products are blood and semen. Infertility clinics buy sperm for about fifty dollars a donation. Some sperm donors have "fathered" hundreds of children. Women who provide eggs for in vitro fertilization are also paid thousands of dollars. Surrogate mothers sign commercial contracts committing them to produce children for a fee.

Are these practices moral? Should the human body be subject to commercial transactions?

One of the most profitable body parts is fetal tissue. Though the sale of fetal organs is against the law, abortion clinics receive a so-called "service fee" for every fetus they hand over. Brokers in turn demand a sizable "handling fee" for every specimen they deliver to doctors and researchers. According to Kimbrell, unregulated brokers in the U.S. reap close to a million dollars a year in fetal tissue sales.

But the big money may soon come from transplants into animals. Human fetal tissue has been implanted into mouse organs—creating so-called "humanized mice," which are used to test certain drugs. What do we think about implanting human tissues into animals? Is this morally acceptable?

Then there's genetic engineering, which has developed a way to use human cells as miniature "factories" to produce profitable medical products. In 1980 the Supreme Court decided these human cell lines could be patented—just like a new toaster or lawn mower. Should the law treat the human body like a patented invention? What does that mean for human dignity?

In all these developments, biotechnology is raising severe challenges to our traditional respect for the human body. The body is no longer treated as God's creation, deserving special respect. Instead, it's just another commodity in the medical marketplace.

The result may be a complete dissolution of ethical considerations. Frank Williams, the director of the American Parkinson Association, once remarked that most people "couldn't care less about the ethical questions" connected with fetal tissue research; "they just want something that works"—as though we were talking about a machine (*New York Times*, 16 August 1987).

What we're seeing is the triumph of a completely mechanistic philosophy. The human body is regarded as a purely physical object to be taken apart, sold, and used—just like any other physical object.

The Bible teaches that we are made in the image of God, but the mechanistic view portrays humans in the image of the machine. This is nothing but idolatry—people bowing down to the work of their own hands.

And like every form of idolatry, it dehumanizes all who worship at its shrine.

The "Baby Cons"

There's a Cost When Virtue Is Lost

THE YOUNG man announced that he was conservative, and sure enough, he was for all the conservative issues: a free market, low taxes, welfare reform. Then one day he started dating someone he had met at work—a very attractive teenage . . . boy.

Yes, the young conservative was gay.

This story really happened, and according to John Miller in *Diversity* magazine, it's not unusual. Today's young adults are growing up in a liberal society. Often they get involved in sex and drugs long before they're old enough to be thinking about a personal life philosophy.

Later, when they do find a personal philosophy that's more traditional, their new values wage a lively battle with their old habits. "Contrary to all the fuss about America's cultural war," Miller explains, "the most crucial battles were fought and lost in the 1960s." Today's young conservatives grew up when sleeping around was no longer a sign of rebellion. It was the accepted norm. Using drugs was no longer a means of expanding consciousness. It was simple recreation. Relativism wasn't an abstract moral theory. It was the unquestioned assumption in most classroom instruction.

Young conservatives—or "baby cons," as one writer calls them—have been hardwired as social liberals.

On economic issues, it seems everyone today recognizes the dark side of the welfare state. Many young people are embracing the concepts of a limited government and a free-market economy. But when it comes to social issues, they are much more ambivalent. So the editor of a conservative student newspaper may moralize about teenage pregnancy—but then sleep with his girlfriend. A young Republican may rail against rampant drug use—then smoke pot with her dormitory friends.

Poll data show the same ambivalence. Many self-described young conservatives favor abortion, gay rights, drug legalization, and pornography—to name just a few. It's not just the baby cons either. The idea that you can be a political and economic conservative and at the same time a social liberal is spreading across all age groups.

This is an idea Christians need to nip in the bud—and fast. The truth is that a society that is socially liberal eventually loses its political and economic liberty.

A society that smiles on sexual relations outside marriage undermines the institution of the family. And family breakdown contributes to increases in depression, health problems, school failure, drug use, crime—virtually every kind of social pathology. When that happens, government feels called upon to expand its services—more welfare, more crime control, more social services. As government acquires more functions, it exerts more control over its citizens. As it runs up higher operating costs, it digs deeper into your pocketbook.

In short: less liberty, higher taxes.

This is the connection we need to help "baby cons"—and other social liberals—to grasp. The loss of personal virtue always leads to an erosion of political and economic liberty.

When people do not exercise internal controls, the government will impose external controls—while asking all of us to foot the bill.

Cannibal Justice

....

Your Tax Dollars at Work

IF YOU tuned in to one Smithsonian Expedition Special on television, you got a real eye-opener. The program highlighted a tribe in New Guinea called the Korowai, never before studied. The program presented the Korowai as enlightened people living in harmony with their environment.

Oh, yes, they also happen to practice cannibalism.

The program was hosted by Paul Taylor, a curator of the Smithsonian's National Museum of Natural History. The narrative begins by telling us that the goal of anthropology is to make local customs seem "logical, reasonable, rational, and understandable."

And that's just what Taylor is eager to do. He tells us that the Korowai live in tree houses that can rise as high as a six-story building—which Taylor describes as "a major architectural achievement for any place in the world." The Korowai also practice equal pay for women—which, Taylor says, "feminists in any country in the world would very much agree with."

Things get a little trickier when it comes to equal rights in other areas—for example, the question of who will be killed and eaten. The Korowai practice cannibalism not only against enemy tribes but also against their own people—as punishment for serious crimes. For men, that includes sorcery and murder. Women may be eaten for stealing bananas and other food.

The Korowai were happy to describe the ritual in detail. The victim is first bound and shot with arrows. The body is then carefully cut into six pieces—while the people, we are told, "have a good time and sing." Finally, the pieces are cooked over the fire and eaten.

This gruesome ritual is presented to the viewer as something

Westerners should not condemn but rather try to "understand." Many things about the Korowai may seem baffling, the narrator says, "until they are seen from within—like cannibalism."

Within Korowai society, we are told, cannibalism is not "mere violence"; instead it is a "well-functioning example of how a complete criminal justice system works." In fact, the program was titled, "Treehouse People—Cannibal Justice."

In his ardor to make cannibals appear "reasonable" and "logical," Taylor never mentions whether they insist on a fair trial before someone is condemned to the cooking pot. In fact, he carefully refrains from making any moral judgments of the practice at all.

The entire program is an exercise in cultural relativism—an effort to deny that Western culture is better than any other. Many anthropologists today will defend even the most barbarous customs as sensible and legitimate practices, which no Westerner is allowed to judge. And through programs such as the Smithsonian's television specials, the message of cultural relativism is channeled to the public at large.

Paid for by your tax dollars and mine.

Perhaps it's time we started holding public institutions like the Smithsonian accountable to the public that supports them. American culture is suffering a moral deficit that is destroying our families and our cities.

The last thing we need is to see smiling scientists on the TV screen telling us we cannot make moral judgments on even the most barbarous behavior.

The Eye of the Beholder

Brave New Bodies

"EVERYBODY at school calls me shrimp," complained eleven-year-old Marco. "I feel like a loser."

Just what is Marco's problem? He's short. Marco stands several inches below the average for his age. To solve the problem, his parents inject him every day with the genetically engineered human growth hormone (*New York Times,* 16 June 1991).

It's a stark example of modern technology literally creating a new category of disease.

Genetic engineers experimented with the human growth hormone not because it was desperately needed but simply because the molecule is easy to work with in the laboratory. Once scientists had found a way to *produce* the hormone, however, the pressure was on to find a way to *market* it—to make money from it. The hormone became a cure searching for a disease.

At first it was used only to treat pituitary dwarfism, a congenital disease where the body is unable to manufacture its own growth hormone. But dwarfism is quite rare; not much of a market there.

So gene companies began to aggressively target another market: kids like Marco, who have no disease or disability but are simply short. Researchers targeted the bottom 3 percent on the height scale—the low end of normal—and redefined it as *ab*normal. They declared shortness a disorder. And to "treat" the disorder, kids like Marco are receiving daily shots of the genetically engineered human growth hormone.

What makes this disturbing is that there's no proof the drug actually increases these children's ultimate height. Nor is there any evidence that it alleviates feelings of inferiority that short kids might have. Even worse, studies show an alarming link between the hormone treatments and the development of leukemia. Yet once treatment is started, it cannot be stopped without stunting a child's growth.

These are significant risks, yet gene companies are enjoying blockbuster sales of the hormone. It's a dramatic example of technology *creating* our sense of what we need instead of being a *servant* to human needs.

The original impulse for modern technology was thoroughly Christian. The early scientists in the sixteenth and seventeenth centuries regarded technology as a gift of God—a means of alleviating the destructive effects of the curse recorded in Genesis 3.

The Bible teaches that human sin caused disruption and discord in nature itself—including our physical bodies. The early scientists believed that science could be a means of healing and restoring nature. The application of science through technology was permeated with religious concern to help the poor and the sick.

But today technology has been divorced from its Christian roots. As Andrew Kimbrell puts it in *The Human Body Shop,* the secular religion of America is that science will allow us to *know* everything, that technology will allow us to *do* anything, and that the market will allow us to *buy* anything we want.

You and I can help bring technology back to its Christian roots by scrutinizing our own lives. Do our gadgets and gizmos serve genuine needs—or do they create new and superfluous needs?

Whether it's old-fashioned machines or the new genetic technologies, we should not let them lead us to worship at the altar of science.

We All Want to Change the World

A Matter of the Soul

FOR generations, school children have recited the little spelling ditty, "the principal is your pal." But at a Manhattan grammar school, students discovered that their principal was *not* their pal. School officials discovered that the principal of Public School 142, Antonio Bilbao, had stolen more than eleven thousand dollars that students had raised through bake sales and school plays.

It is "appalling," said school commissioner Edward Stancik, "that the principal would betray the trust of the children for his own personal greed" (*Newsday,* 7 April 1995).

More attention and research have been devoted to teaching moral education in our schools than at any other time in history, according to William Kilpatrick in *Why Johnny Can't Tell Right from Wrong.* Yet these efforts are failing—not only with kids but obviously with teachers and administrators as well.

Why? Because schools are teaching the wrong *kind* of moral education. Instead of teaching students what constitutes good character, they're inviting children to discover their *own* values. In fact, the only time this type of curriculum is directive is when it involves trendy liberal causes like environmentalism, where kids are pressured to recycle, or feminism, where girls are told they're so oppressed that they need special holidays like Take Your Daughter to Work Day.

What these educators don't understand is that virtue is not a matter of social causes. It's a matter of the soul, and that's where moral education must begin.

The point was beautifully illustrated in a story told by Christina Hoff Sommers, a philosophy professor at Clark University in

Massachusetts. Sommers published an article some time ago urging ethics teachers to focus as much on *private* virtue as they do on *public* ethics—to teach things like personal honesty, decency, and responsibility.

One of Sommers's colleagues, an ethics professor, scoffed at her argument. "You're not going to have moral people," the colleague insisted, "until you have moral institutions." She informed Sommers that in her own classroom, she planned to continue talking about social ethics issues, such as women's rights, protecting the rain forest, and the corruption of big business in multinational corporations.

By the end of the semester, however, Sommers's colleague was singing a different tune. To her shock, more than half the students in her ethics course cheated on a take-home final exam. With a self-mocking smile, she told Sommers, "I'd like to borrow a copy of that article you wrote on ethics without virtue" (*Chicago Tribune,* 12 September 1993).

This professor learned the hard way that we can deal with the moral malaise in American life only when we begin to cultivate personal virtue.

It's easy to focus on social causes. As the Beatles sang, "We all want to change the world." But *real* change starts in our heart and soul—in the cultivation of personal character. Otherwise we end up with students who can glibly recite all the accepted liberal mantras on social causes—and then cheat on tests.

Plato taught that the order in society depends on the order of the soul. In a day when even school principals can't seem to figure out right from wrong, it's time to bring Plato's dictum back to the classroom.

The Good Little Kittens

....

Bill Bennett Teaches Virtue

ONCE upon a time, there was a book on the best-seller list that wasn't a steamy romance or a kiss-and-tell government memoir. It wasn't even a new diet book. It was a whopping eight-hundred-page collection of inspiring stories, fables, and poems designed to illustrate good character and virtue.

The volume was *The Book of Virtues* by William Bennett. The fact that it spent eighty-eight weeks on the *New York Times* best-seller list may tell us something about the longing for goodness that drives the human heart even in our jaded times.

In these pages readers can rediscover the old poems and tales we all heard and loved as children, from *Aesop's Fables* to "Jack and the Bean Stalk," from *Robin Hood* to Shakespeare—all grouped according to the values they teach. See if you can identify the following simple child's poem, which teaches personal responsibility.

The episode begins when three small kittens, due to some unspecified carelessness, have lost their mittens. We learn that there was a direct negative outcome to the kittens' irresponsibility: Their mother announced that they would not be allowed to eat any pie. The blame for the lost mittens was placed firmly on the kittens themselves. They were not allowed to shift the blame onto their parents or society or anyone else.

The rule was firm: No mittens, no pie.

With a clear knowledge of the consequences of their behavior, the kittens were quick to remedy the situation. The next time we meet them, three small pairs of mittens are hanging on the rack where they belong, and three small kittens are enjoying the rewards of their efforts: a rich, sweet piece of pie.

It's a simple story, aimed at very young children, yet it illustrates a profound truth. Stories like these do what scolding and didactic lecturing can never do: They make us *want* to be good. They don't just give us ideas to believe in; they show us characters to emulate. They reach into our imagination so that we vicariously experience the shame of wrongdoing—and then the thrill of picking ourselves back up and setting things right again.

In *Why Johnny Can't Tell Right from Wrong,* William Kilpatrick recommends stories as the best way to teach character. Stories impart a sense that life has meaning, that it makes sense. As Kirkpatrick writes, "the surest foundation for morality . . . is the belief that you have a role to play in life"—that your life has a purpose, like a story with a well-constructed plot.

Perhaps this is why Jesus taught so many moral lessons in the form of parables. The stories of the Good Samaritan and the Prodigal Son illustrate abstract spiritual truths through the actions of flesh-and-blood characters.

The Book of Virtues by William Bennett is not explicitly Christian, but it can help you teach your child good character. Even tiny children need to learn that you can't shift blame for misbehavior onto someone else.

That if you want to have some pie, you'd better hang on to your mittens.

Science and Sex

....

What's the Connection?

PHILLIP JOHNSON is a pugnacious law professor who travels to campuses challenging Darwinian evolution. But something funny often happens to Johnson: Debates over genes and fossils suddenly switch to sex and morality.

What's the connection between science and sexuality?

Here's how Johnson describes it in *Reason in the Balance:* "I have found that any discussion with modernists [or liberals] about the weaknesses of the theory of evolution quickly turns into a discussion of politics, particularly sexual politics." Why? Because liberals "typically fear that any discrediting of naturalistic evolution will end in women being sent to the kitchen, gays to the closet, and abortionists to jail."

In other words, in the debate over creation and evolution, people instinctively sense that much more is at stake than a scientific theory. What you accept as *scientific* truth shapes your view on a host of *moral* issues.

Darwinian evolution purports to show that the appearance of living things on earth can be explained by natural causes alone—that we don't need God to explain life. Darwinism thus acts as the linchpin in a philosophy known as naturalism—that nature is ultimately all there is. And if nature is all there is, then there is no God, and ethical ideals and standards are not based on what God says; instead, they're based on what human beings think.

As Johnson writes, "The famous 'death of God' is simply the modernist certainty that naturalism is true and that human beings must therefore create their own standards rather than take them from some divine revelation."

Think how this affects debates over, say, sex education. If God created us for a purpose, then the most rational thing a person can do is to find out what that purpose is. A person who ignores the Creator is ignoring the most important part of reality—clearly an irrational thing to do. The most rational approach to sex ethics is to ask what the Creator has revealed about his purpose in creating humans as sexual beings, and what we must do to fulfill that purpose.

By contrast, if naturalism is true, then God didn't create us, we created God—or rather, we created the *idea* of God. God exists only as an idea in the minds of religious believers. In that case, the most rational course is to relegate religion to the realm of wishful thinking and to base sex ethics squarely on our own experience. And so the nondirective approach to sex education, which teaches students to judge for themselves what is right and wrong, is completely logical—once you accept the framework of naturalism.

Clearly, the debate over evolution and creation is at the heart of the "culture wars" we hear so much about. It's about worldviews that govern all of life. In Johnson's words, Darwinian evolution has become the "culturally dominant creation story," the foundation for liberal theories in law, ethics, and education.

That's why there's a profound connection between science and sexuality. The only basis for the Christian sex ethic is the opening lines of Genesis 1: "In the beginning God created the heavens and the earth."

Coming Out

Hope and Healing for Homosexuals

IT WASN'T just any wedding. The bride was a former lesbian. The groom was a former homosexual, male prostitute, and female impersonator. But even though John and Anne Paulk had been involved in the gay lifestyle for most of their adult lives, the Good News of Christ's love brought them out of homosexuality. "The

Lord's transforming power was so evident during our wedding," John said later, "that my mother and stepfather prayed to receive the Lord that night."

That's a powerful testimony, and it demonstrates a powerful truth: The gospel *can* free homosexuals to live in monogamous, heterosexual relationships.

Campus Crusade sponsored a series of ads in college newspapers all over the country, featuring John and Anne along with three other former homosexuals who came to Christ. The ads promised students a way out of homosexuality through the Good News of the gospel. Sadly, on some campuses students were denied the opportunity to read John and Anne's testimony. Gay students at Southwest Texas State University called the ads "hurtful" and demanded that the university censor the content.

What's really hurtful is the gay lifestyle itself. It exacts a heavy personal cost. According to Bob Davies, executive director of Exodus International, a ministry to homosexuals, 25 to 33 percent of homosexuals are alcoholics, compared to 7 percent of the general population. And homosexual men are six times more likely than straight men to attempt suicide.

Counselor Paul Brenton relates that, for many men struggling with homosexuality, molestation or emotional abuse is at the root of the problem. They have twisted images of themselves as less than real men. Benton says, "Many of them feel trapped in their lifestyle and genuinely want to get out" (*The Other Way Out,* 1995).

That was certainly the case for John Paulk. His life as a homosexual was a misguided and painful attempt to deal with the emotional pain of rejection. He says, "In my past there were many masks I hid behind to protect myself." His wife, Anne, agrees. It was her underlying need for love and acceptance that drove her into lesbianism, until Christian friends reached out to her with genuine friendship (*Every Student's Choice,* 1995).

The statistics tell a brighter story for those who are able to come to grips with the emotional and physical abuse they have suffered. According to Bill Consiglio, director of Hope Ministries, 40 percent of homosexuals who seek change "move into full heterosexuality, with many entering marriage and parenthood." An additional 40 percent are able to commit themselves to living as celibate Christian singles.

That's a success rate worth cheering about.

Exodus International teaches churches how they can reach out with compassion to homosexuals. Anne Paulk says, "As a lesbian I found hurt people just [looking for] love. As a Christian I found loving people just wanting to heal my hurt."

Many more like John and Anne are waiting to hear the message of unconditional love, forgiveness, and restoration.

New Genes for Old

Breakthrough in Gene Therapy

SCIENTISTS have finally discovered how to do therapy on our genes.

Until now, science has been busy uncovering the genetic basis for several diseases: the gene that causes sickle-cell anemia, the gene that causes cystic fibrosis, the gene that causes colon cancer. But actually *fixing* all these defective genes remained an elusive dream.

That is, until a few months ago.

The case involved Francine, a young Canadian woman who suffers from an inherited disease causing superhigh cholesterol levels, often leading to early death. The culprit is a gene that codes for the production of a particular protein in the liver—a protein that pulls cholesterol from the bloodstream and breaks it down. In Francine's body that gene is defective; as a result, her liver cannot produce the crucial protein to break down cholesterol.

Doctors decided to insert functioning genes into Francine's liver cells. They removed a slice of the liver, broke it down into individual cells, then injected the cells with laboratory-grown genes. The engineered cells were fed back into Francine's liver through a tube. Only a fraction of the engineered cells were taken up by the liver, but that was enough: They began producing the missing protein, and Francine is on her way to a more normal life.

Genetic engineering is one of the fastest-growing new technologies today, and Christians need to understand both its promise and its perils. Genetic technology—like all technology—is sanctioned by what Christians call the "cultural mandate": the command in Genesis to fill the earth and subdue it. Learning how to work with genes is one way to subdue the earth.

Genetic therapy has additional biblical justification in the doctrine of the Fall. Historical Christian doctrine teaches that the world was created good and that death and disease began with Adam and Eve's fall into sin. Hence the Bible sanctions efforts to relieve suffering and reverse the destructive effects of the Fall.

The life of Jesus gives us a model: He not only pronounced forgiveness of sins, he also healed the sick.

From the early church until our own day, Christ's ministry of healing has inspired Christian work among the sick and suffering. Today that work can include genetic therapy.

But genetic technology also raises frightening possibilities. There's the danger of genetic reductionism, which regards people as merely walking DNA. There's the threat of eugenics, which treats people with genetic diseases as though they had no right to live. There's the strange issue of patenting, which reduces life to the legal status of a machine. There's the eerie prospect of cloning and mix-and-match children.

Genetic technology is raising new and sometimes dangerous issues that we as Christians have an obligation to understand so that we can take moral leadership in a confused culture.

You and I can make the difference in whether genetic engineering is used for a ministry of healing—or for creating a brave new world of scientific manipulation of human life.

Genetic Justification

The Search for the Gay Gene

THE *New York Times* called it a "politically explosive study of the origins of human sexuality." Gay activists were elated, holding up the study as definitive proof that homosexuality is biologically determined and hence as "normal" as heterosexuality.

The hoopla was generated by a 1993 National Institutes of Health study, authored by Dean Hamer, reporting the alleged existence of a genetic marker that predisposes individuals to homosexual behavior. It was news that gay activists have long hoped for. Within minutes of the release of the NIH study, the National Gay and Lesbian Task Force issued a statement claiming that it "shows that homosexuality is a naturally occurring and common variation among humans."

As it turns out, the euphoria was premature. It has since been revealed that Dean Hamer is himself a homosexual activist whose agenda may have biased the results of his research. One of Hamer's colleagues accused him of deliberately excluding data that did not support his thesis. Geneticist Evan Balaban, of the Neurosciences

Institute in San Diego, criticized Hamer's research as seriously flawed, both in its methodology and in its basic assumptions. As a result, Hamer is under investigation by the Office of Research Integrity. Perhaps the most devastating criticism is that many of the gay men in Hamer's own study did not even have the genetic marker he claims is linked to homosexual behavior. These men must have had some *other* influences in their lives that contributed to their homosexuality. In other words, we're not talking about genetic *determinism* but a genetic *predisposition*—a predisposition that can be resisted through moral choices.

Dr. David Persing, of the Mayo Clinic, is a molecular genetics researcher who accepts the biblical teaching that all of nature is fallen. That includes our genetic heritage, Persing says. As a result, we *all* have inborn tendencies toward various forms of sinful behavior. With some it may be chemical addictions; with others it may be a tendency to ruthlessness or cowardice; with still others, it may be a weakness for certain sexual sins.

Yet our genes give us no excuse for sin, Persing says. We still have room for making real moral choices. Everyone is dealt a different genetic hand in life, but we're each responsible for how we play it.

Christians need to stand against the philosophy of genetic determinism that makes people the pawns of their genes. The life-giving message of the gospel is that despite our fallen nature, we can still respond to divine grace.

Emotional Responses

....

Moral Sentiment Is Not Enough

ARE you pro-life? And if you are, can you explain *why* you're pro-life?

It turns out, most Americans cannot. When sociologist James Davison Hunter interviewed people for his book *Before the Shooting Begins,* he discovered that most Americans base their moral beliefs entirely on private feelings.

Take a young man named Scott, a former Catholic. Scott argues fiercely that the fetus is a human being, yet he insists that abortion should be legal. Why? The fetus is a person to me, Scott says, but it "might *not* be a person to that mother."

What Scott fails to see is that personhood is an objective fact: The fetus either is or is not a person, regardless of what you and I think. But Scott is typical of Americans today. They base their moral views on sentiment, not conviction.

On the pro-choice side, Hunter asked an architect named Paul why he supports the right to abortion. Paul became agitated. "I don't want to get into philosophical or theological wrangling," he said. "My feelings are based on experiences that are mine alone, and you can't tell me they are wrong."

Notice how Paul begs off from any objective discussion of abortion based on philosophy or theology, even at the most elementary level. Instead, he treats private experience as the final court of appeal. You know, if Paul ran his architectural firm the way he makes moral decisions—if he based his construction blueprints on sheer feelings—his buildings would collapse. To be a good architect, Paul treats physical facts as though they were qualitatively different from moral values.

But when we separate facts and values, genuine moral debate

becomes impossible. If morality is merely a matter of private feelings, then any attempt to reason with people is perceived as a personal attack.

Listen to the words of a young mother named Karen. Karen told Hunter she would never dream of getting an abortion herself, yet she could not bring herself to say that abortion is morally wrong for everybody. "I don't know how [other people] feel," she said defensively. Apparently Karen's greatest fear is that if she says abortion is wrong, she will hurt someone's feelings.

The majority of Americans, Hunter discovered, are just like Karen: pro-life in their personal lives, yet pro-choice politically. Many are even hostile to the organized pro-life movement because, in their words, pro-life activists "are trying to impose their views on everyone else."

Hunter's book does us a great service by delving into the way most Americans really think about abortion—or I should say, how they *feel*. Those of us who base our opposition to abortion on conviction instead of sentiment need to know what we are up against: not just the highly articulate pro-choice movement but also the *in*articulate, inchoate opposition of most pro-lifers— those who have lost a sense of objective moral truth.

For the battle is no longer just over the status of the unborn; it's over the status of truth itself.

You and Euclid

The Loss of Certainty

FIND "the ideal mate of your dreams," promised the flyer in the mail. Just fill in the enclosed questionnaire and our computerized dating service will find you a perfect match.

Isn't it amazing what mathematics can do?

The computerization of courtship is just one way modern culture is dominated by mathematics. In science, industry, and even social policy, operations are quantified and subjected to mathematical treatment.

Is there a Christian view of mathematics? Most of us would say no. After all, 2 plus 2 equals 4 no matter what we believe about God. Yet there are very different ideas about what *kind* of truth mathematics gives.

Think back to the scientific revolution. The early scientists—Copernicus, Galileo, Newton—were Christians who believed that God created the world on a mathematical pattern. As mathematician Morris Kline explains in *Mathematics: The Loss of Certainty*, "The search for mathematical laws of nature was an act of devotion which would reveal the glory and grandeur of [God's] handiwork."

But science proved so successful that scientists began to think they could get along *without* belief in God. Enlightenment philosophers declared that science alone, armed with mathematical formulas, would lead mankind into all truth.

Of all the branches of mathematics, Euclidean geometry seemed the most certain. For two thousand years, its theorems had fit perfectly with physical facts. Its deductive structure seemed to provide absolute truth. Euclidean geometry was set up as the paradigm for all fields—even the study of ethics, law, and society. Mathematics became an idol.

But then, in the nineteenth century, disaster struck. Mathematicians were shocked to discover *other* kinds of geometry—*non*-Euclidean geometries—that are equally valid. Which one was true? Suddenly the most absolute form of human knowledge turned out to be relative. It was as though truth itself had shattered.

Today many mathematicians don't even describe math as "true" any longer. Instead they speak of it as a game—like bridge or baseball. The rules of mathematics are not "true," we're told; they are merely arbitrary conventions to make the game work.

The revolution in mathematics had an enormous impact. Non-Euclidean geometry became a metaphor for sweeping away *all* established truths. Professors of ethics denounced Christian ethics as "Euclidean" and old-fashioned. Professors of law dismissed traditional legal theory as "Euclidean." Political scientists denounced the American political system as "Euclidean" and called for new systems.

If there was no single truth in *mathematics,* it seemed there was none *anywhere.* Non-Euclidean geometry became a symbol to promote radical relativism across the board.

The history of mathematics shows what happens when we try to find truth apart from God. Mathematics was elevated into an idol, and when that idol fell, it created waves of relativism that swept across the entire intellectual landscape.

This is a powerful example we can use in defending our faith in a secular world: If we separate *any* area of life from Christianity—even mathematics—we cut it off from truth itself.

The New Math

....

How Much Is Human Life Worth?

CHEMISTRY teachers tell us the human body is made up of chemicals worth only ninety-eight cents. Today it seems that many abortion advocates take that analysis at face value: They want public policy to apply a strict cost/benefits analysis to the worth of human life.

For example, Eve Gartner, an attorney with the Center for Reproductive Law and Policy, won a case forcing Arkansas to pay for abortions for victims of rape or incest. She argued that abortions are cheaper than providing public services for children after they are born. In Gartner's words, by funding all Medicaid abortions, we can "save more money."

Nancy White of the National Abortion Rights Action League is even more forthright than Gartner. In *American Feminist* magazine, White was quoted as saying that single mothers "have bad children." "Black children born to unwed mothers," she went on, "are not productive members of society." Unless these women's pregnancies are ended by taxpayer-funded abortions, White warned, "the government is going to have to provide social programs like education and welfare" for all those unproductive children (*American Feminist,* fall 1994).

These statements bring into the open the terrifying logic of many proabortion advocates. Gone are self-righteous appeals to "a woman's right" to an abortion or to any supposed constitutional "right to privacy." Now there's just the cold calculus of the bottom line: Because children are expensive to raise, taxpayers should take the cheap way out and urge unmarried women to abort their babies instead.

An argument of this kind by abortion advocates is a startling example of utilitarianism. Utilitarianism is a philosophy of ethics that teaches that the worth of a thing can be measured solely in terms of its utility—what it can *do* and at *what cost*.

But can utilitarianism really figure the worth of human life? Can human qualities like faith, hope, and love be measured on a calculator? Abortion advocates want to answer these questions only in terms of social programs and tax dollars.

But there's another answer, an old one and the right one. It is that human beings are of such inconceivable worth that God sacrificed his own Son to save us from sin.

That is an estimation of human worth beyond our comprehension. It is based on the fact that each of us is made "in the image of God." Each of us is destined to live for eternity. As C. S. Lewis put it in *The Weight of Glory*, nobody has ever met "a mere mortal."

That is the cost/benefits analysis that puts abortion in the correct perspective.

You and I need to keep reminding ourselves of the right answer to the question of the worth of human life: that in God's sight it is priceless.

At What Price?

....

Human Embryo Research

IN THE beginning of each human life there are two cells, then four, then eight—multiplying right up to adulthood in a continuous process. But recently a government panel stood astride that process and drew a thick, black line putting the embryo in a lower category from the rest of life.

Until a human embryo is fourteen days old, the panel said, it can be subject to a host of scientific experiments—at taxpayer expense.

The recommendation was issued by the National Institutes of Health (NIH) and would reverse a fifteen-year ban on federal funding of human embryo research. During that period, embryo research was conducted only in privately funded fertility clinics. But the NIH recommendations permit government-funded research to go far beyond that: to create embryos in the laboratory for no purpose other than conducting experiments on them and then destroying them.

The panel's recommendations were presented in the loftiest moral tone. They spoke of concern for the "appropriateness" of certain experiments, of strict "guidelines," and of "moral considerations." But the panel's real considerations turned out to be purely utilitarian: a crass calculation of risks and benefits.

The report waxed eloquent about all the benefits that will accrue from human embryo research: from improving infertility treatments to diagnosing lethal diseases, designing new contraceptives, and even understanding cancer. The only negative factor noted is that many Americans harbor what one panel member called "deep apprehensions" about human embryo research.

Yet the panel never addressed the genuine moral concerns that *underlie* those "apprehensions." The truth is that the way we treat the human embryo is a microcosm of the way we treat human life itself. As bioethicist Nigel Cameron puts it in *The New Medicine,* we must start by asking, "What kind of being is the human embryo?" The answer is obvious: It's a *human* being at its earliest stages of development. When human beings reproduce, they reproduce *themselves.*

In short, Cameron concludes, the human embryo is "the same kind of being as I am and you are. It is . . . one of us."

Therefore, whatever our society permits in embryo research reveals our view of what it means to be human.

This explains why a host of social commentators has risen up in horror over the NIH recommendations. Even the liberal *Washington Post* editorialized that "the creation of human embryos specifically for research that will destroy them is unconscionable" (*Washington Post,* 2 October 1994). There's something about the deliberate creation and destruction of human life for purely utilitarian purposes that strikes everyone as wrong.

We ought to speak out loud and clear to tell the government that it has no business using our tax dollars to fund these unethical experiments. The most frightening thing is that once laboratories start conducting the experiments—and once the medical benefits start rolling in—eventually public opinion will come to accept it.

That's why you and I need to start now, teaching in our own homes and churches the full dignity of the human being. Even when that human being is only two cells, four cells, or eight cells.

Ten

CHALLENGES
FOR THE
CHURCH

Costly Grace

....

The Legacy of Dietrich Bonhoeffer

HALF a century ago a young Lutheran pastor named Dietrich Bonhoeffer was involved in a failed plot to assassinate Adolph Hitler—and was executed by the Nazis for treason. Astonishingly, fifty-one years later Bonhoeffer's reputation was resurrected when he was officially exonerated by a court in Berlin.

But Bonhoeffer was more than a leader of the Resistance under the Third Reich. He was also a powerful voice for the church. In his book *The Cost of Discipleship*, Bonhoeffer paints a vivid picture of what it means to be true to the Christian faith under a hostile regime. Under persecution, Bonhoeffer discovered that even though God's grace is freely given, it also exacts a high cost.

It was costly grace that led Bonhoeffer to leave a safe haven in America and return to Nazi Germany so he could suffer with his fellow Germans.

It was costly grace that led Bonhoeffer to continue teaching and preaching the Word of God even though the Nazis tried to suppress his work.

Costly grace led Bonhoeffer to stand against a turncoat church that mixed Nazi doctrine with Christian truth. Along with other faithful believers, Bonhoeffer signed the Barmen Declaration, which boldly declared independence from both the state *and* a co-opted church.

Costly grace led Bonhoeffer to attempt to smuggle Jews out of Germany even though it led to his arrest.

Costly grace led the young pastor to set aside his commitment to pacifism and join the assassination plot against Hitler—which finally led to his execution by the Nazis.

Even in prison, Bonhoeffer's life shone with divine grace. He comforted other prisoners, who looked upon him as their chaplain. He wrote many moving letters that were later collected in a volume called *Letters and Papers from Prison,* a book I read during my own stay behind bars, finding strength and encouragement. On the morning of April 9, 1945—less than a month before Hitler was defeated—Bonhoeffer knelt and prayed and then followed his captors to the gallows, where he was hanged as a traitor.

Today, Bonhoeffer is finally receiving the official recognition to match the spiritual veneration he has inspired in so many believers. The late British journalist Malcolm Muggeridge wrote a tribute to Bonhoeffer in his book *The Third Testament.* "Looking back now across the years," Muggeridge wrote, "what lives on is the memory of a man who died, not on behalf of freedom or democracy or a steadily rising gross national product, nor for any of the twentieth century's counterfeit hopes or desires, but on behalf of a cross on which another man died 2,000 years before.

"As on that previous occasion on Golgotha," Muggeridge goes on, "so amidst the rubble of 'liberated' Europe, the only victor is the man who died. There can never be any other victory or any other hope."

The lesson of Bonhoeffer's life and death is that God's grace is never cheap. It demands from us everything—even our lives—but in return it gives us a *new* life that transcends even the most oppressive political conditions.

Like Bonhoeffer, we may at times be called traitors by an earthly regime, but our true citizenship is in heaven.

Joan of Arc Was Not Noah's Wife

Biblical Illiteracy on the Rise

DID you know that Joan of Arc was Noah's wife?

No, this isn't a joke. One in ten Americans thinks the French saint *was* Noah's spouse.

Such unlikely answers were all too common in a survey conducted recently by Christian pollster George Barna. The results showed that while most Americans have a Bible and even accept its authority, they know very little about what's *in* it.

The good news is that 59 percent of those surveyed told Barna that "the Bible is totally accurate in all of its teachings." Seventy-two percent believe that "all of the miracles described in the Bible actually took place," and 85 percent believe that "Jesus Christ was born to a virgin."

But the bad news is that Americans are reading the Bible less than ever before. Less than 50 percent open the Bible in any given week, and even then they only skim a few verses. As a result, 64 percent—or two out of three Americans—don't know that Jesus was descended from King David. Almost 40 percent think the *"entire* Bible [including the Old Testament] was written several decades *after* Jesus' death."

As Barna writes, "There is virtual total ignorance of the history of the Bible" among Americans. And "the content of the Old Testament is a mystery to most adults" (Barna Research Group, November 1994).

Biblical illiteracy on this scale hasn't existed since before the Reformation—more than four hundred years ago. At that time, many people wanted to read the Bible but either didn't own one or weren't permitted to do so. By contrast, the Bible is a best-seller every year, but many of us never open it.

American culture today largely rejects the very concept of truth. False ideologies and even neopagan religions are multiplying. The only way Christians can withstand these cultural forces is to be rooted in God's Word. Bible reading is now a "survival skill," and only Christians steeped in biblical knowledge can defend the faith in our age of relativism.

It isn't enough to wring our hands about the decline of morals or Christian influence in society. Christians are called to be disciples. We are called to be disciplined in studying God's Word. Only then can we also lead disciplined lives.

We can meet this high calling only if we are grounded in the Word—and when our own habits not only protect us *from* the world but are also an example *to* the world.

Islamic Evangelism

Competition for Christianity?

WHEN heavyweight boxing champ Mike Tyson was released from prison after serving time for rape, he announced that he was a changed man. Had he converted to Christianity? No. He had become a follower of Muhammad.

"I believe in Islam," Tyson announced. "The Koran gives me insight into the world" (*Observer*, 12 June 1994).

Well, Tyson has plenty of company. From Africa to London, from the Russian Steppes to America's inner cities, Islam is emerging as Christianity's major competitor. In the U.S., Islam is on the brink of replacing Judaism as the second largest religion. And America's six million or so Muslims aren't just immigrants from the Middle East. Well-financed Muslim missionary programs are winning thousands of converts among native-born Americans—even those who were raised as Christians.

The Islamic revival is especially successful among African Americans. The black church is now facing keen competition from Islamic groups like Louis Farrakhan's Nation of Islam. The result is that today, one out of every fifteen African Americans is a Muslim (*PFUSA Research Summary,* January 1995).

In an age of moral relativism, what is it about the harsh, legalistic moral code of Islam that makes it so attractive to its followers?

Ironically, it's the *loss* of moral bearings that leads people to embrace Islam's authoritarianism. Humans cannot live long in a state of personal and social chaos. The Reverend Carl Ellis heads up Project Joseph, a ministry that helps black churches respond to the challenge from Islam. As values in society break down, Ellis explains, "people are left to make order out of the chaos." And then, he says, "along comes Islam, with its emphasis on discipline [and] making order out of chaos" (*Urban Family,* spring 1994).

With Islam's emphasis on male leadership, strong families, and the rejection of drugs and alcohol, it gives young black men something they may have never experienced before: social role and self-respect.

Understanding *why* people are attracted to Islam will make Christians more effective in witnessing to them. We can explain the crucial differences: Whereas Muslims attempt to resist temptation through discipline alone, Christians have a far more potent weapon. Through the transforming work of the Holy Spirit, Christianity gives people the *power* to live out God's moral law.

A dozen years ago, one Muslim leader announced: "In the next fifty years we will capture the Western world for Islam." Based on the number of Americans converting to Islam today, this is no empty boast.

You and I must redouble our efforts to hold up the rigorous truth of God's Word—before the false message of Islam fills the spiritual void.

A Hero for Our Times

Baroness Caroline Cox

I RECENTLY met someone who brings back the old-fashioned meaning of *heroism:* Lady Caroline Cox, of Queensbury, England. The petite, fifty-five-year-old baroness sits on the board of Christian Solidarity International, an organization committed to humanitarian aid and human rights.

If you're picturing a woman in well-cut tweeds and pearls who does nothing but attend meetings, think again. Like the Energizer Bunny, Baroness Cox keeps going and going—straight into the world's deadliest danger zones.

For example, she's made two dozen trips to war-torn Karabakh, where 150,000 Christian Armenians are defending their land against 7 million Azeri Muslims. On one of these trips, Lady Cox's jeep was jolted by a rocket-propelled antitank missile. Her driver quit, but Lady Cox returned, bringing food, medicine, and Christian love.

She's done the same in southern Sudan, where millions of Christians have been persecuted, killed, or enslaved by Islamic soldiers of northern Sudan. While other relief agencies were forced out, Lady Cox engaged in what she calls a little "unofficial drug running." In other words, she defied government policy, chartered planes, and flew in medicine—even bringing in a bishop so her brothers and sisters in Christ could celebrate at a service with the first clergy they'd seen in years.

In Leningrad, Lady Cox investigated orphanages and helped rescue children living in inhumane conditions. Flying back to Armenia for the umpteenth time, the baroness visited a little boy blinded by shrapnel from a cluster bomb, and she wept with a nurse who had watched soldiers murder her son.

Lady Cox reminds us of Paul's message to the church at Corinth: When one part of the body of Christ suffers, all suffer. That brings us to the Christian definition of *heroism:* a willingness to suffer and sacrifice on behalf of others.

It's a definition we need to bring back in a day when too many people confuse celebrity with heroism—when even violent criminals are lauded as heroes just because they're famous.

A Dose of Prayer

It Could Save Your Life

AN ELDERLY woman checked into Georgetown University Hospital with a serious diagnosis: congestive heart failure. But just one week later she had bounced back dramatically. Her doctor declared himself "astounded."

What caused such a rapid recovery? Was it the result of round-the-clock nursing or the latest medical gadgetry? No. The doctor credited the woman's amazing recovery to intercessory prayer. The patient's family had prayed with her, a deacon from her church had prayed, and the physician himself, Dr. Dale Matthews, had prayed for her regularly (*Washington Post,* 1 April 1994).

Was this just coincidence, or can we really detect the results of prayer in people's lives?

Skeptics say answers to prayer are nothing more than the power of suggestion. A group called the Committee for the Scientific Investigation of Paranormal Claims lumps prayer in with things like spoon bending. It argues that any evidence that prayer produces real benefits comes from believers who "fudge information, consciously and subconsciously" in their efforts to support their faith.

But some of the latest studies prove that it's the skeptics who may be fudging the evidence—or at least ignoring it. These new studies demonstrate that prayer has a measurable impact on a patient's recovery—even if the patient doesn't know he's being prayed for.

Cardiologist Randolph Byrd reports a dramatic experiment in prayer. Byrd asked prayer groups to intercede for nearly four hundred of the patients in the coronary care unit at San Francisco General Hospital. To avoid any placebo effect (where patients feel better for purely psychological reasons), neither the patients nor their doctors knew which patients were the objects of prayer. Byrd found that the patients who were prayed for had fewer complications and were five times less likely to require antibiotics than patients not prayed for (*Southern Medical Journal* vol. 81, no. 7, July 1988).

Psychiatrist David Larson of the National Institute for Healthcare Research makes it his specialty to collect data on the health effects of religious beliefs and practices, including prayer. For example, one documented study shows that religious commitment is associated with lower blood pressure and lower rates of hypertension. Larson has even developed a study manual teaching medical practitioners how to respond when a patient wants to pray or talk about spiritual matters.

Of course, this is not to say that religious believers automatically get miraculous recoveries whenever they pray. After all, prayer is not a magical incantation that puts God in our power. Prayer is communication with the living God, who responds to each of us individually.

Yet it's exciting that medical science can actually detect the impact of the spiritual world on the physical world. Many Americans think of religion as something confined to the internal realm of feelings and experience. We simply don't conceive of faith connected with the so-called real world, the world confirmed by science.

That's why studies that track the power of prayer on physical healing are so important. When we talk to our non-Christian neighbors, we can demonstrate that faith has real and measurable results in the everyday world.

It's evidence that even skeptics can't ignore.

"Like Lambs to the Slaughter"

The Persecution of Christians

IT BEGAN as a typical worship service at a large evangelical church in Oromo, Ethiopia, but the sermon was abruptly interrupted when government soldiers burst through the doors. Many worshipers were arrested, and some later died in jail. The pastor was set free—but only after his eyes were plucked out.

This horrific story was recounted in an article by Michael Horowitz, a fellow at the Hudson Institute in Washington, D.C. Around the globe, Horowitz writes, Christians are being persecuted and often killed for their faith (*Wall Street Journal,* 5 July 1995).

In Pakistan, speaking against Muhammad is punishable by death. In Sudan, Christian children as young as six are sold into slavery. In Egypt, Christian converts are imprisoned and tortured. In Saudi Arabia, citizens are paid a bounty of $3,000 for exposing home Bible study classes.

Instead of helping these people, the U.S. government often makes their plight worse. When Christians escape from oppressive regimes, they often contact U.S. embassies. Our laws demand that the Immigration and Naturalization Service (INS) investigate claims of religious persecution. Instead, the INS usually sends these Christians back home. They are literally delivering them up like lambs to the slaughter.

Ironically, evangelicals are not leading the fight to defend persecuted Christians. Instead, much of the frontline fighting has been done by Michael Horowitz, an American Jew. In the summer of 1995, Horowitz fired off letters to 150 American mission boards asking them to help him do something about the persecution of Christians worldwide.

Their response? So far, a resounding silence.

"If I'd written an article about anti-Semitism in Islamic countries, by now I'd be overwhelmed with calls from Christian groups," Horowitz says. "Why is the Christian community so indifferent about fighting for the human rights of its own people?"

More than three hundred years ago, the Puritans fled to America because of religious persecution. And one hundred years later, Quakers dropped anchor here for the same reason. In the early twentieth century, Armenian and Assyrian Christians who fled Turkey were welcomed here with open arms.

Why, then, are we now slamming the door on Christians from Iran, Egypt, Pakistan, Ethiopia, Saudi Arabia, and China? Why are we turning a blind eye to violations that lead to the torture and murder of millions of our brothers and sisters in Christ?

Perhaps instead of sitting in our comfortable churches, lifting our voices in song, we ought to be on our feet howling in outrage. We ought to be calling our leaders in Washington, demanding that something be done about the INS violations that betray the very people America has historically welcomed: victims of religious persecution.

Five-Star Churches

America's Church Critic

BEFORE seeing a movie, do you ever read the movie reviews to see what the critics are saying? Before buying a book, do you read what the book reviews say? Well, today there's a new kind of critic on the scene—a church critic.

The Reverend George Exoo is America's first paid church critic. His reviews are a regular feature on a Pittsburgh radio station, where he rates churches by giving them up to five stars. He also visits cities around the country, publishing reviews of local churches in area magazines.

So what does it take for a church to earn five stars? In an article in *Milwaukee,* Exoo praises churches that are "innovative," "flexible," and friendly; churches where the leaders are easygoing and engaging; churches with dynamic worship services, easy-to-follow programs, and trained greeters. Most important, churches rate high if they're geared to filling social and emotional needs—churches that, in his words, "heal hurts and meet needs" (*Milwaukee,* February 1994).

This all sounds very appealing. After all, who *doesn't* want a church that meets people's needs? What's wrong with Exoo's rating system is that he fails to consider what *Scripture* teaches about the essential functions of a church: biblical teaching, the sacraments, and discipline.

For example, in one review, Exoo praises a church member for leaving behind "a church of dogma and obedience" and choosing instead a church that "enhance[s] his self-image" and offers "an emotionally satisfying experience." That's a five-star church in Exoo's book. But notice there's not a word about the things that Scripture tells us to look for in a church—a church that teaches the truth and that equips believers to live out the truth in every aspect of their lives.

The reason Exoo ignores the question of truth is that his ratings are based on a market system where the overriding consideration is pleasing the consumer. As he himself puts it, it's "a buyers' market." People no longer attend out of spiritual duty. Instead, he says, "they want product." Exoo goes so far as to praise one church for relying not on "theology" but on "marketing"—the ability to sell to the public.

Unfortunately, Exoo's views are not unique. Many Americans choose a religion not on the basis of what they believe is *true* but what they *like*. For them, religion has become just another service industry; worship, another form of leisure and entertainment.

If we want our own local church to be a real warrior in the battle against the evils of our age, we need to treat it as more than a weekend retreat. We need to treat it as a place to be trained in spiritual combat, a place to put on the full armor of God, a place to renew our commitment to live lives of holiness and purity.

That may not earn five stars from the church critic, but it will be pleasing to God. After all, he's the only critic who really matters.

A Knock in the Night

China's Religious Persecution

IN THE dead of night, a knock was heard on the door. Before Dennis Balcombe could even get out of bed, Chinese police kicked his door in, swarmed into his room, and arrested him.

Balcombe is an American pastor who was visiting churches in China when the authorities ordered his arrest—along with several other Christian leaders. As police led him away, Balcombe could hear the screams of local Chinese Christians still in the house, as police rounded them up and beat them.

According to a report by Roy Maynard, Balcombe and two other Americans spent the next four days and nights behind bars in a detention center. Their account reads like stories from the Soviet gulag: They were refused permission to contact their embassy; they were jerked awake in the middle of the night and dragged out for interrogations; they were pressured to betray their fellow Christians (*World,* 5 March 1994).

Ironically, all this was taking place just as debates were raging in the United States over whether to renew China's Most Favored Nation trading status. China is trying to convince the U.S. that its human-rights record is improving. In fact, it's much worse.

Not long ago Chinese authorities issued two new edicts that forbid evangelism and outlaw any congregations not sanctioned by the government. Like the former Soviet Union, China has churches that are government-approved and controlled. As a result, an underground church has blossomed, meeting primarily in homes. As Marxist ideology is discredited, growing numbers of young people are turning to Christianity to fill the vacuum.

But Chinese authorities have vowed to wipe out the underground churches, closing them down and arresting or killing their leaders. Some Christians have been sentenced to labor camps just for listening to gospel radio programs broadcast from Hong Kong.

The crackdown is motivated by Chinese officials' awareness that religion has the power to topple repressive regimes—like their own. The *Christian Science Monitor* says Beijing is acutely conscious of the role Christianity played in the collapse of communism in Eastern Europe. Chinese authorities are determined not to let the same thing happen in their country (*Christian Science Monitor*, 9 March 1994).

The tragedy is that few Americans are following this drama. Reports about Pastor Balcombe showed up in only a handful of newspapers. Compare that to hundreds of stories about the caning of an American teenager in Singapore. Apparently, our press is more interested in one rebellious teenager than in devout Christians being persecuted in China.

The writer of Hebrews commands us to remember those imprisoned for their faith, as though we were there with them. That means we need to empathize with our brothers and sisters in China and pray for them.

We need to imagine what it's like to hear a knock on the door in the dead of night.

Grassroots Health Care

A Church-Based Model

AN ELDERLY woman—I'll call her Laura—needed medical attention for a mysterious lump in her breast. But she was frightened by the thought of seeing a strange doctor and going to the hospital, so she kept putting it off.

Laura might not have received the treatment she needed until it was too late. But she was lucky: Her church had just hired a congregational nurse, who was able to examine her in the familiar setting of her own home and give her medical advice.

Laura's church is part of a new movement called Congregation-Based Health Ministry. It's a fast-growing movement challenging the common notion that the government should take over health care.

Of course, churches have always regarded health care as part of their mission. That's why so many hospitals bear names like Presbyterian General Hospital or Sisters of Mercy. Many hospitals were founded in the nineteenth century by churches. They aimed to provide poor and middle-class Americans with the advanced health care that wealthier citizens received back then in the privacy of their homes (*Wall Street Journal,* 5 July 1994).

Today churches are looking for creative new ways to follow the biblical command to care for the sick and suffering. As so-called hard medicine becomes more high-tech, churches are picking up the softer aspects of medicine, such as mental health, long-term care, and home nursing.

These things were traditionally considered part of pastoral care, so perhaps it's no surprise that churches are spearheading the most innovative developments. In geriatric medicine, Roman Catholics and Lutherans have led the way in social-service programs that enable older folks to live independently. Episcopalians, Baptists, and Presbyterians have pioneered the design of humane and technically sophisticated retirement facilities.

Today many churches are focusing on mental health as well, and even constructing their own counseling centers. In Alabama, Frazer Memorial United Methodist Church has established a freestanding mental-health clinic to offer professional care at a reasonable price.

One of the most creative innovations is the parish nursing movement. Started by a Lutheran pastor, it bases nurses in individual churches. Since these programs can call upon an enthusiastic corps of volunteers, they're able to offer emotional support and follow-up care relatively cheaply.

A hundred years ago, when churches felt called to care for the sick and needy, they founded hospitals. Today churches are reviving that heritage in new ways, yet many politicians continue to insist that only the government can solve the problem of health-care coverage. Perhaps it's time to rethink whether government programs are really the best way to reform health care—or whether they will actually *block* the innovative health-care movement blossoming in churches.

You and I ought to work within our own congregations for programs to care for the sick and suffering. When church members fulfill their calling, they minister not only to the body but also to the spirit.

That's more than any government bureaucrat can do.

Black and Beautiful

....

Renewing Churches and Neighborhoods

WHAT'S an inner-city church to do when it's located right next to a convenience store whose main attractions are liquor, lottery tickets, and the drug deals taking place on the sidewalk in front?

Well, Metropolitan Baptist Church in Washington, D.C., knew what to do: It purchased the store.

Church members hauled away the liquor signs, tossed out the rotting food, and painted over the graffiti. Today the store is renamed Fish and Loaves. Alongside the cheese and salami, shoppers can browse through Christian books and magazines.

The point of buying the store is not to turn a profit, says the church's senior pastor. The point is to spread the gospel and revitalize the neighborhood. It's part of a holistic vision of ministering to the entire person and the entire neighborhood—a vision that's spreading to inner-city churches across the nation.

In the Anacostia section of Washington, Ambassador Baptist Church bought an apartment building that it uses for a preschool, a food distribution center, and a home for hospital outpatients.

In Detroit, Hartford Memorial Baptist Church bought eight blocks of inner-city decay and turned it into a bustling shopping complex, with several fast-food restaurants and auto shops.

In Queens, New York, Allen African Methodist Episcopal Church turned dilapidated stores into a thriving shopping district and built a housing complex for seniors.

Our inner cities have become spiritual and cultural wastelands. High crime rates have driven out businesses, shops, recreation centers, and other community resources. In this wasteland, however, many black churches are building an oasis where people can rediscover normal community life—places where people can work, shop, eat, or take classes without the shadow of constant fear.

Historically, of course, the church has always been the center of the black community. But during the civil-rights movement of the '60s, many young black people diverted their hopes to politics. Thousands of young people joined the civil-rights movement, starry-eyed with the dream of freedom. There followed civil-rights legislation and government-funded community-development programs. As these programs sprang up, the church began to cede much of its advocacy role to them.

But instead of getting better, the decay in the inner cities worsened. Today the hard truth is hitting home that government programs can't do the job. Real change comes only from inner transformation; it's a product of spiritual renewal, and that's something only the church can offer. By running desperately needed businesses and social services, inner-city churches are demonstrating that spiritual renewal is the path to practical renewal.

Christians ought to boldly point out what churches are doing to restore the inner cities. They're doing it not by begging for federal money but by building communities that express God's love in concrete, practical ways.

Whether it's buying a convenience store, running low-income housing, or tutoring school children, churches are showing that God's Word is tough enough to bring new life even to our dying inner cities.

Evidence for the Exodus

Moses Was Not a Pious Invention

"THE EXODUS and Moses Are Merely Myths." So ran the headline of a story in London's *Daily Telegraph*. The article dismissed the biblical account as part of Israel's "falsified heroic legends" (*Daily Telegraph,* 12 December 1995).

But new research demonstrates that the events of the book of Exodus really *did* happen.

Liberal scholars have long scoffed at the story of the Exodus. They insist that Israelites weren't even living in Egypt at the time when the Bible records their slavery.

What does the evidence tell us? Recently, archaeologists working in the Nile Delta unearthed the remains of a house that is completely different from the Egyptian houses around it. Lo and behold, the house follows the pattern of houses that the Israelites later built in Canaan. In fact, the floor layout is known as "the Israelite-type house." It was discovered in Tell el-Dab'a—the location of the biblical city of Ra'amses. That's where, according to the biblical text, the Israelites lived as slaves under Pharaoh—striking confirmation of the biblical account of the Israelites' sojourn in Egypt.

In another example, the Bible says that on their way out of Egypt the Israelites camped at the ancient city of Dibon. Skeptics have long insisted that Dibon didn't even exist at the time of the Exodus. But then archaeologists in Egypt discovered inscriptions at the temple of Amon, at Karnak, that described an ancient trade route from Egypt into Palestine. One of the cities lying along this route at the time of the Exodus is none other than Dibon.

In short, the evidence shows that the Israelites actually followed a heavily trafficked Egyptian road that very clearly *did* exist at the time of the Exodus. Professor Charles Krahmalkov concludes that "we have irrefutable primary historical evidence for the existence of the city of Dibon" in the time of the Exodus (*Biblical Archaeology Review* September/October 1994).

There's an interesting historical corroboration for one puzzling detail mentioned in the biblical text. There were at least two possible routes that the Israelites could have taken out of Egypt. According to the book of Exodus, God specifically directed the Israelites *not* to go along the coastal route by the Mediterranean—even though it was the shorter and most direct route back to Canaan. Scholars have recently unearthed the reason why: The shorter coastal route was studded with Egyptian military garrisons. The Israelites would have walked right into the jaws of the lion.

The growing list of historical confirmations should come as

welcome news to Christians, because the Exodus is one of the pivotal events of the Bible. It is the paradigm of God's miraculous deliverance of his people, and if it isn't true, then the veracity of the rest of the Bible is compromised along with it.

Christians need to be aware of the factual foundations of our faith. Contrary to the skeptics, the archaeologist's spade is steadily unearthing new evidence for the Bible's historical accuracy.

Trumpets and Tremors

The Destruction of Jericho

ONE of the most dramatic battles in the Bible is the story of Joshua's trumpets bringing down the walls of Jericho, but until recently many scholars denied that it ever occurred. New evidence dramatically confirms the biblical account.

Charles Pellegrino discusses the fall of Jericho in his book *Return to Sodom and Gomorrah*. Pellegrino is an agnostic who set out to examine the archaeological remains of the ancient Near East. During his investigations he was surprised to discover evidence supporting many of the events recorded in the Old Testament. One of the greatest surprises was the discovery of the biblical city of Jericho, lying under layers of dirt and rubble.

For decades skeptical scholars had assumed that Jericho did not even exist in Joshua's time. In fact, the alleged absence of the biblical Jericho was cited in archaeological textbooks as proof that the Bible is not historically accurate. But Pellegrino pulls together evidence from archaeology showing that Jericho existed during the time of Joshua after all. Even more exciting, it shows that the walls surrounding Jericho fell down in a very unusual manner: *out* from the city and down flat—forming a perfect ramp for an invading army.

This is exactly what a student of the Bible would expect to find. According to the book of Joshua, when the priests of Israel blew a blast on their trumpets, the walls of Jericho collapsed, allowing the Israelites to enter and conquer the city.

Moreover, an examination of the fossilized food supplies indicates that the city fell after a very short siege. Curiously, the invaders didn't steal the food supplies. Instead, they scattered the grain and then burned it along with the city, an action one scholar calls "unique in the annals of Palestinian archaeology." Again, this fits with the biblical account: The Bible states that Joshua and his men didn't steal the grain because God told them to destroy the city *without* looting it.

Finally, after the Israelite conquest, Jericho sat empty for hundreds of years—as shown by several feet of silt lying above the ancient ruins. This is consistent with the biblical account of Joshua cursing the city: "Cursed before the Lord is the man who undertakes to rebuild this city, Jericho" (Josh. 6:26).

Of course, as an agnostic, Pellegrino doesn't accept the Old Testament's explanation of the archeological data. For example, he suggests that the walls of Jericho were felled by an earthquake. The Christian's response should be that it's entirely possible for God to use the forces of nature to accomplish his purposes. But if you leave God out of the picture, it becomes nearly incredible to think that an earthquake just *happened* to take place as the Israelite priests blew their trumpets.

In short, it takes at *least* as much faith to accept a naturalistic explanation as it does to accept the biblical account. As for the centuries that Jericho lay empty, Pellegrino admits that he is stumped: "Cities located near major watercourses are never abandoned for all time," he says, "but something unusual happened" at Jericho.

The findings at Jericho are one more reminder that Christians don't need to take a backseat to the biblical skeptics. Why not use this stunning archaeological evidence from Jericho to answer those who deny that the Old Testament is rooted in historical fact.

The story of Joshua's men blowing their trumpets to bring down the walls of Jericho is *not* just a lot of hot air.

The House of David

It's Not a House of Cards

FOR biblical skeptics, David was a mythical figure like King Arthur. His kingdom was no more real than the mythical Camelot. But the skeptical attitude is crumbling under the sheer weight of the facts.

Many scholars consider the Bible to be myth until it is confirmed by other sources. Since the ancient Philistine or Aramean records did not mention David, skeptics assumed that he had never actually existed. Until recently, King Ahab was the earliest biblical character to appear in secular historical records. Ergo, no biblical character prior to Ahab—including King David—was considered historical.

But in the summer of 1993, a great shock hit the biblical skeptics. Avraham Biran, an archaeologist at Hebrew Union College, discovered an ancient Aramean inscription at the biblical city of Dan in northern Israel, dating from the ninth century B.C., and bearing the name "David." The inscription refers to a battle described in 1 Kings 15:16-22.

The biblical account goes like this: The kings of Israel and Judah were at war with each other. The king of Judah, fearing defeat, took the gold and silver from the temple and used it to bribe the king of the Arameans to fight on his side. The Arameans agreed: They took Judah's gold, attacked Israel, and captured the Israelite city of Dan.

Just a myth? The inscription at Dan proves otherwise. It mentions the Aramean victory over Israel, referring specifically to the king of Israel and the "House of David."

There's more. First Kings tells us that the king of Aram was named Ben-Hadad, which means "son of [the storm god] Hadad." Interestingly, the inscription discovered at Dan credits the pagan storm god Hadad with the victory over Israel—another confirmation of the historical accuracy of the biblical account.

The meaning of these exciting archaeological discoveries has not been lost on Christians. In an article on the historical accuracy of the Bible, *Time* magazine stated that "believers around the world are attuned more than ever to the significance of archaeological finds . . . in establishing the reality of the events underlying their faith" (*Time,* 18 December 1995).

The next time someone tries to tell you that the Bible is a collection of myths, tell them about the latest archaeological evidence. Again and again, the Bible proves true on all levels—historical as well as spiritual.

The Great Cover-Up

Evidence for Christ's Crucifixion and Resurrection

UNDERNEATH an ancient church in Jerusalem is found one of the most powerful evidences for the truth of the Gospels. Ironically, the ancient enemies of Christianity were attempting to cover up the evidence—yet all they did was preserve it for later generations.

Our story begins in the year A.D. 135. The Roman emperor Hadrian had just subjugated Judea after the Second Jewish Revolt. Hadrian was determined to impose Roman religion upon the Judeans. After destroying the Jewish synagogues in Jerusalem, he turned his attention to the Christians.

What better way to squelch this upstart religion than to obliterate its holy places? The site of Christ's crucifixion and resurrection was known and venerated by Christians at the time. So Hadrian concealed the site under a massive concrete platform and built a temple over it to the pagan god Zeus.

Nearly two centuries later, the political tables turned: The emperor Constantine converted to Christianity and decided to build a magnificent church in Jerusalem to commemorate Christ's crucifixion and resurrection. He insisted that the church be built upon the actual site, which was easy enough to spot since it was marked by Hadrian's temple.

Constantine's builders set to work demolishing the pagan temple, and sure enough, underneath they found the ancient quarry called Golgotha. Nearby were the remains of Christ's tomb. Today, the Church of the Holy Sepulchre in Jerusalem's Old City still marks the site of Christ's crucifixion and resurrection.

The early Christians knew their faith was rooted firmly in historical events. They built churches throughout the Holy Land for precisely that reason—to mark the actual locations. The Church of the Holy Sepulchre isn't the only example. The Gospels say that Jesus was tried before the high priest Caiaphas and then taken to the procurator of Judea, Pontius Pilate. Not long ago, the tomb of the Caiaphas family was discovered in Jerusalem. Inside were the very bones of the infamous high priest mentioned in the Gospels. As for Pontius Pilate, a first-century inscription discovered at Caesarea confirms that he was indeed procurator of Judea from A.D. 26 to 36.

In addition, the second-century Roman historian Tacitus confirms that Christianity was founded by a man named Christus, whom he says was "put to death as a criminal by Pontius Pilate, procurator of Judea, in the reign of Tiberius."

What does all this mean for us? It demonstrates that our faith is based squarely upon the acts of God in human history. God himself became human and walked among us to redeem us.

Share the story of "the great cover-up" with those who question whether the Bible is really true. Tell them of the botched attempt to hide the site of Christ's crucifixion.

Like the resurrected Christ himself, the truth could not remain buried for long.

Scars That Heal

A Lesson in Forgiveness

IT WAS one of the most poignant snapshots of the Vietnam War: a little girl running naked down the street, screaming in pain, her eyes squeezed shut with terror.

At the time, I was President Nixon's assistant in the White

House, dealing with decisions involving the Vietnam War, and I was horrified by that picture.

Twenty-four years after that picture was taken, Americans finally found out what happened to that little girl. Another photo, taken on Veteran's Day, reveals a poised young woman laying a wreath at the Vietnam Veterans Memorial in Washington, D.C.

As a child, Kim Phuc brought home to Americans the horrors of war. Today, she's teaching us another lesson: the healing power of forgiveness.

As she laid the wreath at the wall, Kim told the assembled veterans: "As you know, I am the little girl who was running to escape from the napalm fire. I have suffered a lot from both physical and emotional pain. Sometimes I thought I could not live, but God saved my life and gave me faith and hope" (*Washington Times,* 12 November 1996).

Speaking to America's Vietnam veterans is the latest chapter in an extraordinary life story. In the moments after the napalm attack, Kim was taken to a hospital by Nick Ut, the Associated Press photographer who had just snapped her picture. Years of painful burn therapy followed.

After the war, Kim enrolled at a university in Saigon, hoping to become a doctor. Unfortunately, she was far too valuable as a propaganda tool. When government officials found out that she was "the girl in the photo," they yanked her out of school and put her to work as a secretary in a government office. There she was expected to roll up her sleeves and show her scars to any visitor who dropped by.

In 1986 the Vietnamese government sent Kim to Cuba to study and to mount goodwill missions. There she met and married Bui Huy Toan, an evangelical Christian, and Kim herself became a believer.

In 1992 on their way home from their honeymoon in

Moscow, Kim and her husband defected to Canada. The couple now live in Toronto with their two-year-old son.

Kim recently told National Public Radio that she and her husband hope to raise enough money to attend Bible college together. Their goal is to equip themselves to share the gospel with the Vietnamese people.

Well, Kim has already shared the meaning of forgiveness with thousands of toughened soldiers. At the Veteran's Day ceremony, Kim publicly forgave the unknown pilot whose load of napalm seared her skin and killed her two younger brothers.

"Even if I could talk face-to-face with the pilot who dropped the bomb," Kim said, "I would tell him we cannot change history, but we should try to do good things for the present and for the future to promote peace." At that point, according to one newspaper account, many of the veterans present began to weep.

Kim Phuc's story reminds us of what only the gospel can provide: the basis for forgiveness and reconciliation. Kim Phuc was able to forgive the soldiers who nearly destroyed her life because she knows that at the cross, God not only reconciled us to himself, he also reconciled us to each other.

ABOUT PRISON FELLOWSHIP

BreakPoint is the radio ministry of Prison Fellowship, an inter-denominational ministry to prisoners, ex-prisoners, their families, and the victims of crime. The ministry was founded in 1976 by Charles W. Colson following a seven-month prison term for a Watergate-related offense.

Today, some 300 employees and nearly 50,000 volunteers labor on behalf of Prison Fellowship across the country. In addition, Prison Fellowship International is involved with prison ministry groups in more than 70 countries around the world.

Chuck Colson went on the air with *BreakPoint* in 1991. *BreakPoint with Chuck Colson* is a daily radio commentary program offering a Christian perspective on news and trends. Its purpose is to equip listeners and readers with a biblical worldview that enables them to contend for truth in modern society. Carried on 359 radio stations nationwide, *BreakPoint* can also be heard on the Internet at www.breakpoint.org.

Prison Fellowship Ministries relies on the generosity of thousands of donors. We hope you will prayerfully consider supporting one of our programs. You may specify one of the ministries listed below.

( ) Angel Tree (Christmas gift-giving program for inmates' children) [7ATGN00]
( ) *BreakPoint* [7RDGN00]
( ) Justice Fellowship (Public-policy arm of Prison

Fellowship that works for criminal justice reforms)
[7JFUN00]

( ) Neighbors Who Care (Provides practical and
emotional assistance to crime victims) [7VMGN00]

( ) Prison Fellowship in-prison programs [7UNGN00]

( ) I am interested in learning more about Prison
Fellowship's programs. Please send me information.
[BCAL0]

To make a donation or for more information about Prison
Fellowship programs, write to the following address:

Prison Fellowship Ministries
P.O. Box 17500
Washington, DC 20041-0500

Prison Fellowship is a charter member of the Evangelical
Council for Financial Accountability. For a copy of our audited
financial statement, you may write to the address above. You
may also request a copy of our financial statement from the
Virginia State Division of Consumer Affairs.

You may contact Prison Fellowship at our Web site at
www.pfm.org.

You may contact *BreakPoint* at our Web site at
www.breakpoint.org.

INDEX

Charles Colson, chairman of Prison Fellowship Ministries, is the 1993 recipient of the Templeton Prize for Progress in Religion. He is a highly respected author, speaker, and columnist and serves as a distinguished senior fellow of the Christian Coalition of Colleges and Universities. Among his best-selling books are *The Body, Loving God, Kingdoms in Conflict,* and *Born Again,* which details his experiences as President Nixon's assistant, his conversion in the midst of Watergate, and his ordeal in prison.

Anne Morse is managing editor for BreakPoint Radio. She earned a bachelor's degree in communications from Seattle Pacific University. Her articles have appeared in several newspapers, magazines, and journals, including *Virtue, The American Feminist,* and *The ARP,* the magazine of the Associate Reformed Presbyterian Church.